Hippocrene U.S.A. Guide to

IRISH AMERICA

Hippocrene U.S.A. Guide to

IRISH AMERICA

RUSS MALONE

HIPPOCRENE BOOKS
New York

For information, contact:
HIPPOCRENE BOOKS, INC.
171 Madison Avenue
New York, NY 10016

Library of Congress Cataloging in Publication Data
Malone, Russ.
  Hippocrene U.S.A. guide to Irish America / Russ Malone.
     p.   cm.
  Includes index.
  ISBN 0-7818-0173-7
  1. Irish Americans — History.   2. Historic sites — United
States — Guidebooks.   3. United States — Guidebooks.
  I. Title.   II. Title: Irish America.
  E184.16M25 1994   93-42116
  973'.049162—dc20   CIP

Printed in the United States of America.

Acknowledgments

I am grateful for the research assistance given by James Quintus; Fr. Vincent J. Keane; Gretchen Tangeman; Nancy Ferguson; Robert Pyle; Eammon McKee of the Irish Embassy; Charlie Diggs, Mary Schieder, Joanne Jessen, Tom Smith, and Steve White, American Speech-Language-Hearing Association; Frank Buhrman, Mount St. Mary's College; and the staff of the American Irish Historical Society, New York; and to my editor, Michelle Gagne. A special thanks to the staff of Malone's Irish Pub for their help and encouragement—Marty, Erin, Pat, Kelli, and Sean.

Photographs were provided by Callahan Associates, Philadelphia; Jesse James Bank, Liberty, Missouri; National Archives; National Historic Site, Brookline, Massachusetts; National Park Service; New York Convention and Visitors Bureau; Jim Burke, University of Pittsburgh; James Quintus, Oklahoma City; and Washington Convention and Visitors Association, District of Columbia.

To
Francis and Rose Malone—
the beginning,
Kelli, Erin, Sean, Shannon-
the future,
Margueritte Shehan Malone—
for all time.

Contents

Éire

The areas where Irish is regularly spoken are known as **An Ghaeltacht** and are shown by black shading.

Failte! Welcome!

They came mainly from the Irish County Societies and the Catholic Athletic Clubs. A number of the latter Irish had distinctly German, French, Italian or Polish names. They were Irish by adoption, Irish by association, or Irish by conviction.

Father Francis Duffy, Chaplain
Fighting 69th, *Diary*

*T*here are forty million Irish Americans, give or take a hundred thousand or so. Whether by reason of adoption, association, conviction, or ancestry, one out of five respondents to the 1990 U.S. Census listed identifcation as Irish American. In a day when most Americans have multi-ethnic heritage, it is significant that so many elect to be Irish. Significant, but not surprising. Less than 100 years ago, when to be Irish meant to be scorned and persecuted at home and abroad, Irish took great pride in being Irish. They always knew they were beautiful!

The *Hippocrene U.S.A. Guide to Irish America* is written for you, the Irish American, who wants a better understanding of the world your ancestors shaped. And for you, the Irish, who may, like many of your family and friends before you, plan to visit the United States. And for you, the armchair or peripatetic adventurer who wants to find new sites to visit and new insights to familiar places. To enhance your appreciation of the sites you will visit, I've suggested a few films. Most are in your video store, all can be seen on television from time to time.

The information in this guide is accurate as of the time of writing, but call for an update before you go. Hours do change, and institutions do move on to the Isle of the Noble.

Today, there is concern that the Irish have been assimilated, that their distinctive characteristics have been submerged in the great melting pot of America. More likely, history has simply repeated itself. Centuries after the Normans invaded Hibernia, it was realized that the Normans had not conquered the Irish, the Normans had become Irish. As G.K. Chesterton explains, "Some countries conquer other countries, the Irish conquered nations." The greening of America, believe many sons and daughters of Erin, refers to the influence Irish Americans have exerted over many facets of life in the United States.

The U.S. A. Guide to Irish America takes you on a great adventure. From the shanty towns of Boston to the mansions of San Francisco, from the bright lights of Broadway's Great White Way deep into the blackness of a Pennsylvania coal mine, from the boxing ring to the Oval Office, from Western vigilante justice to the Supreme Court, and from a battlefield in Virginia and cannibalism in California to a cathedral in New York.

After more than a millennium of fighting for survival, the Irish were prepared and enthusiastic to join in the defense of their new home against the English, whose domination of Ireland had been long and brutal. They eagerly joined in the Revolutionary War and the War of 1812. Although there were Irish fighting on both sides during the Civil War, the Union received the greater numbers, less because of moral conviction than because most had settled in the North; the English were supporting the Confederacy. In later years, the Irish Americans served with honor in World Wars I and II, in spite of English allies.

Irish heroism in the early American wars, when they were represented out of proportion to their numbers, won them sufficient respectability to enter politics. Their mastery of words and understanding of the British system of government, combined with the number of votes they could deliver, gave them an edge in New York's Tammany Hall and the smoke filled back rooms of Boston, Chicago, New Orleans, and Philadelphia. Their political successes were not limited to the cities, but extended to the White House, where at least twelve Irish Americans occupied the Oval Office before the election of the first Irish Catholic president.

The White House, modeled after a home which now serves as the seat of the Dail, the Irish parliament, was designed by an Irishman. It stands as testimony to the creative talent of the Irish—a talent more readily recognized when expressed in theater, the concert hall, film, and literature.

The "fighting Irish" was a appellation used long before it was adopted by Notre Dame for its football team. Often describing the channel which Irish used to give vent to theirdaily frustrations, the term is equally appropriate when applied to the confrontations which took place within the boxing ring. With such names as "Boston Strong Boy" John L. Sullivan, "Gentleman" Jim Corbett, "Manassa Mauler" Jack Dempsey and "Pittsburgh Kid" Billy Conn, the sport was dominated by the Irish until other immigrant minorities—or new to the ring—took over.

Irish Americans have left their fingerprints on both sides of the law—moral and legal. The religion they brought with them from across the ocean was both a source of pain and comfort. It is uncertain whether the Irish suffered in America because they were Irish or because they were Catholic. Most likely the combination. But they remained steadfast in their religious conviction, as they had when they were victims of English oppression in their homeland. And they quickly ascended to dominant positions in the hierarchy of the American Catholic church.

The Irish American also became identified with law enforcement. How many Irish actually entered the police forces is unknown, but the stereotypical police officer always came armed with a brogue. Some of the bad guys these cops were chasing were Irish American— at times in black cars with running boards, other times on horseback, riding under the names of Billy the Kid or Jesse James.

Hungry and unskilled, Irish immigrants eagerly sought the jobs which others did not want. "Paddys" built the railroads, mined the coal, and dug the canals. "Bridgets" cooked the meals, cleaned the houses, and raised the children of the middle and upper classes. About the time that Irish Americans were assuming leadership positions in the unions, their brothers in eastern Pennsylvania were resurrecting vigilante methods that had been used in Ireland against abusive landlords. The Molly Maguires represented a tragic effort to achieve justice for the men and children working in the coal mines— an effort which ended on the gallows.

While their years in Ireland had been a combination of heaven and hell, the early years in America for most Irish was purgatory. Suffering was nearly as great as it was across the ocean, but it lasted for only a generation or two, not a millennium.

And in good times and bad, there has been the comfort of *ceàd mile fáilte*—100,000 welcomes—at the local pub, a social center for the Irish of yesterday and today. The Irish pub is a phenomenon in America. No other ethic group is as readily identified as professional purveyors of good cheer. You'll find the occasional English pub, and the less occasional Scotch watering hole. For a short period of time, the German rathskeller provided a popular retreat. I've even found a Thai tavern in Maryland, but how many French, Italian, or Russian bars do you know?

The Hippocrene U.S.A. Guide to Irish America invites you to travel the paths taken by Irish Americans before you. There are byways, even highways, that we don't include in this book. Their absence can be attributed to limited space and, I reluctantly confess, knowledge. We can't do much about the space, but you can let me know about places I should add to the next edition.

The journey we have planned will take you to all parts of the land. And when you need a rest, as surely you will, there's likely to be an Irish pub just down the street and around the corner.

Slainte!
Russ Malone

Part I

St. Patrick's Day!

Nature seemed to sympathize with the feel-
ings of the exiles of Erin....Morning began
with ear-piercing fifes and spirit-stirring
drum [and] uniforms of green and gold and
bright scarlet fringes....The very beautiful
and appropriate banner...floated gaily on the
wind, and the steps of the volunteers and the
hearts of our citizens beat time to the music
of the Philadelphia band."

An Account of the Proceedings of the
Celebration of St. Patrick's Day, 1837
Anonymous

When the 200 citizens of Shamrock, Oklahoma, turn out to see Mrs. Jones, now in her eighth decade, march the parade down Ireland Street, they are carrying on a 250-year American tradition. This tradition, says John D. Crimmons in his 1902 publication *St. Patrick's Day*, can be traced back to March 17, 1737. Boston Protestants, "Irish gentlemen and merchants," celebrated the day by forming the Charitable Irish Society.

Twenty years later, during the French and Indian Wars, another celebration of the day was taking place at Fort William Henry, Lake George, New York. The French anticipated that this would be a great

17

time to attack. A forced march from Ticonderoga brought the French to the fort by the evening of March 17, 1757. The garrison holding the fort, including a large numer of Irish, took a break from their St. Patrick's Day festivities and forced the French to retreat, leaving with a much smaller force than they came with.

The first written report of a celebration of the day in New York was published by the *Mercury* in 1762. It told of a gathering at the home of John Marshall at Mt. Pleasant.

In 1763, St. Patrick's Day was celebrated at Fort Pitt, now Pittsburgh. Extra grog was issued to the men to "drown the shamrock." Capt. S. Ecuyer stood in for "Crogham" in preparing the daily report: "We had St. Patrick's fetes in every manner so that Crogham could not write by this express."

In 1766, the New York papers reported that the Day was ushered in with fifes and drums and the evening, at the house of Mr. Barden, was passed with the presentation of twenty toasts. The nineteenth toast spoken was, "May the Enemies of Ireland never eat the Bread nor drink the Whiskey, but be tormented with Itching without the benefit of Scratching."

It is known that the day was commemorated by both sides during the Revolutionary War. March 17, 1776, provided the Irish Americans in Boston with particular satisfaction. It was on this day that Gen. Henry Knox, son of an Irish immigrant and member of the Charitable Irish Society, surprised the British at Dorchester Heights and drove them from the city. Gen. George Washington had selected "Boston" as the password of the day and "St. Patrick" as the countersign. The victory is marked by the Dorchester Heights National Historic Site.

The New York *Gazette* observed that St. Patrick's Day 1779 was greeted with the "accustomed Hilarity." The parade was led by the Volunteers of Ireland, formed that day to help the British. By the following year, the Irish Volunteers were switching to the side of the revolutionists in such large numbers that their commander was offering 10 guineas for the head of any "deserter," but only 5 guineas for each man returned alive.

On March 16, 1780, Washington took note of the proceedings

of the Parliament of Ireland, which he said was taking steps "calculated to remove those heavy and tyrannical oppressions...and to restore to a brave and generous People their ancient Rights and Freedom." Accompanying his proclamation to the army at Morristown, New Jersey, was the order that "all Fatigue and Working Parties cease for tomorrow, the 17th, a day held in particular Regard by the People of that Nation." Extra rum was issued.

The following year, Col. Israel Angell of the 2nd Rhode Island regiment wrote of "a great parade this day with the Irish," held at West Point.

By the late 1700s, the first St. Patrick's Day celebration had been recorded in South Carolina, Maryland, and Kentucky. In 1771, the *Gazette and County Journal* stated that the day was celebrated by a number of Charleston gentlemen "with mirth and jollity, ever conspicuous to the natures of that country." The day was commonly observed in Baltimore with parades, banquets, and balls. In 1798, the *Baltimore Telegraph* reported that the parade started in the morning with Captain Stewart's Irish brigade and Captain Keating's Irish grenadiers, accompanied by two pieces of cannon. They marched to Federal Hill where three volleys of cannon were fired. "Afterwards, they partook of an elegant entertainment at Captain Stewart's, where mirth and universal good humor prevailed at the festive board."

The New York *Journal and Patriotic Register* published a "Song on the Anniversary of St. Patrick, 1788." The first stanza read:

> *Ye Sons of St. Patrick, come jovially near;*
> *To the banners of Bacchus resort,*
> *On this solemn feast to Irishmen dear,*
> *To mirth consecrated and sport.*
> Matthew Carey

Through the 19th century, celebrations of St. Patrick's Day continued to grow in number, spreading to most cities by the mid-1800s. St. Louis celebrated its first St. Patrick's Day in 1820. San Patricio, founded by several hundred Irish in the late 1820s, became the first county recognized in the Republic of Texas on

March 17, 1836. And on March 17, 1843, the Providence, Rhode Island, papers reported that the parade by the Hibernian Orphan Society stretched one-third mile as it marched to St. Patrick's church. The large influx of Irish in the latter half of the century stimulated further growth in celebrations of the day.

But St. Patrick's Day, like the history of Irish America, has not been without problems. In the 18th century, the "stuffed Paddy" was an effigy used to insult the Irish. It was a figure of a man, grotesquely fat, sometimes with a face of a pig. Crimmins reported that George Washington, at Valley Forge in 1778, observed that some of the soldiers were displaying a "stuffed Paddy" to which the Irish were responding with ire and fists. Washington stopped the fracas by announcing that he, too, was a "lover of St. Patrick's Day," then giving out extra rations of grog. Soon the men "were merry and good friends."

The following St. Patrick's Day, a crowd of unruly men gathered in St. Mary's cemetery in Philadelphia, drinking, singing, and ridiculing the Irish. Some Irish and French soldiers in the American army decided to show their distaste for the "desecration" by shooting at the carousers. Many were wounded, but the judge dismissed all charges against the soliders when he learned the circumstances.

Recent years have witnessed the development of a new controversy. In 1992, ILGO, the Irish Lesbian and Gay Organization, applied for permission to march under its banner in New York's St. Patrick's Day parade. The parade is organized by the Ancient Order of Hibernians, an Irish Catholic association. The ILGO request, first made in 1991, set off a series of events which have divided Hibernians and other Irish Americans. It has enmeshed the Archbishop of New York, Cardinal John J. O'Connor; New York Mayor David Dinkins; Brooklyn District Attorney Charles "Joe" Hynes; Police Commissioner Ray Kelly; the Human Rights Commission; and Judge Kevin Duffy, among others.

The 1993 New York St. Patrick's Day parade was held, and ILGO did not march in it. Meanwhile, in Boston, an organization of gays and lesbians marched in the parade for the second year. They were greeted with some cheers, but more jeers. Meanwhile, across the seas, gay and lesbian organizations participated without controversy in parades held in Dublin, Cork, and Galway.

Here are excerpts from two letters on the subject written to the editor of *The Irish Voice*:

> *Editor: The fact that homosexuals and heterosexuals have marched side by side in the St. Patrick's Day parade for years under various organizational banners—possibly since 1762—escapes attention in the current brou-ha-ha. Why the breakdown on a sexual basis now? ...if division based on orientation is the order of the day, only four groupings are necessary: homosexual, heterosexual, bisexual and asexual. (January 26, 1993)*

> *Editor: Over eight centuries ago, England conquered Ireland, because the clans didn't unite against a common foe. As a result, the Irish lost Ireland. Today, we have various factions fighting over the parade: the Hibernians and Cardinal O'Connor vs. the Irish Lesbian and Gay Organization and Mayor Dinkins. We also have the Hibernians vs. the Hibernians. Today, we could lose the parade. Is this worth it? (April 6, 1993)*

The effect of this dispute on the parade is hard to measure. Attendance at the parades in New York and Boston was down, but whether this was due to the controversy or the weather is unknown. What is known is that the war is not over. What is also known is that the more than 250 years history of commemoration of St. Patrick's Day in America will continue. The parade may be embroiled in controversy at this time, but St. Patrick's Day is not.

St. Patrick's Day is unique. Its roots are in Ireland, but Americans of all nationalities celebrate it with festivities including more than 125 parades throughout the country. It is a day when Americans, who would "never" take a drink before the cocktail hour, think nothing of stopping by Birraporetti's in Houston for a cool one at dawn. But in Ireland, the people are at Mass, and until recent years, the pubs were closed. It is a day of distinctly Irish identity, but members of all ethnic groups wear the green. It is a day honoring the patron saint of Ireland—even though the saint is English.

But, Leapin' Leprechauns, who's going to tell 40,000,000 Irish Americans and their friends that they're wrong!

Trial, Tragedy...

I met with Napper Tandy, and he took me
  by the hand,
And he said, "How's poor ould Ireland,
  and how does she stand?"
She's the most distressful country that iver
  yet was seen,
For they're hangin' men an' women there
  for the wearin' o' the Green.

Anonymous
The Wearin' of the Green

*T*he Queen was dead. Elizabeth Tudor had finally died. But her death had come too late to help her enemies, the Irish earls, and six days too early to let her savor the achievement of one of her most cherished goals—the conquest of Ireland.

The Tudor dynasty, founded in 1485, consisted of five monarchs over a 118-year span. It is, on the whole, treated kindly by historians, who have given less attention to the founder, Henry VII, than to his son, Henry VIII, and his three children. These four have titillated readers throughout the centuries as much with their personal peccadilloes as their political prowess. Henry VIII, who spearheaded the family's expanded efforts to crush the Irish, beheaded Elizabeth's mother, Anne Boleyn, when he determined that she had been overly generous to some of the men of his court. Subsequently, he divorced one of Elizabeth's four stepmothers and decapitated a second. Elizabeth's tubercular half-brother, Edward VI, died at the age of 16 after sitting weakly on the throne for six years. Her half-sister, Mary I, best known by her unbecoming sobriquet, Bloody Mary, ruled for only five years. She devoted much of her energy to the pursuit of Philip II, King of Spain, who coveted the English throne, but not Mary. She also fantasized a pregnancy, which was heralded throughout both kingdoms, but never bore fruit.

Yet, by 1603, this dysfunctional family managed to succeed where previous predators had failed—they conquered Ireland.

The wonder is not that Ireland fell, but that it stood so long against the hordes of invaders. Unlike the rest of Europe, Ireland never had been united, although it had more than its share of kings and queens. The number of monarchs reigning at one time or another in Ireland has been estimated to be as high as 200. It is a rare Irish American who can not claim a drop of royal blood without a fair chance of being right. There was a hierarchy of kings ascending from petty kings and over kings to high kings. Petty kings paid tribute to the over kings and the over kings paid tribute to the high kings. But the over kings had limited power over petty kings and none over the petty kings' subjects. The high king, or provincial king, frequently did exert authority, and he was held responsible for the protection of the Church.

An integral part of reigning was warring. The "fighting Irish" is a term which has been well, if not always wisely, earned by the Irish throughout their history on both sides of the ocean. But it was not until the end of the 8th century that outsiders joined in the fray.

Ireland, of course, had been visited long before the 8th century. The first visitors could have walked over to England from Scandinavia, a walk made possible by the land connection which existed in 6000 B.C. From Britain it is thought that they crossed over narrow straits of water to Antrim and Wicklow in Northern Ireland. These Middle Stone Age people—Mesolithic—left only limited cues to their culture. They apparently were controlled by their environment, competing with animals for what food existed.

More is known about the new Stone Age people—Neolithic—who date to around 3000 B.C. They were masters of their environment as planters, herdsmen, and craftsmen. Among the more impressive artifacts they left are the large stone—megalithic—tombs found in many parts of Ireland and the Continent.

By 2000 B.C. other visitors were arriving, visitors who had learned the art of shaping metals into tools and jewelry. The Bronze Age was brought to Ireland by people who were searching for metallic ores.

The stage was set. The curtain raised and the Celts charged onto the Irish scene. Large, fierce, fair of skin, red of hair, the Celts who had swept across Europe arrived in Ireland to assume their role as rulers of the realm. By 150 B.C., the Celts were settled into their new home, having come in two waves, one from Northern Britain, and another from Spain. They brought with them a new metal, iron, and a new language (Celtic) from which the current Irish language is derived, and a dialect (Q-Celt), which is distinguishable from that spoken in Scotland and Wales. More than 100 tribes fanned out over the country, establishing their kingdoms of petty kings, over kings, high king and several lower social classes.

The kingdoms of Ireland differed from those which developed in Europe in several ways. The royalty consisted of four generations of males, any one of whom was a candidate to succeed the king. Below the king were the nobles, followed by the priests (Druids) and lawyers (brehons). The Druids included among their skills the ability to foretell the future. Poets were honored; artisans, only slightly less so. War was a continual activity, sometimes lasting for years, sometimes for an afternoon. Brehons, regardless of what tribe they belonged to, were free to rove among all tribes, even those at war with one another.

This was the Ireland into which Christianity was introduced in the fifth century A.D. St. Patrick's arrival marked the beginning of Irish history, since he wrote in Latin the first documents known to have been authored in Ireland. Ireland had an earlier written language, Ogham (pronounced *ahm*), an alphabet of lines and notches usually used for short inscriptions, especially on tombstones.

When St. Patrick came to Ireland in 432 A.D. as a bishop, he returned to an island which he had left as a runaway slave. A native of Roman Britain, Patrick had been captured by Irish raiders at the age of 16. He tended sheep in the west of Ireland until he escaped to France, where he may have obtained his ecclesiastical education. Responding to a vision, he returned to Ireland. Few people can visit Ireland only once.

In Ireland, Patrick is credited with converting the people to Catholicism. One of his most famous converts was Cormac, the King of Cashel. This conversion took place very late in St. Patrick's life, when he was using a staff to help him walk. The story is told that when conducting the baptismal ceremony, he leaned heavily on his staff. Unknown to Patrick, it was resting on the king's foot. The staff penetrated the foot causing great pain. The king, believing this to be part of the ritual, repressed a scream. St. Patrick conducted many other conversions; few among the observers at Cashel.

Part of St. Patrick's success is attributed to his ability to blend Christian teaching with some of the mystical beliefs and practices which had been part of Celtic culture. His choice of the shamrock to explain the trinity recognized the Celtic connection to natural products of the land.

The kings, while not letting their new faith interfere with their daily activities, including warfare, were generous in their gifts to the clergy, enabling the building of magnificent churches and monasteries. These became centers for intellectual pursuits. While the rest of Europe was submerged in the dark ages, Ireland was enjoying its greatest period of intellectual enlightenment, attracting many scholars from the continent.

Then the Vikings came not to learn, but to plunder. As the 8th century drew to an end, Vikings struck along the coast of Ireland, looting and pillaging and carrying away the Irish as slaves. As the century progressed, these Norsemen advanced farther and farther into the country. In order to protect themselves and their possessions, the clergy erected round towers with several floors and an entrance high above the ground. When the Vikings threatened, they would climb a ladder to the entrance, pull it up, and continue this procedure with each level of the tower. This strategy worked well at first. Then the invaders discovered a way to get the churchmen out of the tower. Fire.

Through time, the Vikings built many towns, including Dublin, and intermarried with the Irish. They became more and more involved with Irish affairs, to the point where they joined this or that king in his battles. When the illustrious Brian Boru—arguably the only high king (he preferred the title "emperor") to unite most of Ireland—defeated the Vikings outside of Dublin in 1014, he also defeated their allies, the soldiers of the Irish king of Leinster. Boru achieved his victory with the help of Viking tribes. This marked the end of the Viking wars in Ireland, shifting the focus of aggression to Irish Britain. It might also have ended the Irish internal wars, except that Brian Boru died from wounds sustained in what is called "Brian's Battle."

Now let me tell you the story of a lovely Irish queen and the two warrior kings who vied for her love, one her husband, one her lover. It's a tale of honor and dishonor; seduction and abduction; death and destruction; kingdoms won and lost. It's also the story of how the Normans came to Ireland.

Dervorgilla was a princess of Meath, a wealthy inland province. She was the wife of Tighearnan O'Rourke, the one-eyed king of Brefine. O'Rourke aspired to become king of Meath, but he had a problem. Another warrior king, Dermot MacMurrough, king of Leinster, had the same desire. They could not come to an amicable agreement, so MacMurrough abducted O'Rourke's wife. But was it abduction? It certainly sounded that way as MacMurrough galloped off, Dervorgilla in tow, sobbing hysterically. Or was it seduction? There are those who claim that Dervorgilla had actually enticed MacMurrough into carrying her away. Perhaps this behavior could be dismissed as simple youthful indiscretion, except that all of the participants in this escapade were in their forties. In any event, husband O'Rourke wasn't happy. He vowed to get his wife back. Devorgilla returned to him the following year, and thirteen years later, O'Rourke had his chance for retribution. When his friend and ally Rory O'Connor became high king, O'Rourke used his influence to have his old enemy dethroned. Now, it was Dermot MacMurrough who wasn't happy. He sought help from King Henry II, the Norman ruler of England, to get his throne back. Henry liked the idea. He had thought about invading Ireland when Pope Adrian IV, the only English pope—for which Ireland has reason to be grateful—had generously given Ireland to Henry. The Pope had done so in his position as "lord of all the islands of the sea."

Henry didn't want to get personally involved with MacMurrough's invasion, but he granted him the authority to raise an army. Foremost among the Normans to join him was Strongbow, the Earl of Pembroke, who gave his help on two conditions. First, he would receive the hand of MacMurrough's daughter in marriage, and second, he would succeed MacMurrough as king upon his death.

Fortunately for MacMurrough, Strongbow's men were successful. They defeated high king O'Connor, and MacMurrough was restored to his kingdom. Unfortunately for MacMurrough, he died shortly thereafter, and Strongbow became king. Strongbow was so successful that Henry II decided he should invade Ireland and show everyone he was the real king.

The Normans arrived, and they stayed. They built towns and cathedrals. They settled in to their new land. The English parliament attempted to keep them English by forbidding them to dress like the Irish or speak like the Irish. However, as invaders before and after them, they intermarried with the Irish and ultimately became Irish. (If the Irish kings had devoted their energies to ousting the Normans rather than killing one another, they probably would have succeeded.) But as it was, things were rather calm. Calm, that is, for Ireland.

When Henry VIII ascended the throne of England, he initiated an effort to remove Ireland as a threat to Britain. Henry feared that Ireland would become a channel through which foreign enemies could attack him. Certainly, Ireland had conspired with France and Spain in the past. Henry VIII also wanted to expand the holdings of England to spread his religion—the Church of England he established when he broke with the Pope in order to divorce his first wife, Catherine of Aragon, to marry Anne Boleyn.

Henry hoped to achieve his goals in Ireland peaceably, but some of the Irish earls did not cooperate. Thomas Fitzgerald, earl of Kildare, (known as Silken Thomas because of the colorful scarves he wore) and some of his friends rebelled. They were defeated when Henry's men attacked them at Maynooth Castle. They were given the "pardon of Maynooth"—they were executed. So much for Henry's "peaceable" efforts.

In 1541, Henry accepted the crown of Ireland offered by the English-dominated Irish parliament. Trying, more successfully this time, politics of peaceful coercion, he achieved the obeisance of many of the Irish earls. When Henry died in 1547 he left his son, Edward VI, an Ireland which had a new coinage, a new symbol—the harp—a land which had largely resisted the Reformation.

Edward VI, weak and sickly, did little to carry on the Irish campaign during the few years he wore the crown. His half-sister, Mary, was more successful. She expanded the domination of Ireland during the five years that she ruled, but as the Catholic daughter of Catherine of Aragon, Henry's divorced first wife, she reversed the Reformation in Ireland.

Elizabeth, the last of the Tudors, ruled for 45 years and completed the work begun by her father. She used her armies to accomplish what negotiation failed to achieve. At the battle of Kinsale in 1603, the nine years war finally ended with the defeat of the Ulster earls. The earls had fervently prayed for Elizabeth's death, but when it came only days before the battle of Kinsale ended, it was too late.

With the conquest of Ireland, the old Irish world came to an end. The "flight of the earls" to Europe in 1607 removed Irish leadership and left the people to the mercy of the English.

Over the years, ownership of the land changed by the simple process of "plantation," taking land from the Irish and giving it to the English. The idea was that the Irish would be restricted to small sections of the country. In fact, the Irish continued to work the lands, but as tenant farmers, not as owners. The "Old English," although Catholic, were English by descent and loyal to the English crown. They had lost control of the government, but still owned one-third of the land. They resisted plantation. When Charles I came to power, he needed their money for foreign wars, so he supported their claims to their lands. When the wars ended, he withdrew his support.

Things could not have been worse. But, thanks to Oliver Cromwell, they became so. England's parliament, disenchanted with Charles I, expressed its dissatisfaction by removing his head. The monarchy was abolished, and Oliver Cromwell became the uncrowned king. Unhappy with the failure of the Irish to accede in great numbers to giving up their religion, and upset by tales that the Irish had been less than courteous to the English who took their lands, Cromwell mounted an army and invaded Ireland. He was intent on teaching the Irish a lesson they wouldn't forget. In fact, an estimated 30,000 Irish had precious little time to remember—he slaughtered them at Drogheda in 1649.

Eleven years later, Cromwell was dead and Charles II had become king. Some of the lands confiscated under Cromwell were returned to the Irish. Greater progress was expected when, after a reign of twenty-five years, Charles was succeeded by his Catholic brother, James II. As it turned out, James was more of a problem than a help. He was driven from his throne by William of Orange. James fled to Ireland, William followed, James escaped again, and the Irish were left to the wrath of William. It looked like they were going to do all right when they signed the Treaty of Limerick, which assured them the ownership of their lands and the right to worship as they chose. But instead of these freedoms, they were subjected to the notorious Penal Laws, promulgated by the English parliament. Catholics could not vote, hold office, intermarry with Protestants, serve in any legal profession, or own a horse worth more than 5 pounds. Upon their death, they were not allowed to will their land to the oldest son, which was the traditional way to hold on to the land in one parcel, but were forced to split it up among all male heirs. Priests were not allowed to say Mass or leave their parishes. The Catholics were required to pay enormous rent for small patches of land to live on and raise potatoes.

The Irish seemed finally and completely subjugated, but once again, as with the Normans and the Norsemen, the Protestants who had been placed in Ireland gradually became Irish and wanted independence from English domination. "Freedom from England, an independent Ireland" became their cry, and Protestant Theobald Wolfe Tone, their leader.

Tone was welcomed by both the northern Ulsters and the southern provinces. He and his compatriots founded the Belfast Society of United Irishmen and the Dublin Society of United Irishmen. The Catholics became active again, held a convention in Dublin, and formally requested that England abolish the penal laws which remained on the books. The English parliament responded favorably and conditions improved. Catholics were even granted the right to vote. England's motivation was born not of Christian sympathy, but from the expectation that they soon would be at war again with their historic enemy, the French, who were at the time ridding themselves of King Louis XVI and his "let them eat cake" queen, Marie Antoinette.

The Irish wanted more reform, so they sought support from France. They offered the French a warm welcome to use their isle as a jumping off spot for an invasion of England. Wolfe Tone passed this invitation on to a French agent who had come to Ireland. The agent was accompanied by a friend who, in turn, passed the information on to the English. The agent was imprisoned and committed suicide. Wolfe Tone, who was not found guilty of treason, went to America and from there to France, where once again he urged the French to move troops into Ireland. France sent a fleet, but like other fleets sent by Spain and France, it failed in its mission.

The United Irishmen remained determined that Ireland would achieve its independence and in 1798 rose in armed rebellion. France by this time was busy invading Egypt and was of little help. The insurrection was put down. Wolfe Tone was captured by the English, found guilty, and committed suicide. The name of this illustrious patriot has become popularized in recent years by an Irish folk singing group known as the Wolfe Tones.

In 1880, England established the Act of Union, formally incorporating Ireland as a part of England. Now, surely Ireland would be subdued, but three years later Robert Emmet led a new rebellion. It failed, and he was executed.

In 1823 Daniel O'Connor began a focused and peaceful effort to achieve Catholic emancipation. He founded the Catholic Association. All members were asked to donate a penny a month to the cause. In 1828, O'Connor was elected to Parliament, and a year later, he accomplished one of his goals—the restoration of all important rights to Catholics. His second goal was the repeal of the Act of Union. He was not successful, and in 1847, O'Connor died.

One of O'Connor's legacies was the establishment of the Young Ireland organization, a group of young men who were involved in an aborted insurrection in the midst of the great famine. One Young Irelander, Thomas Francis Meagher, will turn up later as an illustrious Irish-American soldier and politician.

In the Ireland of the 1800s the potato stood between life and death for many. It could be grown in quantity on the small portions of land available to the tenant farmer. In 1845, when a disease was discovered on the potato crop, anxiety swept the land. In 1846, it became clear that a major blight had struck and panic ensued. As the disease lasted through several years, it caused the death of 1,000,000 people and the emigration of another million, most of them to America.

Films

Captain Boycott, Stewart Granger, Kathleen Ryan, Robert Donat(as Parnell). Irish farmers attempt to combat brutality of English landlords in 19th century; effort fails, but introduces new word into vocabulary. (1947)

Cromwell, Richard Harris, Alec Guinness. Sweeping historical drama about Cromwell's effort to dethrone Charles. (1970, video)

Far and Away, Tom Cruise, Nicole Kidman. Depicts Ireland of the 1800s, coffin ships, problems upon arrival in America, and Oklahoma land rush. Spectacular photography. (1992, video)

The Field, Richard Harris, John Hurt. Ireland of the 1930s and a man's fight to retain his land. (1990, video)

Parnell, Clark Gable, Mryna Loy. Biography of the great Irish nationalist was major flop as a movie. (1937)

Private Life of Henry VIII, Charles Laughton. Academy Award-winning performance by Laughton. (1933, video)

Private Lives of Elizabeth and Essex, Bette Davis, Errol Flynn. Not good history, but very entertaining. (1939, video)

Young Bess, Jean Simmons, Stewart Granger, Charles Laughton. Elizabeth survives a traumatic childhood to become queen. (1953)

...*Tribulation and Triumph*

Bring me your tired, your poor,
Your huddled masses yearning
  to breathe free,
The wretched refuse of your teeming shore,
Send these, the homeless, tempest-tost
  to me...

But don't send your Irish!— Perhaps this line should have been added by Emma Lazarus before her poem was placed on the Statue of Liberty.

Americans did not greet the Irish with open arms when they arrived in the late 19th century. Signs appeared in store fronts saying, "Help Wanted. No Irish need Apply." Pennsylvania put a tax on citizens who imported Irish servants. The Irish were not welcomed in the "better" residential areas or among the "better" people. It was not simply a matter of money. Rose Kennedy, the mother of a future president of the United States and the financial beneficiary of husband Joe's gotten and ill-gotten fortune, fifty years later was said to lament that society still did not "accept" them.

The typical Irish immigrant, however, did make immediate contacts after leaving Ireland. He found instant "friends" in Liverpool, from which many Irish sailed to America, and he found them in New York, port of call for most of the immigrants who survived the foul conditions on the "coffin" ships. These contacts had one goal in mind: get whatever money they could from the naive newcomer, steal her purse, hijack his suitcases, take them to a rooming house where they would pay exorbitant rates for abominable space.

There were others, too, who welcomed the Irish. Those who had work to be done which others did not want to do. The Irish would do any task which would earn them survival money. The women, "Bridgets" they were called, were able to get jobs as nannies and maids. This work assured them respectable housing and food. The men, "Paddys," were most likely to be employed as laborers, mining coal or digging canals. These men and their families lived in hovels, gathered together in "shanty towns." Irish were accused of grouping together, rather than mixing with others. It was only with their fellow Irish, however, that they could be sure they were welcome.

The Irish, most of whom had been farmers in the old country, brought with them few skills. But they were accustomed to working long and hard. Their new bosses appreciated this willingness and took advantage of it. Since there were no child labor laws, and since the families desperately needed money, it was common to see small children working along with the men in the coal mines of Pennsylvania. My father was one of them.One of thirteen children, he left school in the 6th grade to take his place, along with his brothers, in the coal mines of Allegheny County. After working long hours, six days a week, in damp, dusty, dangerous underground areas, often not high enough to let a man stand, the workers would receive only a fraction of the pay they had earned. As Tennessee Ernie Ford sang in later years, "I owe my soul to the company store."

The mining companies owned stores where the men were expected to shop for their food, clothing, and other needs. Although the items sold at excessive prices, the company made it easy to buy, by offering charge accounts; and easy to pay, by taking the money out of the weekly earnings. With the right connections, like an uncle who ran the store, they'd even hire one of the miner's underage daughters to clerk in the store forbelow average wages. My sister earned a few dollars that way one summer.

What was good for the company was bad for the miners. The merchandise in the company stores was so overpriced that the miner would receive little cash for his labor, too little to enable him to shop for competitively priced items elsewhere.

To many of the miners, working conditions in the mines were no better than those in their homeland, working for the landowners. So they fell back upon the same methods of dealing with the bosses that they had tried in Ireland. The Molly Maguires, a secret organization introduced in Ireland to fight corrupt landlords, was resurrected in the 1890s in the anthracite coal region of eastern Pennsylvania to fight for improved working conditions. The ultimate result of their struggle was the same as in Ireland. Failure. By the time the campaign ended, nine mine foremen were dead, and twenty Irish-American miners dangled from the gallows.

Although the Molly Maguires failed, the Irish did not. They mastered different ways of coping, and soon Irish names were showing up high in the ranks of organized labor. Among them were George Meany, head of the American Federation of Labor; Terence Powderly, leader of the Knights of Labor; Mike Quill, founder of the Transport Workers of America; and Joe Curran, president of the National Maritime Union.

Paralleling the climb to the top of the labor force was the Irish move into the hierarchy of the American Roman Catholic Church. Religion, in the new world as well as the old, was a source of both comfort and anguish. While generally more civilized in their approach than the English, Americans did not welcome Catholics, either. I say, generally, because America, too, had its church burnings. There is a question as to whether the Irish Catholic was discriminated against because of nationality or religion. Most likely each was a problem, but usually they were thought of as one and the same. To be Irish was to be Catholic. That concept gave rise to the expression "Scotch-Irish." Many of the Irish who had come to America before the late 19th century, were from Ulster—northern Ireland—and were not Catholic. Many of these early immigrants preferred to be distinguished from the impoverished new Irish, and the term "Scotch-Irish" helped them to accomplish that goal.

They succeeded so well that many Americans today believe that John Kennedy was the first Irish-American president of the United

States. This is a source of irritation to some Northern Irish who know that the first Irish president preceded Kennedy by more than 150 years. And he came from Ulster. However, John Kennedy does have the honor of being the first *Catholic* Irish American to serve as president.

The Irish won early respect by doing what they did so well on an amateur and professional level—fighting. In 1863, the Civil War broke out, and the Irish responded to the call for volunteers in relative numbers unmatched by any other ethnic group. Although Irish could be found wearing gray and blue uniforms, they were more plentiful on the side of the North. First, the North is where most of the Irish lived, New York, Massachusetts, Pennsylvania. Second, their old nemesis, the British, were known to be aiding the cause of the Confederacy.

One hero of the Civil War was Thomas Francis "The Sword" Meagher, who as a Young Irelander rebelled against the British and was exiled to the then penal colony of Australia. Meagher's stay in Australia was brief. Shortly after arrival, he shipped out for America, arriving in time to recruit and lead his Irish Brigade into the pages of history.

So many Irish were killed in the Civil War, that the Irish community rioted when a draft was announced and the number of Irish to be conscripted in New York was out of proportion to their numbers. A newspaper editor, studying the list of men killed at the Battle of Fredericksburg, urged an investigation as to why Irish names appeared so frequently on the death rolls.

When the war ended, the Irish had lost many of their men, but they had found respect, at least among the military ranks. Even the Irish invasions of Canada, a misguided effort to force Britain to abandon their forced union with Ireland, did not damage their reputation as admirable warriors. The failure of their aggression was more akin to low comedy than to high tragedy.

The Irish American did not confine his fighting to the battlefield and draft riots. Like other downtrodden groups before and after, he at times took out his frustration on those who had even less than he—the Chinese in Los Angeles and the blacks in New York. At the time, these even less fortunate groups were competing with the Irish for the only jobs open to them.

Fighting also took place in the ring. Sometimes, in the pubs, the ring was made up by crowds of people surrounding the fighters. The Irish dominated the early history of American professional boxing— John L. Sullivan, Gentleman Jim Corbett, Jack Dempsey, Gene Tunney, and later, after the golden period of Irish boxers had ended, brief moments of glory with the "Pittsburgh Kid" Billy Conn.

Among those things that the Irish learned from the British was the value of a verbal virtuosity to help them cope with their oppressor. Elizabeth I is credited with giving meaning to the word "blarney." She was frustrated by her attempts to win more than verbal concessions from the Irish Lord Blarney. He would say the things she wanted to hear, but not do the things she wanted done. When reading his latest response, she would cry out in great umbrage, "This is just more Blarney!"

The new Irish Americans had learned their political lessons well and soon applied them to their local governments. Within a generation they had won positions of considerable influence in many cities, including Boston, New York, Philadelphia, and Chicago. Even today, when their political power has waned, candidates find it helpful to find an Irish ancestor in their family tree. Bill Clinton is among the latest to announce that his family has Irish branches.

The Irish American also won respectability through his identification with law enforcement. Police forces all along the Atlantic seaboard were heavily populated with Irish cops. Before the 20th century ended there was an Irish-American woman seated on the United States Supreme Court.

What is not generally known is that the Irish American was active on the other side of the law, as well. Although many of the Irish names associated with the Mafia, such as Frank Costello, were aliases, some of the best known outlaws of American history were Irish Americans. Billy the Kid, Jesse James, Frank James, and, perhaps, Butch Cassidy had Irish roots. There were notorious gangsters, like Vince "Baby Killer" Coll and Owney Madden, George "Machine Gun" Kelly,

Charles Arthur "Pretty Boy" Floyd, and John Herbert Dillinger were among hoods appearing on wanted posters.

Probably the earliest inroad that gained the Irish power in their new country was the Church. Many Catholic priests came to America, and for decades, Irish names predominated in seminaries. Finally, the Irish influence in the American Catholic Church became so pervasive that leaders of other ethnic groups, like the Germans and Poles, demanded equity. Even today, the bishops of Chicago, San Francisco, and New York are Irish Americans.

The entertainment world helped shape the image of the Irish American, for better and for worse. Some vaudeville entertainers made their living by perpetuating the negative portrait of Irish as lazy, fighters, and drunks, which had been fostered by prejudice. The more successful entertainers offered an image of wit and charm, while singing sentimental songs. George M. Cohan, singer, dancer, composer, was one of the most talented of the early 20th century entertainers. He popularized many Irish-American tunes and helped polish the image of the Irish. It was most fitting that when James Cagney, movie super star before the phrase had been invented, won an Academy Award, it was not for his convincing portrayal of gangsters, but for his role of George M. Cohan in *Yankee Doodle Dandy.*

Cohan's and Spencer Tracy's and Pat O'Brien's and Bing Crosby's and Maureen O'Hara's portrayals of the Irish helped modify the negative stereotype of the Irish in America, but nothing to change the idea that the Irish are known to enjoy the surroundings of a drinking establishment. And well they didn't! The Irish pub is a noble part of the history of the Irish on both sides of the Atlantic. While a pint of dark, brooding Guinness will often be found in the hand of the Irish, the pub has traditionally been a social center for family and friends and remains so today in Ireland, where the entire family often visits the pub following Saturday evening Mass.

When the Irish come to America, one of the first places they head for companionship and help is the Irish pub. They find them in abundance in America, particularly in those areas to which the Irish continue to emigrate—Boston and New York. As in Ireland, the Irish pub usually offers one-hundred thousand welcomes, good conversation, traditional music, games, and, of course, a selection of Irish beers. Cards, popular in pubs in Ireland have been replaced in America by darts. And the emphasis in Irish-American pubs is less on family participation and more on adult interaction. I recently spent a week in Killala, a village on the northern coast of County Mayo. Killala has a population of about 800 people and, at last count, nine pubs. We can't match that ratio here in America, but in the chapter "The Happy Hours," I'll tell you about some Irish-American pubs—some great, many good, and just a few that you might want to avoid.

How did the Irish overcome all of the obstacles in their way to success in America? Most came only prepared to work the land, but they stayed in the cities. They came as Roman Catholics into a country which not only was essentially Protestant in the 19th century, but which was anti-Catholic by heritage. They were poor, unskilled, naive, and unwanted. Yet, within three generations they were leaders in every phase of American life. They had four very important assets which many other immigrants lacked. They spoke the language, they looked the same, they had mastered the political system, and they had learned to co-exist with the Anglo power structure. They invaded every aspect of American life, becoming so interwoven in the fabric that 150 years after the Great Famine, there are fears that they have lost their identity.

There is some evidence to support this contention. Although there are still some Irish communities, the Irish no longer live in ghettos by necessity. They are no longer categorized as servants, miners, or policemen. As they moved up, they moved out into all occupations. Even being Catholic does not restrict them any longer. John F. Kennedy and Sumpreme Court Justice Sandra Day O'Connor are proof of just how high an Irish American can climb.

Yet, there is much evidence to suggest that Irish Americans have not forgotten their roots. The number of books, calendars, records, newspapers, magazines, radio shows, festivals, social and cultural organizations, movies, special tours of Ireland, and merchandises—key rings, coats of arms, mugs, leprechauns and innumerable other items sold in Irish gift shops throughout the country—the thousands of Irish pubs, and the one out of five U.S. citizens who, selecting from more than 100 categories, identifies his and her heritage as Irish. When the Irish emigrate to America, they become Americans. But even several generations later, their descendants do not surrender their Irish heritage.

In succeeding chapters, we'll look more closely at the Irish Americans as they have shaped America in their image. We'll learn what they did and we'll go where they've been. It's a journey which will take us to the depths of despair and to the heights of success.

Film

Studs Lonigan. Christopher Knight, Jack Nicholson, Dick Foran. Life in a turn-of-the-century Chicago Irish neighborhood, based on James T. Farrell's classic. (1960, video)

Paddy and Bridget

Help Wanted
No Irish Need Apply
Boston Sign Company,
September 11, 1915

When we visited Mullingar, County Westmeath, we stayed with Mr. and Mrs. Cox, a delightful couple whose charm and humor could have been lifted from a script of a 1940s Bing Crosby movie. The Coxes manage one of Ireland's justifiably celebrated bed and breakfasts, where the food makes getting up in the morning an event to look forward to.

Our first night we ate Greville Arms, where the bartender asked if we knew Christy Hughes, owner of Washington, D.C.'s Four Provinces (see "The Happy Hours"). Christy is a buddy of the proprietor. Then the waiter announced that someone would like to buy us a drink. The "someone" turned out to be the Coxes. After dinner, we stopped by their table, where they were sitting with friends.

They told us about Tom Malone—a relative, perhaps? Tom was a grave digger who was either dead—I suppose that's what people might call a "busman's holiday"—or simply disappeared. There was more agreement on another bit of Malone news. It seems there was a large estate, now in ruins, once held by the Malones. Since my grandfather came from the Mullingar area, we took off the next morning to view the remains in the nearby village of Ballynacarrigy. With the help of the local historian, we found its many acres of land surrounded by a brick wall and an iron gate. For the next hour we explored the estate with its crumbling chapel and single wall hinting at the mansion that once dominated the region. Encircling the chapel was a cemetery, still being used, with one section fenced off for the dearly departed Malones and an open tract for the family servants and townspeople. A giant gnarled spreading oak guarded the entrance to the grounds. I could picture generations of Malone children scrambling through its branches. But the picture was out of focus.

Why would my grandfather exchange this comfortable life to dig coal hundreds of feet below the Pennsylvania ground? Although that mystery is yet to be solved, my ancestors, like other Irish of the 19th and 20th centuries came to the States with great hope, but few possessions, and fewer employable skills. Most of them had a desperate need for work, not just to survive, but to send money home to their families.

Often they found locating a job almost as difficult as making a living in the old country. They often heard the message, "No Irish Need Apply." The Irish were no more accepted by the established power structure in the States than they had been in Ireland, and they encountered here the same prejudice towards Catholicism that they had suffered overseas.

So the Irish built the canals, dug the coal, and worked in the steel mills and textile shops. When gold and silver were discovered in the West, the Irish were there to mine it. When the railroads crossed the nation, the Irish were there to lay the track. When the children and the homes of the wealthy needed attention, it was the Bridgets that got a job.

The Irish brought another valuable commodity with them across the seas. Experience surviving under tyrannical British overlords. The country had changed, and the work had changed, but the problems were the same—brutal and victimizing treatment. So the Irish drew upon their experience and looked to collective help to solve their problems. In the eastern Pennsylvania anthracite coal mine region, they even imported a name to identify themselves—the Molly Maguires, a secret off-shoot of the Irish brotherhood, the AOH—the Ancient Order of Hibernians. The AOH was going to bring about the end of child labor, unsafe working conditions, long working hours, and the usurper of their miserable wages—the notorious company store. History repeated itself and, as these movements had so often in Ireland, it failed, and the suspected members met their death on the gallows. In recent years, the alleged Molly Maguires—some say they existed only in the minds of the owners who wanted an excuse to keep miners in subjugation—were exonerated.

The Irish were much more successful in some of their other union activities. They are credited with leading the labor movement in the 19th century and continued their prominence into the 20th century. Terence Vincent Powderly (1849-1924) born of Irish immigrant parents began work on the railroads at age 13, later becoming a machinist. In the late 19th century, he served as president of the machinists' and blacksmiths' union. He moved on to become head of the Knights of Labor, the most powerful labor union of its day. In the 1930s, Joe Curran, a New York Irish American, founded and became the first president of the National Maritime Union. Thirty years later another New Yorker, Mike Quill (1905-1966), organized the Transport Workers of America. When the American Federation of Labor and Congress of Industrial Organizations merged into one gigantic union in 1955 (AFL-CIO), George Meany (1894-1980), whose grandfather emigrated during the great famine, was selected its president. Elizabeth Gurley Flynn (1890-19964) led many labor strikes as a member of the International Workers of the World, an extremist labor organization. She later became co-founder of the American Civil Liberties Union and head of the United States Communist Party. Mary Harris Jones (1830 to 1930), who emigrated from County Cork, was an active labor leader into her 90s. "Mother Jones," known as "the elder stateswoman" of the labor movement, died at 100.

Less known, but a man to whom we should all be grateful the first Monday in September, is Peter James McGuire (1852-1906). Called the "Father of Labor Day," he led the drive to establish the United Brotherhood of Carpenters and Joiners, was instrumental in the founding of the Federation of Organized Trades and Labor Unions, co-founded the American Federation of Labor, and in 1894 saw the culmination of his efforts to establish a national holiday honoring labor.

Although the image that the term "Irish immigrant" of the 18th and 19th centuries generally conjures up is of poor, brawling, boozing, shanty town habitues, the Irish were present in all socio-economic classes. An equally colorful vision is that of the smiling police officer, twirling his night stick and whistling an Irish tune as he walks his beat.

And there were the Irish who became businessmen, some who became proprietors of Irish pubs which served the social needs of the people, and a few, like the Mellons, who became enormously wealthy through business investments, particularly in banks. Nor did all the miners spend the rest of their days working underground. Some ended up with fabulous estates like James Flood (1850s) on Nob Hill in San Francisco and Mr. Brown and his wife, "Unsinkable Molly," who beat on the doors of Colorado society with bars of gold, or George Hearst, who founded the fortune that his son, William Randolph (1863-1951), eventually lost, or Tom Walsh (1880s) who bought a place in society with his fortune and an unhappy marriage for his daughter.

Other Irish used their inventive minds to come up with products which changed the world—the car, the submarine, the reaper, and the steam boat.

Today, when job discrimination has essentially ended for the Irish American, there are few people, even those of Irish descent, who are aware that as late as the second quarter of the 20th century, signs could be found saying: Help Wanted—No Irish Need Apply.

Films

Ford: The Man and the Machine, Cliff Robertson, Hope Lange. Life of Henry Ford, automotive genius. (1987, video)

Molly Maguires, Sean Connery, Richard Harris. Tragic efforts by

Irish Pennsylvania coal miners to improve labor conditions. (1970, video)

Nob Hill, Joan Bennett, George Raft. Musical drama hints at San Francisco's 19th century Nob Hill society. (1945)

Pittsburgh, John Wayne, Marlene Dietrich, Randolph Scott. John must choose between coal, steel, and Marlene. Sorry, Marlene. (1942)

Union Pacific, Barbara Stanwyck, Joel McCrea, Brian Donleavy. Stanwyck, complete with Irish brogue, in a story of the building of the railroad. (1939)

The Unsinkable Molly Brown, Debbie Reynolds, Harve Presnell. Musical about a woman wise enough to marry an Irishman who becomes rich from his share of the Comstock mine. (1964, video)

Up in Central Park, Deanna Durbin, Dick Haymes, Vincent Price. Irish Colleen takes on Boss Tweed and Tammany Hall. And who do you think wins? (1948)

Valley of Decision, Greer Garson, Gregory Peck. Lives of Irish-American coal miners in 1870 Pittsburgh. (1945, video)

Irish Nationality Room, University of Pittsburgh, designed, furnished and financed by the Irish government. *(Photo courtesy of University of Pittsburgh)*

Downey's, famed Philadelphia Irish pub and restaurant. *(Photo courtesy of Callahan Associates)*

Shamrock, OK, founded by Irish American Edwin L. Dunn in early
1900s, site of America's smallest St. Patrick's Day parade. *(Photo courtesy
of James Quintus)*

Hughes Log Cabin, Mount St. Mary's College, Emmitsburg, MD,
campus lodging of John Joseph Hughes, future Archbishop of New York
and builder of St. Patrick's Cathedral. *(Photo courtesy of Mount St.
Mary's College)*

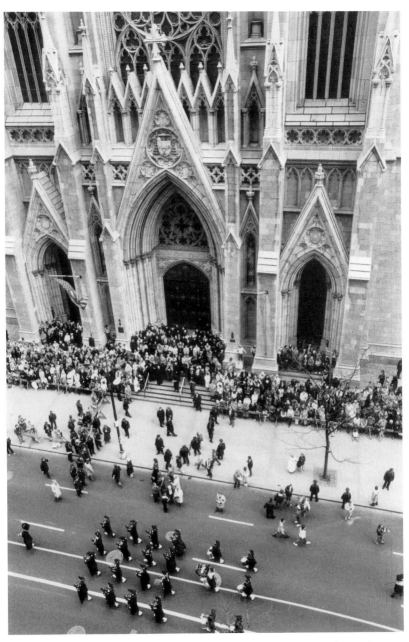

St. Patrick's Cathedral, New York City, built by John Joseph Hughes, and America's largest St. Patrick's Day parade. *(Photo courtesy of New York Convention and Visitors Bureau)*

ABOVE: The White House, Washington, DC, designed by the Dublin-born James Hoban, selected in competition with Thomas Jefferson. *(Photo courtesy of the Washington Convention & Visitors Association)*

RIGHT: John F. Kennedy Birthplace, Brookline, MA. JFK was born and spent his infancy in this seven room, one bath house, with his parents and three siblings. *(Photo courtesy of the National Park Service)*

ABOVE: Stephen Foster Memorial, Pittsburgh, honoring composer of "Oh, Susanna," and other famous American folk songs. *(Photo by Jim Burke, courtesy of University of Pittsburgh)*
BELOW: Jesse James Bank, Liberty, MO, site of bank robbery by Jesse and Frank James. *(Photo courtesy of Jesse James Bank)*

Fredericksburg Battlefield, VA, site of last major Civil War engagement by Irish Brigade, 1862. *(Photo courtesy of National Archives)*

Montpelier, Orange, VA, home and grave sites of James Madison, fourth president of the United States, and Dolley Payne Madison.

Eckley Miners' Village, Hazleton, PA, 19th century anthracite "patch," was the site for the 1970 filming of *The Molly Maguires.*

American Irish Historical Society, New York City, has a library and archive of 25,000 volumes.

Black, Scarlet and Green

In politics, as in religion, their numbers their
strong loyalties, their combativeness, and
their energies carried them to domination of
the organization. Thus, Irish America
brought forth bishops and politicians, not by
accident, but by the same devotion to power.
Edward Wakin
Enter the Irish American (1976)

*N*inety per cent of the Irish (in Ireland) attend Mass each week. That's if you count the men who stand outside the church smoking. Ireland today is moving slowly, very slowly, away from some of the controls which existed when Catholicism held, by law, a special place in the affairs of the country. But when the Irish sailed to the New World in the 19th century, they brought with them a strong bond with the Roman Catholic Church. Despite the concerted and bloody efforts made by England, particularly under Cromwell and the penal laws, to break the Irish ties with the Church of Rome, the Church survived on the Island and gained in numbers in the New World. Meanwhile, the power of the English in America was diminishing.

Both the Church and the newly arrived Irish gained from their relationship. The Catholic Church was in America before the Irish, but its numbers increased dramatically with their arrival in the 1850s.

As these numbers increased, so did the influence of the Irish in the Church hierarchy. The Church attracted large numbers of Irish to the priesthood, and the priests were moving up to positions of influence in the Church. By the mid-19th century, the bishops of Philadelphia and New York were Irish, and one-third of the priests had been born in Ireland. The greening of the Church continued through the century, reaching as high as one-half of all priests and three-quarters of the first 17 cardinals appointed by the Pope, including the first, John McCloskey (1810-1885). Understandably, nativists thought of Irish as Catholic and Catholic as Irish.

The first bishop, and ultimately the first archbishop in the United States, was John Carroll (1735-1815) of the prominent Baltimore Carrolls. He founded the first Roman Catholic university in the country, Georgetown University. There are colleges in Montana, Ohio, and Wisconsin which bear his name. Carroll also began the construction of the first Catholic cathedral in the United States, where he is buried today along with James Cardinal Gibbons.

The best known cathedral in the country is St. Patrick's Cathedral in New York City. It is also a monument to the dedication of Irish-American parishioners who raised the money, and Tyrone-born archbishop John Hughes (1797-1864), who initiated the construction.

Today, the presence of the Irish is still felt, but they no longer are in the majority. Irish Americans among the current 40 archbishops include: John O'Connor, New York; Roger Mahoney, Los Angeles; James Hickey, Washington, D.C.; John R. Quinn, San Francisco; Theodore McCarrick, Newark, New Jersey; and Edward McCarthy, Miami.

The Irish association with Catholicism was a major reason that Irish were persecuted, but the Irish also served as protectors for the Church. When, on one occasion, the nativists threatened to burn a Catholic church, they were advised by the local bishop that, in contrast to past behavior, further destruction would result in swift retribution by the Irish Americans. The church was not burned.

One of the best known names among the clergy is Father Flanagan. He was immortalized when Spencer Tracy portrayed him in the film *Boys Town* and again in *Men of Boys Town.* Father Edward J. Flanagan (1886-1948), of County Roscommon, established Boys Town as a home for troubled and abandoned children.

Wherever their parishioners went, the Church was sure to go, including the Civil War. Father William Corby, first gained prominence as chaplain to the 88th New York Infantry of the famed Irish Brigade, then went on to serve as president of the University of Notre Dame.

Following in his footsteps in World War I was Father Francis P. Duffy, chaplain of the Fighting 69th Regiment, famed for its Irish-Americans.

The Church also was involved in politics, generally as a quiet counselor and as a sideline to the principal work of tending to the flock. Father Charles Couglin (1891-1979) was a notorious exception. Sometimes considered the father of the electronic evangelists, he carried his communist phobia, Roosevelt-loathing campaign over the radio waves and throughout the country.

Many prefer to think of Bishop Fulton J. Sheen (1895-1979) as the "father of electronic evangelists." He achieved high ratings for his nationally televised weekly show. Although he never became a cardinal, he is interred with them today in New York's St. Patrick's Cathedral.

Irish and Catholic were not, of course, synonymous. The city of Berkeley, California, was named for Anglican bishop and philosopher, Dublin-born George Berkeley 1685-1753). Bishop Berkeley also was an architect of sorts, designing a most unusual home in Newport, Rhode Island. Wesley Chapel, the first Methodist church in America, was founded in New York City by Philip Embury (1728-1773) of County Limerick. Augusta Stone Church, Staunton, Virginia, was established by Irish Presbyterians in the mid-18th century. And Pine Hill (now Camden), New Jersey, was founded by Irish Quakers.

But these are exceptions. The history of Irish America and the history of the Catholic Church in the 19th and early 20th centuries were a tautly woven tapestry of black, scarlet, and green.

Films

Boys' Town, Spencer Tracy, Mickey Rooney. Tracy won Academy Award © and film was nominated for "best picture." (1938, video)

Men of Boys' Town, Spencer Tracy, Mickey Rooney. Continuing-story of Father Flanagan's Omaha, Nebraska, refuge. (1941, video)

Going My Way, Bing Crosby, Barry Fitzgerald, Frank McHugh. Winner of six Academy Awards: picture, actor (Crosby), supporting actor (Fitzgerald), script and director (Leo McCarey), and song (Johnny Burke and Jimmy Van Heusen). (1940, video)

Bells of St. Mary's, Bing Crosby, Ingrid Bergman, William Gargan, Ruth Donnelly, Una O'Connor. Father O'Malley back with a passel of Irish American actors, music by Robert Emmet Dolan, and Leo McCarey, director. (1945, video)

A Harvest of Glory

*Never were men so brave. They ennobled
their race by their splendid gallantry on that
desperate occasion. Though totally routed,
they reaped a harvest of glory.*
                    —Gen. Robert E. Lee
                    on conduct of Irish Brigade
                    at Fredericksburg (1862)

*T*he Irish earned their equality by giving their lives for their new homeland. Although Irish had been in this country during colonial days—some even claim that St. Brendan (484-577) was among the very first to discover the continent—it was not until the mid-19th century that their presence began to be felt. More than four million arrived between 1820 and 1920. One in six Irish emigrated to this country. The population of New York and Brooklyn were more than one-third Irish by the end of the 19th century.

Occupants of the first ghettos in America, the Irish were seen as rough and rowdy. With the coming of the Civil War during this period of massive immigration, "rough and rowdy" was modified to "gallant and courageous" among those who fought with or against them. "Fighting Irish" was a term connoting admiration, not derision, won by their courage in battle.

One-fourth of all foreign-born volunteers in the Union were Irish. Eight Irishmen earned the rank of General in the Union Army. Of course, all Irish did not fight on the side of the Union; the Confederacy had five generals of Irish heritage.

The Irish Brigade became the best known of the fighting units, earning its reputation at Bull Run, the Peninsula, Antietam, Fredericksburg, Chancellorsville, and Gettysburg. It was organized and commanded originally by Gen. Michael Corcoran (827-1863) of Sligo, and following his death, by Gen. Thomas Francis Meagher (1823-1867), of Waterford. Meagher, a leader in "Young Ireland," had been banished from Ireland because of his efforts to win repeal of Britain's unilateral Act of Union with Ireland.

It was reported by journalists and noted by the Irish that there was a disproportionate number of casualties among the Irish. This concern was aggravated by the introduction of a draft lottery which required all men between the ages of 25 and 45 to serve in the army unless they found a substitute or paid $300. Since the Irish didn't have access to $300, a larger number of Irish were drafted. On July 13, 1863, a dark period in Irish American history began with the "draft riots." The victims, irrationally, were the relatively small number of Blacks in the New York area. Following four days of fighting, 1,200 people were dead and Manhattan's Colored Orphan Asylum had been burned. The children had been removed before the torching.

Although the contributions made by the Irish during the Civil War are credited with enhancing their image among the nativists, Irish have made important contributions to all of the wars in which the United States has been engaged. One of the five colonists killed by the British at the Boston Massacre in 1770 was Patrick Carr. Wexford-born John Barry (1745-1803), later to become known as the "Father of the American Navy," fought in the Revolutionary War. Sam Houston and Davy Crockett contributed to the independence of Texas. Commander Oliver Hazard Perry (1885-1819), whose mother was from Ireland, announced his naval victory over the British in the War of 1812 with the famous statement, "We have met the enemy, and they are ours." The first hero of World War II was Captain Colin Kelly (1915-1941), the most decorated serviceman was Audie Murphy (1924-1971), and the Sullivan family lost five sons when their ship was sunk in the Pacific. Famed soldiers like Andrew Jackson, Ulysses S. Grant, and Theodore Roosevelt rode from the battleground into the White House. And the only statue to recognize the contributions made by service women, Molly Marine, stands in New Orleans.

When the Western frontier was opened, Irish American Indian fighters and pioneers were there. Most Irish clung to the major cities of the East, but there were notable exceptions. Three of these were Buffalo Bill Cody (1845-1917), Kit Carson (1809-1969) and Daniel Boone (1734-1820). Each has had his accomplishments embellished in books, plays, movies and television, but each made a genuine contribution to the expansion of the country.

When the frontiers of space were expanded, the Irish American was there. Equal in glory to the achievements made by Irish Americans in war were those made by astronauts in peacetime. Kennedy Space Center in Florida contains a memorial to the astronauts, among whom are Irish Americans James McDivitt, Michael Collins, Kathryn Sullivan—the only woman to ever walk in space—and Christa Corrigan McAuliffe, the teacher-astronaut who perished when the space shuttle *Challenger* exploded.

Sacrifices made by Irish-American men and women in the last half of this century were seen as American accomplishments, because Irish Americans were no longer a species apart. Irish American Catholics found few obstacles to progress remaining because of their religion, and fewer because of their heritage.

The glory harvested by Irish Americans in the 19th and early 20th centuries helped open the door to equality in America. But, not wide enough. That was accomplished through the political system.

Films

Alamo, John Wayne. Final battle scenes are worth the price of admission. (1960, video)

Alamo: 13 Days to Glory, The, James Arness, Brian Keith. A well done cliché. (1987, video)

Annie Get Your Gun, Betty Hutton, Howard Keel. "Annie" is

Annie Oakley and Howard Keel is Buffalo Bill and together they make beautiful music with the help of Irving Berlin. (1950)

Annie Oakley, Barbara Stanwyck, Moroni Olsen. Lively and well-liked by film goers. (1936, video)

Buccaneer, Yul Brynner, Charlton Heston. Heston stars as Andrew Jackson who needs pirate Lafitte's help during the Battle of New Orleans. (1958, video)

Buffalo Bill, Joel McCrae, Maureen O'Hara. Fun telling of adventures of Buffalo Bill. (1944, video)

Buffalo Bill and the Indians, Could any Western about Buffalo Bill starring Paul Newman, Burt Lancaster, Joel Grey, and Kevin McCarthy be anything but entertaining? Yes. (1976, video)

Daniel Boone, Trail Blazer, Bruce Bennett, Lon Chaney. Life of scout and Indian fighter. (1956, video)

Davy Crockett, King of the Wild Frontier, Fess Parker. Best of Crockett movies, spun together from three TV segments. (1955, video)

Fighting 69th, James Cagney, Pat O'Brien. Irish-American actors mix it up in tale of famed World War II Irish regiment. (1940)

Kit Carson, Jon Hall, Lynn Bari. Lots of action. (1940; video)

Pony Express, Charlton Heston, Rhonda Fleming. Story of Buffalo Bill and founding of mail routes in west. (1982, video)

Right Stuff, The, Sam Shepard, Scott Glenn, Ed Harris. America's space program and early astronauts. (1983, video)

Sullivans, The, Anne Baxter, Thomas Mitchell. Five brothers lose their lives when their ship is sunk in World War II. (1944, video)

From Tammany to the Oval Office

*To most Irish politicians, government was
more than a public trust; it was an opportunity to set right the economic and social bal-
ance of American society. In short, they spent
public money to insure that the Irish "have-
nots" became the "haves" of urban America.*
—Kenneth Neill, *Irish People*, 1979

When John F. Kennedy (1917-1963) was elected president, it was
not only a triumph for the Kennedy clan, but a validation that it was
finally OK to be an Irish Catholic. It represented the fall of the final
bastion of political prejudice which had begun a century earlier on a
local level, but had been devastatingly derailed during the presidential
campaign of 1928 when, for the first time, an Irish Catholic had won
the nomination of a major political party. The Democrats had selected
Alfred Emanuel Smith (1873-1944) to run against Republican Herbert Clark Hoover. It was a campaign made memorable for its attacks
on the candidate's religion, rather than his policies. Rumors were ripe
that the Pope was waiting in a submarine off the coast of Florida, ready
to lead a triumphant march to Washington, D.C., to seize the reins
of power upon Smith's election. But the "Happy Warrior," a former

mayor of New York City and four-time New York governor, went down in defeat. Only eight states supported his candidacy.

Although the Irish are aware of it, few Americans seem to understand that had he won, Smith would not have been the first Irish American to sit in the Oval Office. Nor was Kennedy. In fact, there's evidence that Kennedy was actually the thirteenth Irish American president. While the "Irishness" of John Adams, John Quincy Adams, and James Monroe are in dispute, there's greater agreement about fourteen others.

James Madison (1751-1836), fourth U.S. president, was the first Irish American to occupy the White House. His maternal grandparents (Conway) had emigrated from County Clare. Madison is credited with helping to establish St. Patrick's Day as a major celebration in the United States. Seventh president Andrew Jackson's (1767-1845) father and mother (Hutchinson) and two older brothers were born in Carrickfergus, County Antrim.

James K. Polk (1795-1849, originally Pollock), eleventh president, was descended from Donegal emigrants on both his mother's and father's sides. James Buchanan (1791-1868), fifth president, had County Donegal ancestry on his father's side and County Antrim on his mother's. Andrew Johnson (1808-1875), seventeenth president, had County Tipperary ancestors on his mother's side (McDonough). Ulysses S. Grant (1822-1885), eighteenth president, and Chester A. Arthur (1829-1886), twenty-first, had Ulster blood from both parents.

Grover Cleveland (1837-1906), twenty-second and twenty-fourth president, and Benjamin Harrison (1833-1901), twenty-third, had Ulster ancestry on their mothers' side. William McKinley (1843-1901), twenty-fifth president, descended from Ulster emigrants on his father's side. Theodore Roosevelt (1858-1919), twenty-sixth president, earned his Irish status from Ulster on his mother's side and County Meath on his father's. Woodrow Wilson (1856-1924), twenty-eighth president, was Irish on his father's side. Richard M. Nixon (1913 -), thirty-seventh president, claimed Irish ancestry (County Laois) from his mother (Milhous); Gerald R. Ford (1913-) thirty-eighth president, from his father (County Monaghan); and Ronald W. Reagan (1911-), fortieth president, from his father whose grandfather emigrated from County Tipperary.

"While the Irish generally practiced politics of passion when it came to Ireland, they practiced politics of pragmatism in their new American home," wrote Ernest Wood in *The Irish Americans.*

The politically ambitious Irish were helped by the large numbers of their kinsman populating cities. During the last decades of the 20th century, when the Irish constituted the largest immigrant group with as high as one-third to one-half of the voters in Eastern cities, 68 municipalities were in the hands of the Irish. The large numbers of Irish in government-patronage positions is credited to the appreciation shown by Irish office holders. Wood points out that in turn-of-the-century Chicago, when Irish males occupied only fourteen per cent of the work force, forty-three per cent of the policemen, firemen, and watchmen were Irish Americans.

Among the more colorful Irish politicians was James Curley (1841-1958), the first Irish-American mayor of Boston. He held political power for fifty years. He is the subject of a 1958 movie, "The Last Hurrah," and a 1992 biography, "The Rascal King." He was followed in the mayor's office by John F. "Honey Fitz" Fitzgerald, maternal grandfather of John F. Kennedy.

Richard Joseph Daley (1902-1976), perhaps more than any other 20th- century metropolitan politician, epitomizes the best and the worst in the Irish office holders. The sixth Irish Catholic to become mayor of Chicago, Daley held onto power for twenty years. During that time he breathed life back into Chicago's economy and earned the short-lived thanks of Democratic politicians and long-term rancor of Richard Nixon. Nixon believed that it was the mishandling of Chicago ballots which resulted in his loss to Kennedy in 1960. In 1968, Daley's forceful response to the riots which marred the Democratic convention lost him powerful allies. When the Democrats met four years later, they refused to accept Daley and his colleagues as delegates from Illinois. Daley remained unbowed and undefeated until a fatal heart attack in 1976. A short-term caretaker mayor was followed in 1979 by the election of Irish Jane Byrne who was ousted from power with the assistance of Richard Daley, Jr., who had his own political aspirations. A decade later, his ambitions fulfilled, another Daley became mayor of Chicago.

Other names which populated the ranks of Irish political city bosses were Jersey City's Frank Hague (1879-1956), Philadelphia's William McMullen, and Kansas City's Tom Pendergast (1872-1945).

The most famous and notorious political institution was the Tammany Society, more popularly known as Tammany Hall, the building housing the Society. The Tammany Society was founded by Thomas Mooney in New York City in 1789 as a patriotic association, but in a short time the national concept was lost and the purpose was rechanneled into a political mission. Although Irish Americans were active in the Society, it was not until the notorious "Boss" Tweed (1823-1878) was jailed that the Irish got a grip on the leadership, beginning with "Honest" John Kelly (1822-1886). Kelly was followed by two other Irish Americans. Tammany had many successes in promoting candidates and causes of its choice until its reputation for corruption created the need for candidates to publicly disavow the Society.

Two of the more colorful and highly regarded Irish Americans in elective office in recent years have been Thomas P. "Tip" O'Neill (D-MA), speaker of the House of Representatives from 1977 to 1986, and U.S. Senator Daniel Patrick Moynihan (1929- , D-NY), who have made significant contributions to the literature on Irish Americans.

A breakthrough for politically appointed offices was achieved when in 1981 Reagan appointed Sandra Day O'Connor to be the first female justice of the Supreme Court. Other Irish Americans who have sat on the land's highest court are John Rutledge, who was appointed to the first court in 1789; Roger B. Taney (1835-1864), the first Irish- American chief justice; Edward D. White, who also served as chief justice; Joseph McKenna (1898-1925); Frank Murphy (1940-1949); William J. Brennan (1956-); and James F. Byrnes (1941-42).

Government service, appointed and elected, has reaped benefits for Irish Americans. It was the most important single avenue leading to equality in America. Irish Americans have made extraordinary contributions toward shaping the America of today.

Films

All the President's Men, Robert Redford, Dustin Hoffman. Superb story of journalists Woodward and Bernstein uncovering the scandal which brings down the Nixon presidency. (1976, video)

Blood Feud, Robert Blake, Cotter Smith, Ernest Borgnine. Conflict between Attorney General Robert Kennedy and Teamster's Jimmy Hoffa. (1983)

JFK, Kevin Costner, Sissy Spacek. Fascinating film of New Orleans D.A.'s obsession with determining truth about Kennedy's assassination. (1991, video)

John F. Kennedy: Years of Lightning, Day of Drama. Documentary on life of JFK won critical raves. (1964, video)

Last Hurrah, Spencer Tracy, Pat O'Brien. Film of Edwin O'Connor's best selling novel based on life of Boston's first Irish mayor, James Curley. (1958, video)

President's Lady, The, Charlton Heston, Susan Hayward. Fictional, but fun story of Andrew Jackson and the First Lady with a past. (1953, video)

Tennessee Johnson, Van Heflin, Ruth Hussey. Andrew Johnson's rise from tailor to president. (1942)

The World Is a Stage

*The critics have missed the important thing
about me and my work, the fact that I am
Irish.*

Eugene O'Neill

We boxed many rounds, hit many home runs, serenaded many
loved ones, bathed in the spotlight amidst thunderous applause, and
never left our seats. All through the power of Irish American artists
and athletes to draw us into their world for brief, never-to-be-forgotten
moments.

Boxing was dominated by the Irish and Irish Americans in the
early days of the sport. John L. Sullivan (1858-1918) was the first
world heavyweight bare knuckle champion. He was followed by
Gentleman Jim Corbett (1866-1933), who was crowned the first
world heavyweight boxing champion fighting under Marquees of
Queensbury rules. In the era of the Irish boxer, men like O'Rourke,
Morrissey, Sullivan, Coburn, McCoole, McCoy, Gallagher, Ryan,
Kilrain, McCaffrey, Dempsey, Kerrigan, Crosby, and McAuliffe
were the gladiators. The end of the era came when Jack Dempsey
(1895-1983), the "Manassa Mauler," was finally defeated. Although
the dominance died, the occasional Irish name continued to emerge,
like "The Pittsburgh Kid," Billy Conn (1917-), who almost KO'd
Joe Louis in their first battle; Sean O'Grady, who moved out of the
ring and into the broadcast booth: and the current Irish hope,

Tommy "Duke" Morrison—John "Duke" Wayne's nephew. You may have caught Morrison in his movie debut, "Rocky V."

The baseball diamond was filled with many Irish names. Among the greatest managers were John McGraw, New York Giants; Joe McCarthy, New York Yankees; Connie Mack (McGillicuddy), Philadelphia Athletics; and Charles Comiskey, Chicago White Sox. The players include Hugh Duffy outfielder; Mike J. "King" Kelly, prince of thieves—bases, that is; and George "Mickey" Cochrane, catcher.

George M. Cohan was one of the first of the Irish to become a genuine star in American vaudeville. His career as a performer and songwriter was told in "Yankee Doodle Dandy," a film starring a later day Irish American, Jimmy Cagney, known for his gangster roles. Cagney received an Oscar for his singing-dancing performance. Many other stars of Hollywood's golden era could trace their talent to their Irish roots, including Alice Faye, Walter Brennan, Bing Crosby, Judy Garland, John Wayne, Maureen O'Hara, Tyrone Power, Geraldine Fitzgerald and Barry Fitzgerald, Gene Kelly and Grace Kelly, and the "singing sweethearts" Nelson Eddy and Jeanette MacDonald.

Bing Crosby introduced "crooning," a singing style emulated by most popular singers for several decades and, even today, has influenced Harry Connick, Jr. Crosby's recording of "White Christmas" remains at the top of the all-time best selling recordings, and his acting in "Going My Way" won him an Oscar for best performance.

If an Oscar had been given for best performance as a bizarre character, it would undoubtedly have been won by Howard Hughes. Hughes, the multi-million dollar owner of Hughes Aircraft, toyed with inventions, movies, and movie actresses whom he often paid for not acting. Although he retained many millions to the end of his life, his emotional stability was long gone.

Stephen C. Foster (1826-1864), whose songs about the South have been sung by generations of school children, grew up in Pittsburgh, Pennsylvania, but spent vacations in Kentucky. His melodies were inspired by his Irish heritage and the spirituals of the African Americans.

Eugene MacDowell (1861-1908), composer and pianist, is memorialized by a summer colony for artists and a music festival on the grounds of his home in Peterborough, New Hampshire. Among his better known compositions are "Woodland Sketches" and "Indian Suite."

Perhaps Irish Americans gained their greatest prominence—not unexpectedly—in the world of words. F. Scott Fitzgerald (1896-1940), whose tempestuous life, with and without his eccentric wife Zelda, often garnered more attention than his talent, left a treasury of writings that created the 20th century legends. But his personification of an era—the roaring 20s—sometimes overshadows his work. Edgar Allan Poe (1809-1849), teller of terrifying tales, continues to frighten and fascinate us through his writings and the films based on his stories. *Murders in the Rue Morgue* has been filmed five times; *The Raven, The Masque of the Red Death* and *The Black Cat,* at least twice. Vincent Price owes much of his longevity as an actor to Poe's work. Memorials to Poe are found in Maryland, New York, Pennsylvania, Rhode Island, and Virginia.

Margaret Mitchell (1900-1949), with one publication, left her mark on the world. *Gone With the Wind,* America's most successful novel, was made into America's most successful film. Through repeated theater and television showings, it has been seen by more viewers than any other motion picture. A long awaited sequel, *Scarlett,* published more than four decades after Mitchell's death in 1992, was a best-seller before it hit the book stores. Georgia remembers Mitchell in many ways. But the world remembers her Irish-American heroine, Scarlett O'Hara.

Inheritor of great wealth, William Randolph Hearst wielded great influence through his chain of newspapers. Today, he is known best by the classic, but unflattering, movie "Citizen Kane," and his magnificent, but outrageous, clutch of castles in San Simeon, California.

Irish-American Georgia O'Keeffe (1887-1986) is remembered as much for her overwhelming personality as for her provocative, erotic paintings. Art critic John Russell said, "It would be difficult to imagine American painting in the first half of this century without the presence of Georgia O'Keeffe."

Br'er Fox, Br'er Rabbit, and Br'er Bear traveled from the the tongues of slaves in Kentucky to a child's ears, then flowed through the pen of a grown up Joel Chandler Harris(1848-1908) into the hearts of readers. The popularity of the Uncle Remus stories grew when they were told in the movie, "Song of the South." Harris memorials are found in Georgia.

Through the last two centuries, Irish Americans have contributed to many aspects of American life, but most certainly an important contribution is their ability to entertain.

Films

Ah, Wilderness, Wallace Beery, Lionel Barrymore, Mickey Rooney.Well done adaptation of Eugene O'Neill's story of a turn-of-the-century small town. See *Summer Holiday.* (1935)

Beloved Infidel, Gregory Peck, Deborah Kerr. Sheila Graham's intimate memories of F. Scott Fitzgerald's Hollywood period. (1959, video)

Citizen Kane, Orson Welles. Classic veiled portrayal of life and loves of William Randolph Hearst. (1941, video)

Dempsey, Treat Williams. Powerful story of Jack Dempsey, heavy-weight boxing champion of the world 1919-26. (1983, video)

Daisy Miller, Cybill Shepherd. Shepherd misinterpets Henry James's novel of an American girl living and loving in Europe. (1974, video)

Desire Under the Elms, Sophia Loren, Burl Ives, Anthony Perkins.Mixed reviews greeted the filming of Eugene O'Neill's play of jealousy and love. (1958, video)

Gentleman Jim, Errol Flynn. Biography of the greatest of the Irish American heavyweight boxing champions is a knockout! (1942, video)

Going My Way, Bing Crosby, Barry Fitzgerald. As Father O'Malley, Crosby picked up an Academy Award ©. Writer-director Leo McCarey picked up two. (1944, video)

Gone With the Wind, Vivien Leigh, Clark Gable. The mother of all movies. (1939, video)

Great Gatsby, The, Robert Redford, Mia Farrow. F. Scott Fitzgerald's novel was much better. (1974, video)

In Old Chicago, Alice Faye, Tyrone Power, Don Ameche, Alice Brady, Brian Donleavy. Story of the days leading up to the great Chicago fire with Oscar ©–winning Alice Brady as Mrs. O'Leary, owner of the country's second best known cow. (1938)

Long Day's Journey Into Night, Katharine Hepburn, Ralph Richardson. Successful interpretation of Eugene O'Neill's novel of New England family's fall into alcohol and substance abuse. (1962, video)

Masque of the Red Death, Vincent Price. Edgar Allan Poe's horrific tale of an evil medieval Italian prince who has an uninvited guest at his grand ball. (1964, video)

Murders in the Rue Morgue, George C. Scott, Rebecca de Mornay.The fifth and probably the best of the many filmings of Edgar Allan Poe's story of murder in 19th-century Paris. (1986, video)

Naughty Marietta, Jeanette MacDonald, Nelson Eddy. Delightfully dated story, and the stars' singing of Victor Herbert's music remains thrilling. (1935, video)

The Outlaw, Jane Russell, Jack Buetel. Billy the Kid gets Jane Russell, but Jane got the publicity. Howard Hughes, engineer and producer, designed a special bra for Russell. The movie flopped, but Jane didn't. (1943, video)

The Raven, Vincent Price, Boris Karloff, Peter Lorre, Jack Nicholson. Poe's epic poem inspired this horror-comedy classic.(1963, video)

Show People, Marion Davies. One of Davies' few successful movies. (1928, video)

Song of the South, James Baskett, Bobby Driscoll. Joel Chandler Harris's characters came to the screen in a joyous combination of animated and live action. (1946)

The Raven, Vincent Price. Some critics consider this to be the best of the films based on Poe's stories. (1963, video)

Summer Holiday, Mickey Rooney, Walter Houston. Musical remake of O'Neill's *Ah, Wilderness.* Not as good, but fun. (1948, video)

Swanee River, Don Ameche, Al Jolson. Enjoy this musical biography of Stephen Foster, but don't take it seriously. (1939)

Wizard of Oz, Judy Garland. This film carried Judy Garland "Somewhere Over the Rainbow" and into the hearts of America. (1939, video)

Yankee Doodle Dandy, James Cagney. The quintessential Irish film with Cagney in his 1942 Oscar©-winning portrayal of George M. Cohan. (1942, video)

The Dark Side

"Oh, well," said Mr. Hennessy, "we are as
th' Lord made us."
"No," said Mr. Dooley, "lave us be fair.
Lave us take some iv th' blame oursilves."
Finley Peter Dunne
Observations by Mr. Dooley
by Mr. Dooley, 1902

*I*rish America has had its troubles. Often as victim, sometimes as witness, and on occasion, as perpetrator. The name which was associated with triumph in 1960 and heartbreak in 1963 was marred by tragedy and disgrace in 1969.

John F. Kennedy ushered in an era of Camelot. The nation's shame that was Al Smith, doomed to lose the presidency in the 30s because of his religion, became the nation's pride when Kennedy was elected, despite his religion. When President Kennedy was assassinated, the admiration in which he was held by many of his countrymen and women grew into adulation.

When his brother Robert (1925-1968) was also martyred during his campaign to wrest the presidential nomination from Lyndon Johnson, the price that the Kennedy family had paid for their place in history weighed heavily on the minds and hearts of Americans.

Then along came Ted (1932-). The youngest brother, the senator from Massachusetts and an aspirant to the highest office in the land.

The last hope for a return to Camelot was lost when something went terribly wrong. Tragedy struck as Ted Kennedy drove his car off a bridge and into the Chappaquiddick. Ted escaped. His companion, a young woman who had worked for Robert, was imprisoned in the car and drowned.

The circumstances following Mary Jo Kopechne's death led to criticism of Kennedy's actions during the crisis. Although found guilty by a local judge only of the infraction of leaving the scene of an accident, the public punished him by denying him a bid for national office.

Politics has generally been a very fruitful ladder for Irish Americans to climb to prominence and great respect. On the dark side, however, many Americans call to mind the senator from Wisconsin, Joseph McCarthy (1908-1957). McCarthy surged to prominence when he announced that the communists were infiltrating the entertainment world. He was the instigator of the infamous black lists, which led to the loss of work for persons simply suspected of being communists and those who refused to cooperate with McCarthy by "naming names" of people to be added to the black list. A new word came into the dictionary: "McCarthyism [after J. McCarthy, U.S. senator (1946-57)], the use of careless, often false, accusations and methods of investigating that violate civil liberties."

Irish Americans have used the power of the pulpit to great good in the shaping of the moral values of America, but there have been some controversial spokesmen. During the 30s and 40s, out of the dark side emerged Father Charles E. Coughlin. He was known to his admirers as the "Little Flower of Fatima" and to his detractors as "a bigot in populist clothing." Just as the children of Salem before him and Joseph McCarthy after him, Coughlin was able to find evil in good and nobility in destruction.

Although movies, television, story tellers, and folk music have popularized the exploits of men who rode the Wild West, they've also created heroes where they didn't exist—for example, Jesse James (1847-1882) and Billy the Kid (1859-1881). Both killers, among lesser things, Jesse could trace his Irish ancestry through his mother, a Cole, and Billy, through his parents, McCartys (variously reported as "McCarthy"), who emigrated from Ireland.

Jesse roamed Missouri and Iowa spreading mayhem along the way. His death came in a house in St. Joseph, Missouri. Or did it? There are those who claim that at the age of 102 Jesse convened a meeting of outlaws in the Meramec Caverns of Missouri.

Billy and other Irish Americans engaged in a five-day battle, known as the Lincoln County War. The war led to his fame, infamy, and death.

Butch Cassidy and the Sundance Kid initially became famous around the turn of the 20th century. Their above the law escapades earned them a reputation in the Midwest, West, and Bolivia. They became even better known in the late 1960s, when they returned on the movie screen in the persons of Paul Newman and Robert Redford.

The 18th and 19th centuries spawned a number of shady Irish organizations, including the Kerryonians. Founded about 1825 and exclusive to natives of County Kerry, it was one of the earliest organized crime gangs.

"Machine Gun" Kelly came on the scene early in the 20th century, roaming and robbing from Memphis to Tupelo and Oklahoma City. "Pretty Boy" Floyd (1901-1934) was active during the same period and is alleged to be the "machine gunner" of the Kansas City Massacre. The real superstar of the Irish American bad guys was John Herbert Dillinger (1903-1934, alias Frank Sullivan, John Donovan). Within twelve months, he is credited with stealing more money than Jesse James did during his entire sixteen-year crime career.

Kit Carson, hero to his generation and to many of us as children, had a dark side, and it came out in Arizona where he drove the Indians from their homes in a 300-mile trudge to new lands. They returned several years later.

One of the greatest tragedies to capture the minds of the public has been told and retold. It's the story of the Donner Party, pioneer families who were trapped in a snow storm as they neared the end of their trek to the golden land of California. The tragedy of death and the horror of survival was chronicled by Irish American Patrick Breen.

Films

Gore Vidal's Billy the Kid, Val Kilmer. Nice kid. Misunderstood. Goes bad. (1989, video)

Butch Cassidy and the Sundance Kid, Paul Newman, Robert Redford,Katharine Ross. Skillful combination of action and comedy. (1969, video)

Cotton Club, The, Richard Gere, Gregory Hines. One of gangster Owney Madden's semi-legitimate businesses is worth watching more for the visual excitement than story. (1984, video)

The Crucible (also titled *The Witches of Salem*), Simone Signoret, Yves Montand. Based on Arthur Miller's parable of the Salem witch trials. Signoret is superb. (1957)

Dillinger, Anne Jeffreys, Lawrence Tierney. Receives a B for production, but an A for action. (1945, video)

Dillinger, Warren Oates, Cloris Leachman. Takes Dillinger from mid-gangster days to his violent death in Chicago. (1973, video)

Donner Pass: The Road to Survival, Robert Fuller, Andrew Prine.Television film handles grim story with delicacy. (1978, video)

Jesse James, Tyrone Power, Henry Fonda. The best of the Jesse-Frank films. (1939, video)

Jesse James at Bay, Roy Rogers. Roy Rogers? Even Trigger blushed! (1941, video)

Kansas City Massacre, Dale Robertson, Bo Hopkins. Crammed full with Irish American gangsters—"Pretty Boy" Floyd, John Dillinger, and "Baby Face" Nelson. (1975; video)

Lady in Red, The, Frances Sue Martin, Robert Conrad. Who, why,and what happened to the woman who betrayed her boyfriend, John Dillinger. (1979, video)

Left-Handed Gun, Paul Newman. Billy the Kid—a pseudo-psychological study with interesting moments. (1958, video)

Manhattan Melodrama, Clark Gable, William Powell, Myrna Loy. Screenplay of gangster-DA friendship won an Oscar, but best known as film seen by Dillinger immediately before he was gunned down.(1934)

Melvin Purvis—G-Man, Dale Robertson. Preguel of *Kansas City Massacre* tells fictional story of pursuit of "Machine Gun" Kelly. (1974, video)

Pretty Boy Floyd, John Ericson. Just another cops and robbers movie. (1960)

Story of Pretty Boy Floyd, The, Martin Sheen, Kim Darby. Action-packed telemovie. (1974)

Tail Gunner Joe, Peter Boyle, John Forsythe, Patricia Neal. Riveting portrait of one of America's foremost demagogues, Joseph McCarthy. (1977 telemovie)

The Happy Hours

*I spent 90 per cent of my salary on good Irish
whiskey and women. The rest I wasted.*
—Tug McGraw, Irish American

*N*o man or woman would question the high regard in which the
Irish hold whiskey. The very word is short for the Irish "usque-baugh."
Nevertheless, it is beer that is seen most often in the hand of the Irish.
And it is to the pub that the Irish have traditionally been drawn to
complement that libation with conversation.

Or is it the other way around? In years gone by, when the Irish
were brewing their poteen at home, they were still gathering in public
houses. Today, there are more than 12,000 pubs on the Island (one
for every 360 persons). Sure'n a little bit of heaven fell from out the
sky one day.

As the more than 5,000,000 Irish left their homes for the New
World, they left behind families and friends, but not their affection
for the public house. Today, the Irish pub is a unique part of the
American scene.

If you've already discovered the Irish-American pub, this will be
your guide to a friendly haven in many of the places your business
or vacation travel takes you. If you are new to the Irish scene, you
will be introduced to a home away from home. The Irish pub is fun,
folksy, friendly and, at times, adventuresome.

Irish pubs cut across class and culture. You'll find them in all neighborhoods and even in combination with Italian and Mexican restaurants. Some Irish pubs attract an exclusively blue- or white-collar following, but the most common and most interesting are those that meld a cross-section of society.

Celebrating St. Patrick's Day in an Irish pub is an experience not to be missed. I've been in the crowds overflowing the sidewalks surrounding a pub in Kansas City, the people forming a beer brigade to make certain that those in the farthest reaches were not neglected. I've been in lines trying to get into Irish pubs in New York City after they had reached their legal limit, vainly trying to convince my buddy, Father Keane, to use his heavenly connections to get us in. I've been part of a seemingly impenetrable wall of celebrants at a Houston pub that gave way to a noted athlete streaking through, and I've been in a Cleveland pub downstairs from an ecdysiast emporium when the dancers abruptly interrupted their gyrations to join the spectators as the St. Paddy's Day Parade passed by.

But it's not just St. Patrick's Day that brings an extra shot of adrenalin to an Irish pub. New Year's Eve in San Antonio's Durty Nellie's is memorable, as is Finnegans Wake in Pennsylvania's Limeport Inn, and September 17th (half way to St. Patrick's Day) in Dave's, Baltimore, Maryland.

Irish-American pubs have been absorbing research. My report is, most often, based on personal impressions, developed during one visit or many. I may have caught the pub on an off night, but if I've visited it, I call it as I found it. This is not a collection of the best or the worst, although there are some of both. And it's not a geographically balanced list, although you'll find all regions of the country represented. My only regret is that I couldn't personally visit each of the pubs referenced here. I'm dedicated to that goal. And if you know about an Irish pub which should be included in my list the next time around—and you will—let me know. But first check the Appendix. There are 293 listed there.

If you don't find a pub in the area that you'll be visiting, don't assume one doesn't exist. We've included only a small portion of the thousands of Irish-American pubs that enliven and enrich all regions of the country.

How can you find one not listed? The most reliable sources are proprietors of Irish gift shops and Irish-American newspapers. If the area can support these businesses, chances are good there will be at least one Irish pub. Another font of all knowledge, always available, is a bartender. But, unless she or he is sophisticated, you could end up in a British or Scottish bar. Not bad, but not Irish. The Yellow Pages are an obvious source, but be careful, names can be misleading. You're probably safe with anything listed under "restaurants," "taverns," or "cocktail lounges" that includes the word Blarney, Dublin, Emerald, Harp, Irish, Leprechaun, Malone, or Shamrock—and Birraporetti's! But be careful of the Shenanigans, Kellys, O'Neils, and O'Gradys. Some are, some aren't.

Many businesses clearly identify themselves as Irish, but sometimes the only clue will be the subtle substitution of a shamrock for an apostrophe in the name.

Part II

Symbols

The following symbols preceeding each entry in Part II refer to the associated chapter in Part I:

Symbol	*Chapter*
HI	Trial, Tragedy ...
HIA	... Tribulation and Triumph
P	Paddy and Bridget
B	Black, Scarlet, and Green
G	Harvest of Glory
T	From Tammany to the Oval Office
S	The World Is a Stage
D	The Dark Side
HH	The Happy Hours

Sites to Visit
Alabama

Birmingham

ℍ𝟙 **Harwell G. Davis Library**, Samford University. 800 Lakeshore Drive. The library contains 19th and 20th century materials on Ireland.

Open Monday-Thursday 7:45 a.m.-11 p.m., Friday until 4:30 p.m., Saturday noon-4 p.m., Sunday 3 p.m.-11 p.m. Information: 205-870-2011.

Montgomery

𝕋 **First White House of the Confederacy**, 644 Washington Avenue. Originally located at Bibb and Lee, the home of the first lady of the Confederacy, Irish-American Varina Howell, and Jefferson Davis, President, is now a Confederate museum. It contains many Civil War artifacts and personal belongings of the Davis family.

Open daily, Monday-Friday 8 a.m.-4:30 p.m., Saturday and Sunday 9 a.m.-4:30 p.m.; closed New Year's, Thanksgiving, and Christmas. Handicapped facilities. Donations. Information: 205-242-1861.

𝕊 **Scott and Zelda Fitzgerald Museum**, 919 Felder Avenue. Montgomery is the hometown of Zelda Sayre, and many of the exhibits relate to her personal and professional life. Those interested in American literature will find some significant items of Scott Fitzgerald's. The Fitzgeralds lived here when he wrote *Tender Is the Night* and she wrote *Save Me the Waltz*. Scott and Zelda were a colorful couple, stereotypes of the time in which they lived. Zelda died in a mental institution, and Scott had a fling with Hollywood writing and movie columnist Sheila Graham before dying in 1940.

Open Wednesday-Friday 10 a.m.-2 p.m., Saturday-Sunday afternoon from 1-5. Donations. Information: 205-264-4222.

Wetumpka

G **Fort Toulouse, Fort Jackson,** 3 miles north of Montgomery, 3 miles west off US 231. Established in 1717, the fort was reopened in 1814 by Andrew Jackson after his defeat of the Creek Nation at Horseshoe Bend. Forts are reconstructed. Of major interest are the Indian mounds dating back to 1100 A.D. Facilities include a museum, nature walks, picnic area, and boat ramp.

Open, except New Year's and Christmas. Free. Information: 205-567-3002.

Alaska

Juneau

HH **The Irish Shop,** 175 South Franklin Street, 2nd floor. It's nice to run across shamrocks in Alaska and here, on one street, you'll find two establishments sporting them: The Irish Shop, filled with good things Irish, and **The Lucky Lady** which displays a few shamrocks and is as close as you're going to get to an Irish pub in this area. If you go, make it during daylight hours. I'm told it can get a bit rough in the evenings.

Information: 907-586-6055 (Irish Shop); telephone operator reported no phone number for The Lucky Lady.

Arizona

Chinie

D **Canyon de Chelly National Monument,** located within the lands of the Navajo Indian Reservation. The monument includes the Canyon de Chelly (de SHAY), the Canyon del Muerto (of the dead), and Monument Canyons. Sheer red sandstone walls, decorated with pictographs, reach 1,000 feet into the sky. Ruins of cliff dwellings, built by prehistoric peoples in the early 4th-century A.D., have been found. Navajos moved in after an earlier people had abandoned the area.

In 1864, Kit Carson drove the Navajos out of the canyon, walking them 300 miles into eastern New Mexico. They returned four years later to farm the land. Today, you can see more than 60 major ruins and many minor ones. Most important are the White House Pueblo, occupied from 1060 to 1275; the Mummy Cave, dating from around 1250, and Antelope House. Most of the ruins are inaccessible (we wonder how the Indians got to them?), but can be viewed from the ground or from a road running along the rim at the top. With one exception, hikes can only be taken with a National Park Service permit and an authorized guide, for which a fee is charged. The one self-guided trail is 2 1/2 miles and leads you to the canyon floor and White House Pueblo. Two drives can be made along the rim of the canyon in private car. Only 4-wheel drive vehicles are permitted in the canyons and must be accompanied by an authorized guide.

A visitor center contains a museum, open daily except New Year's, Thanksgiving, and Christmas. Six-hour and overnight horseback rides, requiring no riding experience, can be taken to Mummy Cave and Antelope Cave,.mid-May through mid-October. Fee. Information: 602-871-4663, or write Twin Trail Tours, Box 1706, Window Rock 86515.

Half-day or all-day jeep tours into the canyons can be arranged throughout the year. Fee. Information: 602-674-5436, or write Thunderbird Lodge, Box 548, Chinie, 86503.

Daviston

D **Horseshoe Bend National Military Park,** 12 miles north of Dadeville on Route 49. Andrew Jackson won more than a military victory here, he won a national reputation which would carry him to the Oval Office. The battle of Horseshoe Bend was fought in March 1914 on the Tallapoosa River. It ended the influence of the Creek Indians who were forced to surrender 20 million acres of land to the United States government and move to Oklahoma. The war ended many years of conflict which followed the Treaty of 1790. The U.S. government had guaranteed the Creek lands, but continued to violate the agreement. Not America's finest hour. You can drive for several miles through the battlefield, passing Tohopeka, where the Creek women and children were hidden during the fighting.

The park contains a boat ramp, picnic facilities, fishing, hiking trails, nature walk, and visitors center with museum. The museum has exhibits, bullet molds, arms, and a diorama of the battle.

Open daily 8 a.m.-4:30 p.m., except New Year's and Christmas. Free. Information: 205-234-7111, or write Horseshoe Bend National Military Park, Route 1, Box 103, 36256.

Phoenix

HH **Dubliner Irish Pub & Restaurant,** 3841 East Thunderbird Road. This is an authentic Irish pub in the heart of the Old West. It has all the usual things which make for a good Celtic time, but it has something special which makes it an excellent choice—the recommendation by one of the staff of the Tucson Leprechaun pub. "The Dubliner," said my informant, "is a real Irish pub."

Open daily. Information: 602-867-0984.

Tucson

HH **Leprechaun,** 5870 East Broadway. The Leprechaun is a third generation Irish pub at this location. The name came with the newest owners. The drawings on the building and the stained glass windows feature the little people. Harp and Guinness are on tap, and Irish stew and corned beef are among the food items. You'll have to wait for St. Patrick's Day if you want to hear live Irish entertainment. It's not what you'd call authentic, but it's a bright, cheerful room with a circular bar and friendly staff.

Open daily. Information: 602-748-2525.

Arkansas

Berryville

D **Saunders Memorial Museum**, 115 East Madison on AR 21. A collection of guns owned by wild men of the West, including Irish-American Jesse James, Pancho Villa, and Wild Bill Hickok, are on display. The museum also exhibits silver, handcrafts, china, rugs, and furniture.

Open daily mid-March to October. Fee. Information: 501-423-2563.

California

Berkeley

B The city of **Berkeley** was named in honor of Anglican bishop and philosopher, George Berkeley.

HI **Bancroft Library**, University of California. Sean O'Faolain (born John Whelan) died in 1991 at the age of 91. He was a full-time writer and, following World War I, a short-time revolutionist. O'Faolain wrote in Irish and English. He is best known for his short stories, many of which were published in 1983 under the title *Collected Stories of Sean O'Faolain*. The library contains manuscripts by O'Faolain, including early drafts and edited material.

Open Monday-Friday 9 a.m.-5 p.m., Saturday afternoon 1-5; closed Sunday. Information: 510-642-6481.

Danville

S Eugene O'Neill National Historic Site. "Long Day's Journey Into Night," "The Iceman Cometh," and "Moon for the Misbegotten," the greatest plays authored by Eugene O'Neill were created when he and his wife lived in this isolated area between 1937 and 1944. The 14-acre site includes their Spanish-style, white concrete home, swimming pool, and landscaped lawns. Even the grave of their Dalmation. Especially interesting is O'Neill's study, the envy of every one who craves isolation. To reach it you must pass through three doors and one closet.

Open by appointment, and the number of visitors is limited. Free. Information: 510-838-0249, or write Eugene O'Neill National Historic Site, P.O. Box 280, 94526.

Lake Tahoe

D Donner Memorial State Park, 2 miles west of Truckee off I-80. The entire event, in horrifying detail, was chronicled by Patrick Breen, Irish emigrant from County Cavan. The fate of the Donner Party, and many Irish families, who attempted to travel the Rockies in the winter of 1846-47, is an oft-told tale of death and cannibalism. The group of 85 people, led by George Donner, was trapped by snow which reached the height of 22 feet. Forty-five survived, nourished in part by the bodies of those who died. The park commemorates the tragedy with a film shown in the Immigrant Museum and by the Pioneer Monument which stands 22 feet tall.

Museum open daily 10 a.m.-4 p.m., mid-May through September; 10 a.m.-noon and 1 p.m.-4 p.m., the rest of the year; park open 8 a.m-dusk, June-September; museum and park closed New Year's, Thanksgiving, and Christmas. Fee. Information: 916-587-3841.

Long Beach

S The Spruce Goose, Long Beach Harbor area. If Irish-American Howard Hughes was not the most eccentric person in Hollywood, it wasn't for lack of trying. His entanglements with screen legends such as Lana Turner and Ava Gardner won him a lot of press even before his neuroses evolved into full-fledged psychoses. One of his most talked about inventions was an airplane named Hercules, better known as the Spruce Goose. The largest wooden aircraft ever built, it has a 320-foot wing-span. It had everything going for it, except one—it didn't fly very well, and it was only in the air once. Hughes earned early recognition for his film *Hell's Angels,* recognized for spectacular aerial shots and remembered as the film that introduced Jean Harlow.

You can visit the Spruce Goose and enjoy a "multisensory entertainment journey" without leaving the ground. The Goose is on a combination ticket with the Queen Mary—the largest passenger ship ever built.

Open daily 9 a.m.-9 p.m., July 4 to Labor Day, and 10 a.m.-6 p.m., the rest of the year. Fee. Information: 213-435-3511.

Los Angeles

HH Casey's Bar and Grill, 613 South Grand Avenue. Casey's is where you come after work if you want to be part of a convivial group of business people; come later in the evening if you want a quiet spot for intimate conversation; if you want a cool Harp or Guinness, don't come weekends, because it's closed. Casey's is a good-looking Irish pub with appropriate touches of Irish decor.

Open Monday-Friday 11 a.m.-11 p.m. Information: 213-629-2353.

G Gene Autry Western Heritage Museum, 4700 Zoo Drive, Griffith Park. Through art and artifact the real and fictional world of the West come together in this museum. A saddle belonging to Buffalo Bill Cody and a saddle and revolver belonging to Teddy Roosevelt are displayed. Cody was the son of an Irish immigrant, and Roosevelt had ancestors from Counties Antrim and Meath. You can also see clips from old Westerns.

Open Tuesday-Sunday 10 a.m.-5 p.m., except Thanksgiving and Christmas. Fee. Senior and children's discount. Information:213-667-2000.

S **Hollywood** was founded in 1903, made part of Los Angeles in 1910, and became home to the first movie studio in 1911. Once the "glamour capital of the world," much of Hollywood has faded along with the golden years. Nevertheless, there is still a fascination to the landmarks of old Hollywood. Irish and Irish Americans played a major role in enticing audiences into the movie palaces. And if you look in the right places, you'll still find them on Hollywood Boulevard.

S **Walk of Fame**, Hollywood Boulevard. The terrazzo sidewalk is inset with names of show business celebrities written on bronze stars. The installation of one of these stars, even today, draws crowds. Fans accept the responsibility of keeping the stars polished.

S **Hollywood Memorial Park Cemetery Mortuary**, 6000 Santa Monica Boulevard. Tombs of many stars, statesmen, and tycoons are located here, including those of Irish-American actors Tyrone Power and Nelson Eddy. Also, interred here are Cecil B. DeMille, Rudolph Valentino, Douglas Fairbanks, Sr., and Norma Talmadge.

S **Hollywood Wax Museum**, 6767 Hollywood Boulevard. Wax models of nearly 200 famous figures, including Hollywood celebrities and presidents. A bit tacky like most of Hollywood Boulevard.

Open daily. Handicapped facilities. Fee. Information: 213-462-8860.

Information on all Hollywood sites can be obtained by contacting the Chamber of Commerce, 6290 Sunset Boulevard, Suite 525, 90028 (213-469-8311); Hollywood Visitors Information Center, 6801 Hollywood Boulevard (213-466-1389).

HH **Irish Molly Malone's Pub**, 575 South Fairfax Avenue, Wilshire District. This is a good, solid, unpretentious neighborhood

Irish pub, populated with good, solid, unpretentious Irish Americans. It's a gathering spot for folks who want Irish music (Wednesday-Sunday), enjoy darts, or just like to huddle with their Guinness in an atmosphere which is unexciting, but comfortable.

Open daily 11:30 a.m.-2 a.m. Information: 818-935-1577.

S Mann's (formerly Grauman's) Chinese Theater, Hollywood Boulevard, near Highland Avenue. Across from the once famous Hollywood Roosevelt Hotel, Mann's was the scene for movie premiers and the setting for the stars' footprints and, when circumstances demanded, other anatomical parts—see Jane Russell's and Betty Grable's contributions.

HH Tom Bergin's, 840 South Fairfax Avenue. Tom died twenty years ago, but his spirit lives on, and so does the tradition of attracting some of the brightest (and not so bright) stars of Hollywood. We visited on a Sunday evening when there were few customers lining the horseshoe bar and a sprinkling of people at the tables in the adjoining room. The decor is typically authentic with green tablecloths, shamrock decorated lamps, and walls lined with photos.

Among the familiar faces we saw were Pat O'Brien and Bing Crosby hanging on the wall and Kiefer Sutherland learning on the bar. If you visit a few times a week, you get your name on one of the shamrocks lining the vaulted ceiling. Don't believe the waiter who insists that the shamrocks represent customers he's executed. Nevertheless, I left a large tip. It was worth it. The food was as good as the people watching. My Irish stew, simmered in Guinness stout, was among the best I've tasted, and my friends enjoyed the pasta putanesca and corned beef and cabbage. Next time I want to try the Irish bacon burger with peanut butter sauce. Don't miss Tom Bergin's, surely a 4-shamrock pub.

Open Monday-Friday for lunch and dinner; weekends for dinner only. Information: 213:936-7151

Newport Beach

HH Shamrock Bar, 2633 West Coast Highway. Here is a new pub which is already building up a strong local following. An authentic pub with an authentic Irish brogue behind the bar, it's making it on a traditionally friendly Irish pub atmosphere, cold Irish beer, and good prices. Breakfast, lunch, and dinner is served in this small setting (maybe *cozy* is a better description). Outstanding is their Irish breakfast served all day Saturday and Sunday, consisting of sausage, bacon, eggs, and black and white pudding. Just $6.95 brings you all this plus brown bread and drink. If you stop by Saturday at 7 a.m., you can enjoy your breakfast while watching live-on-TV English soccer.

Happy Hour, 4 p.m.-7 p.m. Monday through Friday, offers free food and drink specials.

Open daily from 7 a.m. Information: 714-631-5633.

San Diego

HH Blarney Stone Pub, 502 5th Avenue. Located in the Gaslamp Quarter, the oldest section of San Diego, the Blarney Stone has a noble and possibly ignoble ancestry. It sits in the heart of what used to be the "Red Light District." The current owners explain that around the turn of the century, the Acme Saloon occupied the premises. The Acme was operated by a colorful Irishman named Augustes Burnes, who kept a menagerie of monkeys, bears, birds, an anteater, and wildcat outside the door. The pub is nothing so exotic today, but the inside can be just as lively when the Harp and Guinness flow.

An old mahogany bar dominates the photo-lined main room, and you can enjoy breakfast and lunch daily here or in the adjoining dining room. Irish breakfast, priced at $7.95, includes Irish sausages, rashers, black & white pudding, fried tomatoes, eggs, and home fries. Dinner is served Friday and Saturday.

The Blarney Stone has a lot going for it, but the best is their helpful staff who gave us directions to all the Irish pubs in the area.

Bar and kitchen open daily. Information: 619-233-8519.

HH Reidy O'Neill's Irish Bar & American Grill, 939 Fourth

Avenue. O'Neill's identifies itself as a "stately restaurant serving solid American fare with an Irish twist." The Irish is corned beef and cabbage, and the twist is a New York steak flamed in Jameson whiskey.

Open daily. Information: 619-231-8500.

ᚻᚻ **Patrick's II**, 428 F Street. Patrick's is a downtown Celtic house of pleasure, offering New Orleans jazz, blues, boogie, rock, and, of course, Irish traditional music to accompany your Irish beer. Entertainment Tuesday-Saturday evening 8:30-1:00, Sunday evening 5:00-10:00.

Open daily. Information: 619-233-3077.

San Francisco

S **San Francisco**, founded in 1776, is America's favorite city, and often described as its loveliest. It was planned by Dubliner Jasper O'Farrell. O'Farrell owned a huge estate near San Francisco which he named Annaly, for an area in Ireland once owned by the O'Farrells. The city's O'Farrell Street is named in honor of its planner.

ᚻᚻ **Abbey Tavern**, 4100 Geary Boulevard, Richmond. Probably the most popular Irish pub in the city, the Abbey attracts a young, high decibel crowd, who sip the dark one at the horseshoe bar. That's weekends at the Abbey. But during the week, you can have a more calming experience tossing the darts or just drinking a Guinness.

Open daily 11 a.m.-2 a.m. Information: 415-221-7767.

ᚻᚻ **Dovre Club**, 3541 18th Street, Mission District. A neighborhood Irish pub, it will be remembered more for its political philosophy than for its uninspired decor. The first clue is the sign above the door reading, "Let's drink to the final defeat of the British army in Northern Ireland."

Open daily 8 a.m.-2 a.m. Information: 415-552-0074.

ᚹ **James Flood Mansion** (Pacific Union Club), corner of California and Mason Streets, Nob Hill. If you could make it to the top of Nob Hill, you could make it anywhere. Or so the members of high society of San Francisco believed. While most of the Irish immigrants were still living in shanties, James Flood had amassed a fortune which paid for a magnificent block-sized home. Flood was one of the Irish-American Big Four who made it big, really big, by purchasing Henry Comstock's share of a mine in Nevada for the sum of $11,000. Through time, the mine returned hundreds of millions of dollars in silver and gold to its purchasers. Flood's mansion still stands majestically above San Francisco, and it remains unapproachable by the average citizen. It is now the "exclusive" Pacific Union Club.

☺ **Jeremiah O'Brien**, Ft. Mason Center, Buchanan Street and Marina Boulevard. In what is considered to be the first naval activity of the Revolutionary War, Jeremiah O'Brien led the successful maneuver to capture the British schooner *Margaretta*. The only remaining unaltered and still operating World War II Liberty Ship was named for this Cork-born hero.

Open third weekend of each month, except May and December, 9 a.m.-4 p.m. Fee. Senior and children's discount. Information: 415-441-3101.

ᚻᚻ **The Little Shamrock**, 807 Lincoln Way, Sunset District. The Little Shamrock is a survivor. It's been here since 1893, and it's got the bar to prove it. OK, you know that the great San Francisco earthquake occurred in 1906, but do you know the hour? Just look at the old clock on the wall. It stopped ticking at the time of the earthquake. The decor is aged, but the crowds are young and energetic, tending to the athletic types on weekends. Darts and backgammon can keep you entertained if the patrons don't.

Open daily 3 p.m.-2 a.m. Information: 415-661-0060.

ᚻᚻ **Pat O'Shea's Mad Hatter**, 3848 Geary Boulevard, Richmond District. "We cheat tourists and drunks" reads the sign. That message and the business-like waitresses garbed in green could cause you to pass this one up. But what a mistake you'd be making. Here they offer a fine selection of draught beers and good food at nice prices. Ireland's own Guinness and San Francisco's own Anchor Steam are on draught and lamb and fish and nasturtiums are on the menu.

Nasturtiums? Isn't that a flower? And in an Irish pub? You could overdose with continual sports coverage running on several television sets, but the regulars thrive on it.

Open 11:30 a.m.-3 p.m. and 4 p.m.-9 p.m. (obviously restaurant hours, not pub!) Information: 415-752-3148.

⚑ **Robert Emmet Statue,** Golden Gate Park. Robert Emmet, Irish patriot and physician, along with friends, attempted to seize Dublin Castle in 1803. The popular support they had counted on did not materialize. Emmet escaped, but was betrayed to the British who hanged him. His speech from the gallows is recited annually at this site.

𝕭 **St. Patrick's Church,** 756 Mission Street. This is an Irish church through and through! It's the fourth church at this site since the parish was established by Father Magginis in 1851. The interior is finished in translucent green Connemara marble and Caen stone. The stained-glass windows honor Irish saints associated with the 32 provinces of Ireland. Vestments and crucifix are inspired by 6th and 8th century Celtic designs.

Information: 415-421-0547.

⚑ **United Irish Cultural Center of San Francisco,** 2700 45th Avenue. The Center has a large collection of Irish books, newspapers, and magazines relating to Irish literature, history, and genealogy. Information: 415-661-2700.

⚑ **William Andrews Clark Memorial Library,** University of California, 2520 Cimarron Street. Dublin-born British satirist Jonathan Swift (1667-1745) spent much of his life in Ireland. He is best known for *Gulliver's Travels.* Irish Oscar Wilde (1845-1900) won great recognition as a playwright ("Lady's Windemere's Fan," "The Importance of Being Earnest"), but was also a successful poet ("The Ballad of Reading Gaol," written after serving a prison term for the crime of sodomy) and novelist (*The Picture of Dorian Gray*). The library holds a collection of Jonathan Swift manuscripts and first editions and Oscar Wilde manuscripts and printed works.

San Simeon

S **Hearst-San Simeon State Historical Monument**, San Simeon. This whaling village with a population of 50 people attracts visitors who come to view the sea lions, otters, and whales that migrate north in the spring and return south in the winter. But the most amazing site in San Simeon is not in the water, but up on the hill.

William Randolph Hearst, publisher-politician-movie dabbler, was a controversial figure from the late 19th to the mid-20th century. Born in San Francisco of Irish ancestry, he followed in the footsteps of his father by getting elected to the U.S. House of Representatives in 1903. However, he lost more elections than he won, and earned his greatest fame as publisher of the nation's largest newspaper syndicate. He used and abused this power. Franklin Roosevelt experienced both his love and hate. Marion Davies, his mistress and a modestly talented movie actress, won his love, praise in the "Hollywood" columns of his newspapers, and keys to his castles on "Enchanted Hill."

Mansions, pools, tennis courts, gardens, wild animals, and trainloads of movie stars from nearby Los Angeles filled the grounds of the vast estate. With the help of his wife, he collected magnificent works of art and furnishings from around the world, many of which are now on display in the compound, a State Historical Monument.

Various tours of nearly two hours each are offered. You need more than one day to see it all. Considerable walking and climbing are required, but wheelchairs can be handled with 10 days notice. Open daily, except New Year's, Thanksgiving, and Christmas. Fee. Information and tickets: 800-444-7275 or write MISTIX, P.O. Box 85705, San Diego, 92138.

S **Jack Smith's Hearst Castle Show**, San Simeon Lodge, 3 1/2 miles south at 9520 Castillo Drive. A two hour video presentation consists of a 90-minute slide show on the personal and professional life of William Randolph Hearst and a 30-minute compilation of films starring Marion Davies. This is an easy way to gain some insight on the Hearsts and heighten your enjoyment of the Castle.

Open Wednesday-Monday at 8 p.m., March-November. Fee. Senior and children's discount. Information: 805-927-4601.

Yorba Linda

T Richard Nixon Library and Birthplace, 18001 Yorba Linda Boulevard. Richard Milhous Nixon, 37th president of the United States, and the former first lady, Patricia Ryan, both claim Irish ancestry. The ex-president says his great-great-great-great-grandfather Thomas Milhous was born in Carrickfergus, County Antrim, and later moved to the hamlet of Timahoe, near Dublin, and finally to Pennsylvania. Mrs. Nixon's grandfather emigrated from Ballinrobe, County Mayo.

The small house where Richard Nixon was born and a museum are located at this site. The house is furnished in the style of an early 20th century, middle-class home. The museum includes videos and personal memorabilia associated with his personal and professional life.

Open Monday-Saturday 10 a.m.-5 p.m., and Sunday 11 a.m.-5 p.m.; closed New Year's, Thanksgiving, and Christmas. Fee. Senior and children's discount. Information: 714-993-3393.

Colorado

Central City

T Teller House, Eureka and Pine Streets. When President Ulysses Simpson Grant visited the Teller House in 1872, he strode up to the front door over a walk of solid silver. In honor of his visit, the stones had been replaced with silver bricks. Note the painting of the "Face on the Barroom Floor" inspired by the poem.

Open daily 11:30 a.m.-4 p.m., May through November, and by appointment other times. Fee. Senior and children's discount. Information: 303-582-3200.

Colorado Springs

T **Hall of Presidents**, 1050 South 21st Street. With more than 100 wax figures, the Hall includes all U.S. presidents and first ladies, prepared by artists in the London studios of Josephine Tussaud. Models are presented in 23 room-size sets. Also, models of characters from fairy tale stories are displayed.

Open daily 9 a.m.-9 p.m., June-September; limited hours other months. Fee. Children's discount. Information: 719-635-3553.

T **Pikes Peak Ghost Town**, 2 miles west of Colorado Springs at 400 South 21st Street at US 24. Personal items of 23rd president Chester A. Arthur are among the large collection of items in this authentic town of the Old West, created under one roof. Arthur's father was born in Antrim, Ireland. Included in the town is a general store, blacksmith shop, jail, hotel, drugstore, firehouse, livery stable, Victorian home, saloon, and the bulletproof car used by Franklin D. Roosevelt. You can also enjoy nickelodeons, arcade movies, and an 1890 shooting gallery.

Open May through mid-October. Fee. Information: 719-634-0696.

Creede

D One of the wildest of the wild towns of the West, **Creede** came late to the mining business. Silver was not found until 1890. It earned its reputation for hell-raising with the help of such institutions as Frank James (Jesse's brother), Bob Ford (killer of Jesse), and Bat Masterson. Now down to a population of 400 and a calmer lifestyle, one of the old silver mines has been resuscitated! Stay tuned for the next chapter in the life of Creede.

Denver

HH **Finnegan's Irish Pub**, 1550 Court Place, Raddison Hotel. Finnegan's provides authentic Irish cuisine and entertainment.

There's a full menu with Irish specialties for lunch and dinner. Call for the schedule for live Irish entertainment.

Open 11 a.m.-11 p.m. daily, except Sunday. Information: 305-893-3333.

P **The Molly Brown House,** 1340 Pennsylvania Street, 2 blocks south of US 40. Built in 1889, this is the fabulous home of the equally fabulous Molly Brown, survivor of the *Titanic* and of a marriage which brought her great wealth, when her husband struck gold, but not the social standing she craved. She has become even better known today than she was in the 19th century due to *The Unsinkable Molly Brown*, the movie and stage musical which has starred Irish-American actress Debbie Reynolds in endless revivals over the past several decades. The Molly Brown house has been restored to its original— quite original—decor.

Open Monday-Saturday 10 a.m.-4 p.m. and Sunday afternoon noon-4, June through August; Tuesday-Saturday 10 a.m.-4 p.m. and Sunday afternoon 12-3, other months. Fee. Senior and children's discount. Information: 303-832-4092.

S **Museum of Western Art,** 1727 Tremont Place, Old Navarre Building. Georgia O'Keeffe is among the outstanding artists shown in this exhibit of American Western art.

Open Tuesday-Saturday 10 a.m.-4:30 p.m., except New Year's, Thanksgiving, and Christmas. Fee. Senior and children's discount. Information: 303-296-1880.

Georgetown

P **Georgetown Loop Historic Mining and Railroad Park.** Here's a slice of life as lived by the Irish mine and railroad worker during the 19th century. The park features a mine, crushing mill, and reconstructed buildings. You can ride a train on the reconstructed Georgetown Loop Railroad on a 7-mile tour. The railroad joined Georgetown to Silver Plume during the boom years of the late 1800s.

Open daily. Fee. Information: 303-670-1686.

Golden

G **Buffalo Bill's Grave-Museum**, summit of Lookout Mountain, on Lariat Trail. The museum details the life of William F. Cody and displays memorabilia of the Old West.

Open daily 9 a.m.-5 p.m., May-October; Tuesday-Sunday 9 a.m.-4 p.m., rest of the year, except Christmas. Fee. Senior and children's discount. Information: 303-526-0747.

Leadville

P **Leadville**, located in central Colorado, is a town with a story as lively as that of one of its most famous citizens, the "unsinkable" Irish American, Molly Brown. And it's had about as many ups and downs. Molly is one of the people who made her fortune here during one of its ups. Leadville was once the producer of gold and silver, then a decaying mining town until the late 1950s, when the remaining local citizens resuscitated it without destroying its past. The story of Leadville is told in the opera "The Ballad of Baby Doe."

But who is Baby Doe? A friend of H.A.W. Tabor. And who is H.A.W. Tabor? Tabor was one of the men who backed the right prospectors. He became outrageously wealthy and spent his money freely. His wife Augusta didn't like this, but Baby Doe did. So, H.A.W. said, "Goodbye, Augusta. Hello, Baby!" Tabor lost his money in the Panic of 1893 and died six years later. Baby Doe heeded his death bed instruction, "Hang onto the Matchless Mine." She did, and lived in a nearby cabin for the next 36 years until she died in poverty.

Leadville, with a population of 2,600, survives and so do some of the special sites, including the "Matchless Mine Mine Cabin," which can be visited daily between June 1 and Labor Day.

Manitou Springs

T **Colorado Car Museum**, 135 Manitou Avenue. Antique cars and limousines used by Presidents Kennedy, Truman, and Eisenhower and Queen Elizabeth II are on display, along with a 1900 Locomobile steamer and the first car to climb Pike's Peak.

Open daily, May to mid-October. Handicapped facilities. Fee. Information: 719-685-5996; Chamber of Commerce, 354 Manitou Avenue (719-685-5089).

Trinidad

G **Carson Park and Statue.** Once a busy trading post along the Santa Fe trail, Trinidad had Irish Americans Bat Masterson for a sheriff and Kit Carson as a frequent visitor. Today, the seat of Las Animas County, Trinidad traces its development through coal mining, ranching, farming, and as a railroad center. A statue of Kit Carson stands in a park named in his honor.

Victor

S At the turn of the 20th century, when gold was found in this area, the population of Victor rose to move than 12,000. Today is a quieter time, and there are more buildings than people. Over 300 structures from Victor's early days (1893) still stand. Among them is the City Hall where the Manassa Mauler, Colorado-born, Irish American Jack Dempsey, world heavy weight boxing champion (1919-1926), once trained.

Connecticut

London

S **Eugene O'Neill Theater Center,** West of New London via US 1 in Waterford. The artists' complex is named in honor of the Irish-American playwright, recipient of the Nobel Prize for Literature. It is a writers' oasis serving the National Playwrights Conference, National Critics Institute, National Opera/Music Theater Conference, and National Theater Institute. Readings of new plays are presented in summer.

Information: 203-443-5378.

S Monte Cristo Cottage, 325 Pequot Avenue. Boyhood home of Eugene O'Neill, it was named for his Irish-born father's best known role as the Count of Monte Cristo. O'Neill included the setting in "Long Days Journey Into Night" and "Ah, Wilderness!" You can view the multimedia presentation, research library, and O'Neill memorabilia.

Open Monday-Friday afternoon 1-4, mid-April to mid-December, except holidays. Fee. Information: 203-433-0051.

Delaware

New Castle

It was in **New Castle**, near what is now Strand and Delaware Streets, that William Penn and his secretary, James Logan of Armagh, Ireland, first laid eyes on his vast land holdings. New Castle, once the county seat, produced two Irish-American signers of the Declaration of Independence, George Read and Thomas McKean. With the loss of the railroad, New Castle settled into a more serene community, which may explain why much of the original Federal architecture can still be enjoyed today.

T George Read II House and Garden, 42 The Strand. An example of Federal-style architecture from the turn of the 19th century, the mansion was built by the son of one of the signers of the Declaration of Independence. The home has period furnishings. The formal gardens date from 1847.

Open Tuesday-Saturday 10 a.m.-4 p.m. and Sunday afternoon noon-4:00, March-December; Saturday 10 a.m.-4 p.m. and Sunday noon-4 p.m., other months; closed holidays. Fee. Senior and children's discount. Information: 302-322-8411.

Wilmington

P Hagley Museum, Route 202 and Buck Road. This was originally the E.I. du Pont's black powderworks, where many Irish immigrants labored. Today, the 200-acre site includes a one-room schoolhouse, a millwright shop, exhibit building with working models, functioning 1875 machine shop, and gift shop. You can tour the 1803 home with artifacts relating to five generations of du Ponts, a barn housing antique wagons, and a 19th-century garden.

Open daily, except New Year's, Thanksgiving, and Christmas. Fee. Senior discount. Information: 302-658-2400.

ℋℋ O'Friel's Irish Pub, 706 Delaware Avenue. Wash down your pub grub with a pint of Guinness or Harp in a jolly, friendly gathering of a cross-section of Wilmingtonians. Folks are attracted to the long, dark unpretentious bar and adjacent dining area, especially after work and Thursday-Saturday evenings when they're likely to hear live Irish music.

Open daily, except Sunday. Information: 302-654-9952.

District of Columbia

In 1900, the chairman of the Committee on the District of Columbia, Sen. James McMillan, invited a group of respected artists to suggest improvements in Washington's parks. The group included Irish Augustus Saint-Gaudens, sculptor; Charles McKim and Daniel Burnham, architects; and Frederick Law Olmsted, Jr., landscape architect. The Mall received the most attention, but their recommendations shaped the future appearance of the District.

G, T Andrew Jackson Equestrian Statue, Lafayette Square, across Pennsylvania Avenue from the White House. The central monument in Washington's most televised square is that of Andrew Jackson on horseback, erected in 1853. The bronze statue is the first equestrian statue created in America. It is frequently surrounded by pickets and protesters seeking to influence the president and gain media attention for their cause. Both of Jackson's parents were born in Carrickfergus, County Antrim.

HH **The Dubliner Restaurant and Pub**, 520 North Capitol Street, N.W. & No.4 F Street, N.W. The Dubliner is one of the two best Irish pubs in D.C. With a pint of Harp or Guinness or a bottle of Guinness Gold, you can sit at one of three bars (one non-smoking!) and enjoy the authentic Irish pub atmosphere of green and wood. Or you can sit in one of the several dining rooms and select from a menu crammed with Irish specialties, like oak smoked salmon imported from Ireland; Irish cut lamb chops; beef stew; veal Donegal; or cheese cake Dublin style. If you time it right, your indulgence will be accompanied by live Irish entertainment, presented nightly. On the other hand, I recommend Sunday morning for the Irish country breakfast.

The Dubliner is popular with families, singles, students, government workers, professionals, and the Irish.

Danny Coleman (from Tipperary Hills, Syracuse) also owns the elegant Powerscourt restaurant upstairs and the adjoining Phoenix Park Hotel to form what he calls the "Center of Irish Hospitality in the New World." This "center" if expanded (as it once was) would include the pub next door, The Irish Times.

Open Sunday-Thursday 11 a.m.-2 a.m., Friday-Saturday until 2:30 a.m. Information: 202-737-3773.

G **Gen. George Meade Memorial**, Pennsylvania Avenue, near the National Gallery of Art. A winged sculpture was created to honor Gen. George Gordon Meade, whose ancestor, Andrew Meade, emigrated from Kerry in 1690. Meade led the defense of Washington during the Civil War and headed the Northern forces to their victory at Gettysburg.

G **Gen. Ulysses S. Grant Memorial**, Union Square, Pennsylvania and Maryland Avenues, N.W. A 17-foot bronze statue of Grant dominates Henry Schrady's monument to the tragedy of war. Schrady, a young, unknown artist, was selected by a group of highly regarded sculptors, including Irish-born Auguste Saint-Gaudens.

B **Georgetown University**, 37th Street & O Street, N.W., Georgetown. The first Roman Catholic college in America was founded in

1789 by Irish American John Carroll. Carroll would become the first bishop and archbishop in the country. Georgetown is recognized as one of the finest Catholic universities in the world.

Information Center in Healy Building. Tours. Handicapped facilities. Information: 202-667-3634.

T **Historical Society of Washington, D.C.**, Heurich Mansion, 1307 New Hampshire Avenue, N.W. The brownstone and brick home, built in the late 19th century, houses the Historical Society, founded in 1894. Among the many impressive items to be noted is a unique desk created for Ulysses S. Grant. Reportedly, the desk was designed and constructed for Grant by a Montana admirer. It combines drawers and a secret compartment into a three-sided 1872 monstrosity highlighted by a pair of antlers. The home was owned by Christian Heurich, an immigrant German brewer, and his wife.

Different parts of the complex are open different hours on different days, but if you visit noon-3 p.m. Wednesday or Friday, you can see the house, library, exhibition gallery, and garden. Free admission to the exhibition gallery and library; fee for house tour. Senior and student discount.

Information: 202-785-2058.

HH **Ireland's Four Provinces**, 3412 Connecticut Avenue, N.W. The 4 Ps is one of the two best all-round Irish pubs in Washington, D.C., a city blessed with many good Irish pubs. Guinness and Harp on draught. Good pub grub, including Irish stew. Darts and live Irish entertainment nightly. Who could ask for anything more? Apparently not the crowds who fill the long bar and cavernous room most nights of the week. All ages flock here, but it's particularly popular with college students, young professionals, and the Irish-born.

Christy Hughes, from Westmeath (the land of my grandfather, bless his soul) transplanted a little bit of Ireland and placed it right here in Washington, D.C.

Open daily from 5 p.m. Information: 202-244-0860.

T **John F. Kennedy Center for the Performing Arts**, New Hampshire Avenue at F Street, N.W. The monumental and official memorial to the 34th president has a concert hall, opera house, two small theaters, movie theater, three restaurants, and library. A 7-foot bronze bust of Kennedy is set in the Grand Foyer.

Tours daily. Free. Information: 202-416-8341.

T **John F. Kennedy Homes**, Georgetown. Kennedy's first bachelor pad after coming to Washington as U.S. Senator from Massachusetts was at 1528 31st Street, N.W. Later, as he became more socially active, he moved to a four-story house at 1400 34th Street. When he married, he and Jackie set up housekeeping (so to speak) at 3271 P Street, moving on to 3307 N Street, then up to the White House. These continue to be private dwellings.

HH **Kelly's Irish Times Pub**, 14 F Street, N.W., looks from the outside as if it barely survived the War of 1812. Inside, blue- and white-collar workers mingle in a rustic setting with walls lined with Irish artifacts and copies of the *Irish Times*. The story is that Sen. Bob Packwood (OR) and the Chief of Staff of the Senate Committee on Finance wrote up the 1986 Tax Reform Bill while huddled over a pitcher of beer in one of these booths.

You can have a pint of Irish beer with a "fresh hot roast turkey platter," once described by food critic Phyllis Richmond as "Best in Class" lunch special. Entertainment, sometimes Irish, is offered Thursday-Saturday.

"Give me your thirsty, your famished, your befuddled masses," reads the sign above the entrance. Join the masses if you're in the area, before or after visiting the Dubliner.

Open Sunday-Thursday until 2 a.m., Friday-Saturday until 3:00 a.m. (202-543-5433).

T **Library of Congress**, 10 First Street, S.E. It was James Madison who initiated what was to become the Library of Congress. He felt that it was "indispensable" that the representatives have ready access to the literature relating to their work. He argued that the ignorance of such material could be observed in some of the legislation that they had passed.

In 1780 a bill was passed authorizing $5000 to purchase books and house a library. Congress bought 740 books, but the books were burned by the British when they attacked Washington, August 24, 1814. This loss must have been particularly galling, since the British had sold these books to Congress in the first place. Congress then bought Thomas Jefferson's library of more than 6,000 books and housed them in the Capitol where they remained until the Thomas Jefferson Building was completed in 1897—the first of three buildings to comprise the Library of Congress. The other buildings were named for John Adams and James Madison.

T **James Madison Memorial Building and Statue**, Library of Congress, First Street and Independence Avenue, S.E. Opened in 1980, this is the official memorial to James Madison, 4th U.S. president, one of three buildings comprising the Library of Congress. It contains the James Madison Memorial Hall, exhibition space, reading rooms, and offices. As the world's largest library building, it stores more than 50,000,000 items, including a collection of more than 13 million photographs. Among these photos are work by Matthew Brady, Irish-American photographer of the Civil War.

For the first time in its 200-year history, Congress is considering charging the public for certain library services.

Open Monday-Friday 8:30 a.m.-9:30 p.m. and Saturday-Sunday 8:30 a.m.-6 p.m. Free. Information: 202-707-5458.

HH **Murphy's D.C.**, 2609 24th St., N.W. Deservedly popular with neighborhood young professionals and tourists from nearby hotels, Murphy's is an authentic Irish pub with two bars which offer not only Guinness and Harp, but Murphy's (not named for the owner) and Mooney (which is named for the owner). A limited menu includes corned beef and cabbage (which I've rarely seen on a menu in Ireland) and Irish stew. Sen. Ted Kennedy is one of the familiar faces that you may see here. Irish entertainment nightly. See Alexandria, VA, and Lima, OH for other pubs owned by Mooney.

Open daily. Information: 202-462-7171.

T **National Archives**, Constitution Avenue between 7th and 9th Streets, N.W. The Declaration of Independence, the Constitution, and the Bill of Rights are on display in the Exhibition Hall. In order to prevent further deterioration, they are enclosed in a glass and bronze case filled with inert helium. The signers of the Declaration of Independence include the names of Irish- born James Smith and George Taylor of Pennsylvania and Matthew Thornton of New Hampshire; Irish Americans Thomas Lynch, Thomas McKean, George Read, and Edward Rutledge, and the only Catholic to sign, Maryland's Charles Carroll III.

On July 8, 1776, John Nixon, from County Wexford, was the first to read the Declaration of Independence in public. The Constitution was signed by Irishman Thomas Fitzsimmons, the only Catholic to sign. Among the more than 6,000,000 still photos on file are Civil War photos taken by Irish American photographer Matthew Brady.

Open daily 10 a.m.-9 p.m., April-Labor Day; 10 a.m.-5:30 p.m., the rest of the year; closed Christmas. Free. Information and tour reservations: 202-501-5000.

T **National Building Museum**, 401 F Street, N.W.; ramp entrance on 5th Street. Built between 1882-1887 as a home for the U.S. Pension Office, it is one of the more striking structures in the city. Twelve inaugural balls have been held here, those of William Howard Taft, Jimmy Carter, George Bush, and six Irish American presidents, beginning in 1885 with Grover Cleveland, then Harrison, McKinley, Theodore Roosevelt, Nixon, and Reagan. The exterior of the building is encircled with a 3-foot high frieze representing a procession of Union army veterans. In 1980, the building was renovated to serve as the home of the National Building Museum.

Tours can be arranged. Open 10 a.m.-4 p.m. Monday through Saturday and noon-4 p.m. Sunday; closed New Year's, Thanksgiving, and Christmas. Free. Information: 202-272-2448.

P **National Gallery of Art**, 4th Street and Constitution Avenue, N.W. The development of the Gallery was made possible as a result of a bequest from Andrew Mellon, Secretary of Treasury under three presidents, ambassador to England for President Franklin Roosevelt, and one of America's wealthiest men. Mellon, whose father and grandparents emigrated from Ireland, made the family fortune through his business acumen, including investments in oil, steel, aluminum, and banks. When he died he left an art collection, worth $6 million, purchased in the Soviet Union in 1931 during a financial crisis, and megamoney to support a national gallery.

Among the holdings of the Gallery of special interest to Irish Americans is a display of photographs of painter Georgia O'Keeffe by her husband, famed photographer Alfred Stieglitz.

Open Monday-Saturday 10 a.m.-5 p.m., Sunday 11 a.m.-6 p.m.; closed New Year's and Christmas. Free. Information: 202-737-4215.

S National Museum of American History, one of the Smithsonian Institutes, Constitution Avenue, between 12th and 14th Streets. A phenomenal display of articles relating to all aspects of American life. Among the show business artifacts with an Irish aura are those of the eternally young Irish offspring of Scandinavian ventriloquist Edgar Bergen–Charlie McCarthy, one of the best known entertainers of the 1940s; also one of the four pairs of ruby red slippers worn by Irish American Judy Garland as Dorothy in the "Wizard of Oz"; and the rocking chair used by Irish American actor Carroll O'Connor as the blue collar worker everyone loved feeling superior to, Archie Bunker.

In order to experience all of the displays of science and technological, political and social history requires more than one visit.

Open daily 10 a.m.-5:30 p.m.; closed Christmas. Free guided tours. Information: 202-337-2700.

S National Museum of Women in the Arts, 1250 New York Avenue, N.W. Georgia O'Keeffe is represented among the more than 500 works of art by established women artists.

Open Tuesday-Saturday 10 a.m.-5 p.m. and Sunday noon-5:00. Donations. Information: 202-783-5000.

S National Portrait Gallery, Smithsonian Institutions, south wing of the Old Patent Office Building, between 7th, 9th, G, and F Streets, N.W. The Portrait Gallery is exclusively devoted to portraits of Americans who have made significant contributions to the history of the country. The Hall of Presidents includes photographs by American Civil War photographer Matthew Brady.

Open daily 10 a.m.-5:30 p.m.; closed Christmas. Free guided tours. Information: 202-357-2700.

Ⓖ **Navy Museum,** 9th and M Streets, S.E. John Barry left County Wexford as a cabin boy. By the end of his naval career, he had served the Continental cause as captain of the *Lexington,* which made the first seizure of a British ship early in the Revolutionary War; also as senior captain of the naval fleet established by Congress following the war; and first commodore of the United States Navy. John Barry is known as the "Father of the United States Navy." He died in 1803 and is buried in Philadelphia.

The museum features a statue of Barry and a model of the destroyer, the USS *Barry.* Through displays, you can follow the history of the Navy beginning with the Revolution.

Open Monday-Friday 9 a.m.-4 p.m., Saturday and Sunday 10 a.m.-5 p.m.; Memorial Day and Labor Day 9 a.m.-5 p.m., other holidays 10 a.m.-5 p.m. Information: 1-202-433-2651.

Ⓣ **The Octagon House,** 1799 New York Avenue, N.W. This six-sided (not eight) house, built in 1801 by Virginian John Tayloe III, was the temporary home of President and Mrs. Madison after the British burned the White House in the War of 1812. The Treaty of Ghent, ending the war, was signed here. The mansion has been restored to its original state.

Open Tuesday-Friday 10 a.m.-4 p.m., Saturday-Sunday afternoon 1-4. Fee. Senior and children's discount. Information: 202-638- 3105.

Ⓢ **The Phillips Collection,** 1600 21st Street, N.W. at Q Street. The gallery features 19th- and 20th-century paintings by Georgia O'Keeffe, Mark Rothko, Paul Klee and other American and European artists. The most famous work is "Luncheon of the Boating Party" by Renoir.

Concerts are performed Sundays at 5 p.m., September-May.Open Monday-Saturday 10 a.m.-5 p.m. and Sunday noon-7 p.m.; closed

New Year's, Independence Day, Thanksgiving, and Christmas. Fee. Senior, student, and children's discount. Information: 202-387-2151.

ℋℋ **Powerscourt Restaurant**, 520 North Capital Street, N.W. Powerscourt reminds the visitor of the elegance that is Irish. It is what would have been described by earlier generations as "lace curtain." It is intimate in size and classic in simplicity. The chef focuses on doing a few things well. Service is attentive and friendly, but not intrusive. Annually, chefs are imported from Ireland to prepare special fixed price dinners. Owned by Danny Coleman, who also owns the Dubliner pub downstairs, it is equally successful. Expensive, but my favorite Washington, D.C., restaurant.

Open daily except Sunday. Information: 202-737-3776.

ℋℐ **Robert Emmet Statue**, S Street and Massachusetts Avenue.

The statue of Robert Emmet, erected in 1966, honors the Irish patriot and commemorates the 50th anniversary of Irish independence.

S **Saint-Gaudens' Statue**, Rock Creek Cemetery, Rock Creek Church Road, N.W. Saint-Gaudens' statue of a woman was commissioned by her husband following her suicide.

T **St. Matthew's Cathedral**, 1725 Rhode Island Avenue, N.W. John F. Kennedy attended mass in the cathedral, the seat of Washington's archbishop. It was here in 1963 that Kennedy's funeral service was held. A memorial to the assassinated president is in front of the main altar.

Open Monday-Friday 7:30 a.m.-6:15 p.m., Saturday 7:30 a.m.-6:30 p.m., and Sunday 6:30 a.m.-7:30 p.m. Free. Information: 202-347-3215.

G **Sheridan Circle**, Massachusetts and 23rd Street, N.W. Erected in 1909, the equestrian statue portrays Irish-born General Philip H. Sheridan astride his horse, Rienzi. Sheridan was a major general during the Civil War.

G **The Society of the Cincinnati**, Anderson House, 2118 Massachusetts Avenue, N.W. Gen. Henry Knox, an Irish immigrant and chief of artillery under George Washington, formed the Society in 1783. It had a membership of nearly 2,400 military officers from 13 states. The officers had served in the Continental Army with the French forces between 1775 and 1783. A 14th society, in France, came to an end during the French Revolution, but was revived in 1925. Today, membership is about 3,300, made up primarily of the oldest son extending back to the original member. The Anderson House, completed in 1905, has 12 rooms with period furnishings, a marble staircase, tapestries originally belonging to King Louis XIII, and a gallery with memorabilia of the life of the original owner of the mansion, Larz Anderson III, former ambassador to Belgium. When Anderson died in 1937, he deeded left his home to the Society of the Cincinnati.

Museum and library hours and days vary, but you can see both if you visit Tuesday through Friday afternoons 1-4. Free. Handicapped facilities. Information: 202-785-2040.

T **Supreme Court Building**, East Capitol Street and 1st Street. Although the Supreme Court was established in Washington in 1800, it was not housed in a permanent spot until 1935. Cass Gilbert designed an imposing white marble structure with double rows of Corinthian columns. Far more impressive, if less fun, than meeting in a tavern as the justices once had. This is the work place of such illustrious Irish Americans as Justice Brennan Roger Taney and the first female Supreme Court justice, Sandra Day O'Connor.

Court is in session Monday-Wednesday, October through April, and the first work day of the week, May-June. If you want to visit when the Court is in session, you must make a choice. One line permits you a few minutes in court, before ushering you out. The other lets you spend the day. The lines start forming about 8:30 a.m.

Open Monday-Friday 9 a.m.-4:30 p.m. Free. Information: 202-479-3000.

T **Theodore Roosevelt Island**, George Washington Parkway near the Theodore Roosevelt Bridge. A 17-foot bronze statue of the 26th U.S. president oversees an 88-acre wilderness island in the Potomac River. It contains trails, marshland, swampland, and a variety of trees and animals. A pedestrian bridge connects the Island to the Virginia mainland.

Information: 703-285-2598.

℗ **Walsh-McLean House,** Massachusetts Avenue and 21st Street. This was once the site of glittering balls presented by Evalyn Walsh-McLean, the last individual to own the fabulous Hope Diamond. Her father, County Tipperary-born Tom Walsh, made the family fortune when he struck silver and gold in Ouray, Colorado. He used his money to buy a place for his family in Washington, D.C. society, more accepting of the nouveau riche in the late 19th century than other eastern cities. Naturally, Evalyn was enrolled in dancing classes and there, at the age of 12, met her future husband, Edward McLean, son of the publisher of the *Washington Post.* This worked out nicely, because when they married, they could afford a proper wedding.

To ensure that the newlyweds wouldn't have to worry about cash during their honeymoon, each of the fathers gave his child $100,000. But the daddies had taught them well. As parents will readily understand, the children soon ran out of their $200,000 and had to wire home for money to cover their hotel. The kids did manage to leave Europe without paying a number of other troublesome bills.

Like other honeymooners, they wanted to bring back a memento of their trip. Unlike other honeymooners, Evalyn brought back the Star of the East. This was the beginning of her diamond collection which reached its zenith shortly thereafter with the purchase of the 45 1/2-carat Hope Diamond, a jewel which was alleged to have brought bad luck to its previous owners. Evalyn scoffed at such "superstition," but the years ahead were not kind. She and her husband drank more and enjoyed one another less. He earned a reputation for doing eccentric things, like putting a damper on a White House party when he urinated into the fireplace. Evalyn spent more and more time drinking and indulging in other less socially acceptable drugs. She existed a number of years after her husband's death, but led a desultory, lonely (her only son was killed in a car accident), and painful life, alternating between drugged states and dementia tremors.

After Evalyn's death, no buyer could be found for the **Hope Diamond**. It was donated to the Smithsonian, where it is the stellar attraction in the Hall of Gems of the National Museum of Natural History. To learn more about the McLean-Walsh saga, consult Stephen Birmingham's *Real Lace, America's Irish Rich.*

The Walsh-McLean House remains a monument to the fortunes and follies of two Irish American families. But few people know it as anything more or less than the Embassy of Indonesia.

T **Washington National Cathedral**, Mount St. Alban at Massachusetts and Wisconsin Avenues, N.W. Completed in 1990, after 85 years of construction, it is the sixth largest cathedral in the world. Woodrow Wilson is buried in "Wilson's Bay," where carvings illustrate events in his life. He is the only U.S. president to be buried in Washington, D.C.

Open Monday-Friday 10 a.m.-9 p.m. and Saturday-Sunday 10 a.m.-4:30 p.m., May-Labor Day; daily 10 a.m.-4:30 p.m. other times. Donations. Information: 202-537-6200.

S **The White House**, 1600 Pennsylvania Avenue. Inspired by the Irish Dail (parliament) and designed by Kilkenny-born James Hoban, the White House was built in 1800, burned by British in the War of 1812, rebuilt by Hoban and remodeled by various presidents. It has been home and office to all presidents except George Washington and Thomas Jefferson.

Tours of five public rooms Tuesday-Saturday mornings, Memorial Day-Labor Day. Tickets can be obtained at the Ellipse Booth adjacent to the White House grounds. Closed New Year's, Christmas, and during presidential functions. If you contact your senator, you can get a more elaborate tour and won't have to stand in line. Free. Information: 202-456-7041.

T **Woodrow Wilson House**, 2340 South Street, N.W. This is the town house where Wilson lived following his second term as president. It contains the original furnishings and memorabilia, including a miniature of the Robert Emmet statue standing on S Street and Massachusetts Avenue.

Closed Mondays, New Year's, Thanksgiving, and Christmas. Fee. Information: 202-387-4062.

Florida

Apalachicola

☉ **Fort Gadsden State Historic Site,** 24 miles northeast via US 98, FL 65. This was a battle site during the War of 1812 and the Civil War. The first fort, built by the British in 1814, was destroyed, but rebuilt by Andrew Jackson, son of Antrim emigres. It was taken by the Confederates during the Civil War. Portions of the fort still stand, and a miniature of the fort and exhibits can be seen. Open daily. Free. Information: 904-670-8988.

Fort Myers

℗ **Fort Myers** has just about everything. Seventy varieties of palms, tropical fruit, a glorious spectrum of flowers, and, imported from the North, the Minnesota Twins—the Twins go there for spring-training. Fort Myers has long been popular with the advantaged, including Irish-American Henry Ford who bought a home here next to his buddy, Thomas Edison, in 1916. Furnished in early 20th century style, the home is part of an Edison-Ford complex. Florida's largest banyan tree is on the grounds.

Both homes are open Monday-Saturday 9 a.m.-4 p.m. and Sunday afternoon 12:30-4; closed Thanksgiving and Christmas. Fee. Children's discount. Information: 813-334-3614.

☉ **Kennedy Space Center,** 15 miles north of Cape Canaveral, via US 1, I-95 to NASA Parkway, then east; north via FL 3. The 140,000-acre space center is one of the most historically significant spots in the world. It is home to all human space flights since 1964, including the first manned flight to the moon. Irish American astronauts were James McDivitt; Michael Collins; Kathryn Sullivan, the first woman to walk in space; and Christa Corrigan McAuliffe.

Two hour bus tours are available. The Red Tour includes the Apollo II Moon Landing Show—Collins piloted the spacecraft which made the first landing on the moon. The Blue Tour includes the Gemini launching pad—McDivitt was one of the Gemini astronauts.

Wheelchairs available. Information: 407-452-2121.

G **Spaceport USA**, 11 miles east of I-95, south of Titusville. Films show space launches on a screen 5 1/2 stories high and 70 feet wide with wrap around sound. Exhibits include moon rock, replicas of space capsules, and the Viking probe.

Handicapped facilities. Free. Information: 407-452-2121.

G **Astronauts Memorial: Space Mirror**, off FL 405, through entrance to Spaceport USA. The memorial is dedicated to the astronauts who have lost their lives in the line of duty. It is made of black granite with reflecting panels behind each name. A computerized turntable revolves the memorial so that rays from the sun shine through the names. Among the names is Christa Corrigan McAuliffe, the first teacher-astronaut, who along with her companions, perished January 28, 1986, when the Challenger space shuttle exploded.

G **U.S. Space Camp/U.S. Astronaut Hall of Fame**, on FL 405, 11 miles east of I-95, south of Titusville. Films, photographs, and memorabilia of Mercury astronauts are displayed. All Space Center attractions are open daily, except Christmas and certain launch days. Information: 407-452-2121 or write SPACEPORT USA, TWS, Visitors Center, Kennedy Space Center, Florida, 32899.

White Springs

S **Stephen Foster State Folk Culture Center**, way down upon the Suwannee River on US 41, near the Georgia border. Stephen Collins

Foster, one of America's most popular and prolific composers, was the great-grandson of Alexander Foster, who emigrated to America from Derry in 1728, settling in Pennsylvania. Foster was born in Lawrenceville, now part of Pittsburgh. Foster's work was influenced by the black spirituals and his Irish heritage. Charles Hamm, in *American Irish Culture*, stresses Foster's familiarity with the work of Irish composer and poet Thomas Moore, pointing out the similarities of some of Foster's work to Irish tunes. Hamm also notes the use of Irish rhythm patterns in Foster's compositions. Foster wrote the words and lyrics to songs familiar to all Americans, such as "Old Folks at Home," "My Old Kentucky Home," and "Oh! Susanna." He also wrote many minstrel songs which show the influence of Black music. Much of Foster's financial reward was invested in liquor, and he died alone and penniless in 1961 in the charity ward of Bellevue Hospital, New York.

The Center features crafts, music, and legends of early and contemporary Floridians. The 97-bell Degan carillon plays concerts daily. A number of musical events are held during the year, including the annual "Jeannie with the Light Brown Hair" auditions and ball.

Guided tours of the center, bell tower, and boat tours are offered. Fee. Information: 904-397-2733.

Georgia

Athens

S **Taylor-Grady House**, 634 Prince Avenue. A beautifully restored 1840 Greek Revival mansion was first owned by Gen. Robert Taylor, who emigrated with his family from Ireland. It was purchased by William Simmons Grady in 1864, while on furlough during the Civil War. Grady was killed shortly after at the Battle of Petersburg. His son, Henry W. Grady, was managing editor of the *Atlanta Constitution* and is credited with the phrase and promotion of the concept of the "New South."

Open Monday-Friday 10 a.m.-3:30 p.m., except holidays. Fee. Under 6 years, free. Information: 706-549-8688.

Atlanta

S Atlanta-Fulton County Public Library, 1 Margaret Mitchell Square. The library displays memorabilia associated with the development and production of *Gone with the Wind*, based on Margaret Mitchell's best seller, and starring the English Vivien Leigh as the South's most famous Irish American, Scarlett O'Hara.

Open Monday-Friday 9 a.m.-6 p.m., Tuesday-Thursday 9 a.m.-8 p.m., Friday-Saturday 10 a.m.-5 p.m., Sunday afternoon 2-6. Information: 404-730-1700.

S Across the street is **Margaret Mitchell Park** with a columned sculpture and waterfall. Where the Georgia-Pacific skyscraper now stands is the spot where *GWTW* premiered in the Loew's Grand Theater.

HH County Cork Pub,56 East Andrews Drive, between Roswell land W. Paces Ferry Roads, offers Irish beer, Irish liquor, and Irish dinners. Green beer, bagpipes, singers, dancers, fiddlers, and Irish fare on St. Pat's Day. Our taxi had some trouble finding it on the upper level in the rear of a shopping center, but it's worth the search for its informal, cheerful, cozy, friendly atmosphere. Passable, but cheap food. Skip the sausage plate (I did my second visit), and stick to the stew or pub grub. Irish entertainment and/or Karioke weekends. Tap beers include Guinness and Harp plus English, German, Scotch, and American. Avoid green beer after St. Patrick's Day. Sometimes offered cheap, but its life slips along with its price. They sell a wide range of T-shirts, one of the greatest—now a classic—was the "Irish Storm" shirt which came out in 1991. Many Atlantans think this is the city's only Irish pub. It isn't, but it may as well be.

Open daily until 2:00 a.m. (404-262-2227).

S Henry W. Grady Monument, Marietta Street near Forsyth Street. A statue has been erected in honor of the Irish American writer-publisher and managing editor of the *Atlanta Constitution,* who was the spokesman for the concept of the "New South." Grady died December 23, 1889, after contracting pneumonia during a trip to Boston where he lectured on the New South.

S **Margaret Mitchell Apartment,** 10th and Peachtree Streets. The apartment house in which Mitchell created the best-selling novel of American history, the Pulitzer Prize-winning *Gone with the Wind,* stands (barely) on this corner. A group of Atlantans is trying to raise money to renovate the building.

S **Margaret Mitchell Grave,** 248 Oakland Avenue. Margaret Mitchell is buried at Oakland Cemetery. She was killed while helping her husband cross Peachtree Street, near 13th, August 16, 1949. The graves of golfer Bobby Jones and many well-known sons and daughters of Georgia are also here. After viewing the graves, you can eat your lunch under the magnolia trees, if the ambiance appeals to you.

Free tours weekends. Information: 404-577-8163 or -522-4345.

S **Margaret Mitchell Square,** Peachtree Street. Named in honor of Atlanta's best known 20th century author, the square includes the Atlanta History Center Downtown.

S **The Wren's Nest,** 1050 Abernathy Boulevard, S.W., off I-20 west, via exit 19. This was the home of the writer of the Uncle Remus Animal Stories, Irish American author/journalist Joel Chandler Harris. The stories, based on tales told to him by slaves when he was a child, were made into the Disney movie, "Song of the South." A diorama from the movie is shown. The Wren's Nest has been used as a museum since Harris's death in 1908.

Guided tours and a picnic area. Open Tuesday-Saturday 10 a.m.-4 p.m.; Sundays 1 p.m.-4 p.m.; closed holidays. Fee. Senior citizen and children's discount. Information: 404-753-8535.

Chickamauga

G **Chickamauga and Chattanooga National Military Park.** The oldest and largest military park in the country, Chickamauga is the site of a victory of Irish-American Gen. Ulysses S. Grant, which opened the heart of the Confederacy to Union forces. The Battle of Missionary Ridge followed several days of intense fighting for the control of Chattanooga. The 8,000 acres of park are dotted with more than 1,600 markers, cannons, and monuments.

Chickamauga Visitor Center, 9 miles south of Chattanooga on US 27, near north end of the Chickamauga Battlefield.

Open daily 8 a.m.-5:45 p.m., June-August; 8 a.m.-4:45 p.m., rest of the year; closed Christmas. Free. Multimedia presentation of Battle of Chickamauga. Fee. Information: 706-866-9241.

Dublin

HIA Dublin's Irish heritage is reflected in its St. Patrick's Day Festival, a rare occurrence in Georgia. Sixteen-thousand citizens party with parades, beauty pageants, arts and crafts, folk dancing, and sporting events.

Information: 912-272-5546, or write Dublin-Laurens County Chamber of Commerce, P.O. Box 818.

Eatonton

S **Br'er Rabbit Marker.** The likeness of Br'er Rabbit can be seen in the center of town on Highway 441 across from the Putnam County Courthouse.

S **Uncle Remus Museum,** 3 blocks south on US 441 in Turner Park. The museum is housed in a log cabin made from two slave quarters. The cabin has been decorated to recreate the setting of the Uncle Remus stories. As a child, Joel Chandler Harris had worked as a journalist apprentice at a nearby plantation, where he listened to the stories told by the slaves. These tales inspired the Uncle Remus Animal Stories. For a time during the earlier days of the civil rights movement, the stories were criticized for their depictions of dialect. In more recent years, Harris's work has been recognized as an important contribution to keeping alive the folklore. The museum includes first editions of Harris's work and woodcarvings and paintings of his characters, Uncle Remus, Br'er Rabbit, Br'er Fox, and Br'er Bear.

Open daily Monday-Saturday 10 a.m.-noon and 1 p.m.-5 p.m., May-September; Sunday afternoon 2-5; closed Tuesdays October-April. Fee. Information: 404-485-6731.

Fitzgerald

HIA Fitzgerald, located in south central Georgia, was the product of its namesake, Irish American P. H. Fitzgerald, lawyer and publisher of Indianapolis, and Gov. William J. Northern of Georgia. It was born of tragedy—a drought in the Midwest—of generosity, a "Friendship Train" filled with food and supplies sent from Georgia, still recovering from the ravages of the Civil War—of vision, the desire of Fitzgerald to establish a colony in Georgia for Union veterans to escape the northern cold—and forgiveness, Georgia's willingness to provide a home for their recent enemy. Today, a century since its founding, Fitzgerald is a thriving industrial city with a population of over 10,000.

Milledgeville

S Flannery O'Connor Room, Dillard Russell Library, Georgia College. O'Connor, in her short life span (1925-1964), enjoyed great renown, especially for her mastery of the short story form. She authored two collections of short stories: *A Good Man Is Hard to Find* (1955) and *Everything That Rises Must Converge* (1965), both of which she wrote while living in Milledgeville. Her work showed the influence of her Southern and Irish-Catholic background. The room at her alma mater displays first editions, furnishings from her nearby home, and memorabilia of her life and work. She is buried in Memory Hill Cemetery.

The Flannery O'Connor Room is open by request Monday-Friday 8 a.m.-5 p.m. Information: 912-453-5573.

Savannah

HIA How would you like to wake up to a plate of green scrambled eggs? Unless you're Dr. Seuss, it's not the sort of thing most of us want to see the morning after St. Patrick's Day. Especially when the eggs are snuggling close to a pile of green grits. Anyway you look at it, you've got to admit they do know how to celebrate St. Patrick's Day in Savannah. There are at least 125 St. Patrick's Day parades held in the United States. New York's is the largest—no surprise— but in second place is Savannah's! It's been going on now for more than 165 years. Nobody knows why and fewer care. They just enjoy.

Savannah is a city that won't disappoint. Ante-bellum mansions, mint juleps, and seductive drawls—they're all here. You'll also find the nation's largest restored historical district, a population of 145,000 people, and a life that retains much of the charm expected of the South. But, the best time of year to come to Savannah is St. Patrick's season.

Information: 912-234-8054, or write 18 Abercorn Street, 31401.

Idaho

Montpelier

D In 1896, Butch Cassidy and his gang robbed the Bank of Montpelier of $7,000. Montpelier, one of the oldest towns in Idaho, was settled by Brigham Young as a Mormon community. He named the area after the capital of his home state of Vermont.

Illinois

Chicago

HH The Abbey Pub, 3420 West Grace. Very active on the local Irish-American scene, the Abbey offers what you'd expect of a good Irish pub—Irish beer, good atmosphere, good conversation, good food, and good entertainment, including televised sports and Irish music. In addition, Irish set dance classes for beginners are held here September-June.

Open 10 a.m.-2 a.m. Sunday-Friday and Saturday until 3 a.m. Information: 312-478-4408.

S **Auditorium Building**, Michigan Avenue at Congress Street. Designed by Louis H. Sullivan, whose father emigrated from Cork, this is one of several buildings created by Sullivan which has won international recognition for its style. When opened in 1889, it contained a 400-room hotel, 17-story tower, 136 offices, and 4,200-seat auditorium renowned for its beauty and acoustics. It deteriorated through years of neglect, but today the auditorium has been restored to its original splendor. Much of the interior has been modified to serve the academic needs of Roosevelt University. Sullivan was one of the founders of the Chicago School of Architecture, which was a style developed for commercial buildings. He was also involved in the development of the modern skyscraper, an answer to the high cost of land.

D **Biograph Theater**, 2433 North Lincoln Avenue. Two gangsters were in the Biograph the night of July 22, 1934—Clark Gable on the screen and John Dillinger in the audience. But while Gable had Mryna Loy to comfort him, Dillinger had Anna Sage, the notorious "Lady in Red." When "Manhattan Melodrama" ended, Sage led Dillinger out of the theater and into the line of fire of the F.B.I. Sage had betrayed her lover who lay dead on the sidewalk.

HH **Butch McGuire's Tavern**, 20 West Division Street. This is reputed to be the first bar in Chicago to introduce singles night. True or not, it is one of the more popular places for singles to mingle. If you've seen the film *About Last Night* with Bob Lowe and Demi Moore, then you've seen Butch McGuire's. *Trendy* isn't a word we often use to describe an Irish pub, but it works for this one. The traditional patron will take comfort in the Irish prints on the wall.

Open daily. Information: 312-337-9080.

S **Carson Pirie Scott & Company**, 1 South State Street. Built 1899-1904, this was the last of the major projects completed by architect Louis H. Sullivan. The outstanding feature of the building is a spectacular round corner entrance. Carson's, one of Chicago's fine clothing stores, is still in business at this location.

Open Monday and Thursday 9:45 a.m.-7:30 p.m., Tuesday, Wednesday, Friday, Saturday 9:45 a.m.-5:45 p.m.

HIA **Chicago Fire**, West Side, including DeKoven, LaSalle, and State Streets. Was it really started by Mrs. O'Leary's uncoordinated bovine? Did her cow knock over a lantern igniting a hay stack in the O'Leary barn? That's the legend, and no one has disproved it. O'Leary's cottage on DeKoven Street was one of the few survivors when flames swept through the area, swallowing up the wooden homes and businesses. The spot where the O'Leary cottage and barn stood is now occupied, appropriately, by the Chicago Fire Department Academy, 558 West DeKoven Street, between West Taylor and South Jefferson Streets.

Artifacts of the Chicago fire can be seen at the **Chicago Historical Society**, 1601 North Clark Street, near West North Avenue. Note the statue of Abraham Lincoln on the lawn, sculpted by Augustus Saint-Gaudens.

The Historical Society is open Monday-Saturday 9:30 a.m.-4:30 p.m., Sunday noon-5 p.m. Free Monday; fee other days. Information: 312-642-4600.

S **Graceland Cemetery**, North Clark Street, near Irving Park Road. Established in 1860, Graceland is the burial site of architect Louis Sullivan. Sullivan designed the bronze gates, considered one of the best examples of his work. Cemetery buildings were designed by Holabird and Roche.

Open daily 8 a.m.-5 p.m.

HIA **Irish American Heritage Center**, 4626 North Knox Avenue. Look first row center, and you're likely to see Chicago's second generation Mayor Richard Daley enjoying an Irish play in the re-decorated auditorium. The Center, formerly occupied by Mayfair

College, serves the compleat Irish man and woman. Reportedly, the North Side Irish pursue the more intellectual aspects of their heritage, such as Irish and Irish-American history, while their South Side cousins emphasize the more fun side. Hence, a Center which has a library and a museum which highlights the contributions of the Irish to America and to Chicago. But it also has an expansive classic-style pub with fireplace. Dedicated by Ireland's President Mary Robinson when she visited in 1991, the Center offers entertainment and a full schedule of classes, including Irish language and dance.

Office open Monday-Saturday 9 a.m.-4 p.m. Information: 312-282-7035.

H Irish Castle, 1024 South Longwood. Copied from an Irish castle, this multi-turreted structure was built in 1866 as a promotion to attract home buyers to the area. Today, it is the home of the Beverly Hilton Church.

S Museum of Broadcast Communications, 78 East Washington Street, Chicago Cultural Center. One of the most popular "Irish" entertainers of the mid-20th century, Charlie McCarthy lives on in the museum (he must commute, because we saw him at the Smithsonian, in Washington, D.C., too) along with his sometime-buddy Mortimer Snerd. The museum contains many early radios and television sets and a large stock of early shows on tape.

Open Wednesday, Friday, Sunday afternoons noon-5, Saturday 10 a.m.-5 p.m. Senior and student discount. Information: 312-987-1500.

B Old St. Patrick's Church, 718 West Adams. Built in 1856 and dedicated on that Christmas, St. Patrick's survived the Great Fire of 1871, which devastated most of the city, including the area surrounding the church. St. Patrick's is Chicago's oldest church. Particularly significant in its design are the two towers, one Gothic and the other Byzantine, which represent the joining of ethnic groups in the parish. Thomas O'Shaughnessy created the nave windows which picture the major Irish Saints Patrick, Brigid, Finbarr, Colman, Brendan, Columbanus, and Columcille. He also designed the window memorializing the revolutionist Lord Mayor McSwiney of Cork who died in 1920 while on a hunger strike. It is made of 150,000 pieces of glass.

Information: 312-782-6171.

H] O'Rourke's, 1625 North Halsted. O'Rourke's pays homage to Irish writers with photos of Brendan Behan, James Joyce, Oscar Wilde, and William Butler Yeats lining the walls and to journalists of any nationality from the Chicago papers sampling the Guinness at the bar. One of the better Irish pubs in the city.

Open daily. Information: 312-335-1806.

T Richard J. Daley Center, West Randolph, West Washington, North Clark, and North Dearborn Streets. Designed by C. F. Murphy Associates, the center houses civil courts, county and city offices. The adjoining plaza contains an eternal flame honoring the late Richard J. Daley, mayor of Chicago for 21 years.

HH Robert's Roadhouse, 9090 Roberts Road, Hickory Hills. The Roadhouse provides a time-honored service for its Irish immigrant patrons. It's a gathering spot for transplanted Irish to seek and give comfort and advice on the basics of a new life in America, like getting a job. As Boston in the East, Chicago is still attracting immigrants, and as in days of old, they still need help finding work.

Open daily. Information: 708-598-8181.

S Saint-Gaudens' Seated Lincoln, Grant's Park, Lakefront between Randolph Street and Roosevelt Road. The park is the setting for Dublin-born Auguste Saint-Gaudens's seated statue of Abraham Lincoln.

S Saint-Gaudens' Standing Lincoln, Lincoln Park, Lake Shore Drive, North Avenue to Hollywood Avenue. This bronze statue is considered by many to be the most expressive memorial portrait of Lincoln. The park also contains a statue of Ulysses S. Grant.

HH Schaller's Pump, 3714 South Halsted. Schaller's is Irish, noisy, crowded, and a century old, with Irish beer and passable food, and loaded with Democratic Ward politicos from across the street. That, plus a friendly staff, is enough to make it one of South Chicago's most successful pubs.

Open daily. Information: 312-847-9378.

Ħ⏌ **University of Chicago**, 1100 East 57th Street. The university library has a collection of materials relating to 17th through 19th century Ireland.

Information: 312-702-8782.

Dixon

⍑ **Ronald Reagan's Boyhood Home**, 816 South Hennepin. The 40th president of the United States and former movie star Ronald Reagan lived in this 2-story, 3-bedroom house from 1920 to 1923. It contains memorabilia from his early life and later work.

Open Monday, Thursday, Saturday 10 a.m.-4 p.m., Sundays and holidays 1 p.m.-4 p.m., from March - November; Monday and Saturday 10 a.m.-4 p.m., other months. Free. Information: 815-288-3404.

Galena

Ꮐ **Vinegar Hill Lead Mine**, 6 miles north on FL 84 at 8885 North Three Pines Road. John Furlong, an Irish soldier, discovered this mine. Captured and forced into the British army, he was shipped to Canada. He escaped to Illinois and financial success.

Open daily 9 a.m.-5 p.m., June-August; Saturday-Sunday 9 a.m.-4 p.m., May, September, October. Fee. Children's discount. Information: 815-777-0855.

Highwood

Ꮐ **Fort Sheridan**, North on Sheridan Road. In the 1880s, Chicago was feeling the anger of laborers who were demanding better working conditions. Clashes with the police were common, the most notable being the Haymarket Square Riot, which occurred May 3, 1886, at the McCormick Harvester Company. Several strikers and seven policemen were killed.

A group of Chicago businessmen, upset by the Haymarket riot, purchased land north of Highwood and donated it to the government to build a fort. Irish-American Gen. Philip H. Sheridan, who had earned a reputation for putting down riots, was hired to maintain order in the area. A total of 94 buildings, erected in the late 19th and very early 20th century serve today as headquarters for the U.S. Army Recruiting Command and headquarters for the 4th Army.

Information: 708-926-2173.

Salem

T **William Jennings Bryan Statue.** The Gutzon Borglum statue of Bryan stands in Bryan Memorial Park.

T **William Jennings Bryan Birthplace and Museum,** 408 South Broadway. Bryan, the great orator, was born here in 1860. The restored home, originally built in 1852, contains much Bryan memorabilia.

Open daily, except Thursdays and holidays, limited hours. Free. Information: 618-548-7791.

Indiana

Corydon

G **Squire Boone Caverns and Village,** 10 miles south of I-64 on FL 135, 3 miles east on Squire Boone Caverns Road. Squire Boone, Daniel's brother, discovered the caverns in 1780 when hiding from the Indians. The caverns contain streams and waterfalls, stalactites, stalagmites, and travertine formations.

The village contains a restored gristmill, petting zoo, craft shops, and restaurant. A 1-mile trail leads to Squire Boone's grave. Cavern tours, hay rides, trails, and a picnic area are available.

Open daily 9 a.m.-6 p.m. Memorial Day weekend through Labor

Day; cavern tours only, the remainder of the year; closed New Year's, Thanksgiving, and Christmas. Fee. Senior and children's discount. Information: 812-732-4381.

Greenfield

S **James Whitcomb Riley Birthplace Museum,** 250 West Main Street. Riley lived here during his childhood from 1850 to 1869. The author of "When the Frost Is on the Punkin," "Little Orphant Annie," and "The Raggedy Ann," Indiana's poet laureate based much of his work on experiences gained during these early years. The tour of his restored 1850 home includes the bedroom occupied by a young girl who boarded with the Rileys. She inspired the Raggedy Ann and Andy dolls; the comic strip, "Little Orphan Annie"; the Broadway musical, Annie, and the movie by the same name; and a sequel to the Broadway show. The house next door features works and mementos of Riley's life.

Open daily Monday-Saturday 10 a.m.-4 p.m. and Sunday afternoon 1-4, April 1-December 21, except major holidays. Fee. Children's discount. Information: 317-462-8539.

Hammond

T **Little Red Schoolhouse,** 7205 Kennedy Avenue. Built in 1869, it was used by William Jennings Bryan as his presidential campaign headquarters and, more successfully, to celebrate the presidential victory of William McKinley. The schoolhouse contains original furnishings, including desks, stove, books, bell, and stove. The last Saturday in June the Schoolhouse Festival is held featuring a corn and potato roast and a parade.

Open by appointment. Free. Handicapped facilities. Information: 219-931-7559.

Indianapolis

S **Eiteljorg Museum of American Indian and Western Art,** 500 West Washington Street, White River State Park. The $14 million building was erected specifically to display the Western and Indian art collected by Indianapolis businessman Harrison Eiteljorg. The work of Georgia O'Keeffe is among the outstanding art exhibited, along with Charles Russell and Frederick Remington. The museum houses work created by the members of the original Taos, New Mexico, art colony, and traveling exhibits of American Western art. An orientation film can be viewed.

Open Monday-Saturday 10 a.m.-5 p.m. and Sunday noon-5 p.m., June-August; Tuesday-Saturday 10 a.m.-5 p.m. and Sunday noon-5 p.m., other months; closed New Year's, Thanksgiving, and Christmas. Fee. Senior, student, children's, and family discount. Information: 317-636-9378.

Indiana — Indianapolis

HH Kelly's Pub & Wine Bar, 5620 Georgetown Road. Kelly's is a solid Irish pub in a part of the country that needs more. Irish beer and Irish stew are on the menu. Irish entertainment is presented Thursday and Saturday, and you may even find some green beer on Irish holidays—that includes St. Patrick's Day and Finnegans Wake (with or without the apostrophe). You'll be rubbing elbows with neighbors, professionals, and college students.

Open daily, except Sunday. Information: 317-297-4404.

S James Whitcomb Riley Home, 528 Lockerbie Street. Riley, known as "the Hoosier poet" and the "poet laureate of democracy," became known through his folk writing for the Indianapolis Journal. Born in 1849, he published many books of poetry. He lived in this Victorian home from 1892 until his death in 1916. On display are many of his personal items, including his pen. The home has been maintained as it was when he lived.

Open daily, except Mondays and most holidays. Fee. Information: 317-631-5885.

T President Benjamin Harrison Memorial Home, 1230 North Delaware Street. Benjamin Harrison, 23rd president of the United States, was descended on his mother's side from emigrants from County Down, Ireland. Built in 1875 for Harrison, he lived here except for the years he was in the White House (1889-93). The home has 16 rooms with original furniture, art, and family memorabilia. There is a garden and gift shop.

Open daily, except January, Easter, Thanksgiving, and Christmas. Fee. Children's discount. Information: 317-631-1898.

Iowa

Chariton

D **Wayne County Historical Museum,** 25 miles south of Chariton on IA 2. Among the artifacts of Wayne County history is a special Jesse James exhibit, including a safe he robbed. The museum also contains an exhibit showing Mormon travel through Iowa in mid-19th century and replicas of a jail, physician's office, toy store and 14 other buildings.

Open April-October 1-5 p.m. Handicapped facilities. Fee. Information: 515-774-4059.

Council Bluffs

P **Golden Spike,** 21st and 9th Avenues. A 56-foot golden concrete spike, erected in 1939, commemorates the junction of the Union Pacific and Central Pacific railroads. This momentous accomplishment was achieved with the muscle-power of Irish-American men. Information: 712-325-1000.

Grinnell

S **Poweshiek County National Bank,** downtown on corner opposite the town square. Built in 1914 in a "jewel box" style, this is one of the finer of the late structures designed by Louis Sullivan. A celebrated architect of major commercial buildings in the mid to late 1800s, Irish American Sullivan fell out of fashion by the end of the century and was reduced to designing modest structures in small mid-Western towns.

Open daily, except Sunday.

Le Claire

ᠭ **Buffalo Bill Cody Museum**, 206 North River Road. Exhibits relate to Iowa's native son William "Buffalo Bill" Cody and local history. Located next to the museum is the steamboat *Lone Star*.

Open 9 a.m.-5 p.m. daily May 15-October 15 and Saturday-Sunday only during the rest of the year. Fee. Information: 319-289-5580.

McCausland

ᠭ **Buffalo Bill Homestead**, 3 miles southwest of McCausland. The restored boyhood home of William "Buffalo Bill" Cody was built by his father, a pioneer settler, in 1847. It is furnished in the style of the mid-18th century.

Open daily 9 a.m.-6 p.m. April-October. Information: 319-225-2981.

Winterset

Ꞩ **John Wayne Birthplace Site**, 224 South 2nd Avenue. This is the birthplace of Academy Award © winning superstar John Wayne, who made many Irish and Irish-American movies. One of his classic films was *The Quiet Man* with Irish actors Maureen O'Hara and Barry Fitzgerald. The home contains Wayne memorabilia. It's partially restored to its 1907 appearance, the year that Wayne charged into the world, reportedly with a six-shooter in each hand.

Open daily 10 a.m.-5 p.m., except New Year's, Thanksgiving, and Christmas. Fee. Information: 512-462-1044.

Kansas

Coronado

Ꞩ **Coronado Museum**, 567 East Cedar Street. Have you ever wondered what become of the Kansas farmhouse where Dorothy lived with her little dog Toto? It's comforting to know that it's still in

Kansas. In the Coronado Museum. *The Wizard of Oz* made Judy Garland, daughter of two Irish Americans, a star. You won't find Dorothy in the farmhouse, but you will find her bedroom, just as it was in the 1939 movie. The interior of the house features period furniture.

Open Tuesday-Saturday 9 a.m.-5 p.m., Sunday 1 p.m.-5 p.m.; closed holidays. Free. Information: 316-624-7624.

Dodge City

G **Fort Dodge**, on US 154. Among history's famous people associated with the Fort Dodge were Irish Americans Buffalo Bill Cody and Gen. Philip Sheridan. The fort was established in 1865 to protect travelers on the Sante Fe Trail from Indians. The fort is now a veterans' home supported by the State of Kansas and contains a library and museum. Original buildings made of sod and adobe are gone; buildings constructed from stone in 1867 are still used.

Library and museum open afternoons 1-5. Free. Information: 316-227-2176.

Kentucky

Bardstown

S **Bardstown**, population 6,200, is proud of its association with composer Stephen C. Foster, who used to come here to visit his cousin. Foster is memorialized in tourist sites and on street signs. It is thought (or hoped) by the locals that his visits to Bardstown inspired one of his most memorable compositions, "My Old Kentucky Home." St. Patrick's Day was celebrated here as far back as theearly 1800s.

S **Bardstown Historical Museum**, Spalding Hall, just off North 5th Street. The museum depicts 200 years of local history, including Stephen Foster memorabilia, a replica of the first steamboat, Lincoln papers, and period costumes.

Open daily 9 a.m.-5 p.m. and Sunday afternoon 1-5, May-October; Tuesday-Saturday 10 a.m.-4 p.m. and Sunday afternoon 1-4, the rest of the year. Free. Information: 502-348-2999.

S **My Old Kentucky Home Park**, 1 mile east on US 150. Owned by Judge John Rowan, the home was frequently visited by his cousin, Stephen Foster. The stately 18th century home is set on 250 acres which contain a picnic area, amphitheater, playground, gardens, tent, and trailer sites. Attendants are dressed in period costumes.

Hours and days vary according to seasons. Grounds free. Fee for guided tour of house. Handicapped facilities on ground floor.

The "Stephen Foster Story" is told in the Amphitheater nightly, mid-June to early September. The musical features 50 of Foster's melodies. An inside theater is used when it rains. Handicapped facilities.

General information for the park: 502-348-3502; information for the musical: 800-626-1563.

Danville

P **McDowell House, Apothecary, and Gardens**, 125 South 2nd Street. Irish American Ephraim McDowell was a well-known surgeon of the late 18th and 19th centuries. His restored 18th century home is furnished in early Kentucky style. The apothecary has a variety of equipment. Medicinal herbs are found in the gardens.

Open Monday-Saturday 10 a.m.-noon and 1 p.m.-4 p.m., Sunday afternoon 2-4, March-October; closed Monday, November-February, New Year's, Easter, Thanksgiving, and Christmas. Fee. Senior and children's discount. Information: 606-236-2804.

Frankfort

G **Daniel Boone's Grave**, East Main Street. Boone died near St. Louis, Missouri, in 1820 at the age of 85. His remains were moved twenty-five years later to the Frankfort Cemetery. There he lies with his wife, Rebecca, beneath a monument to their memory, which depicts Daniel hunting and Indian fighting and Rebecca milking a cow.

Open daily until dusk.

Harrodsburg

G "The Legend of Daniel Boone," James Harrod Amphitheatre. The comedy-drama recounts the life and legend of Daniel Boone Monday-Saturday evenings at 8:30 from mid-June through late August. Fee. Children's discount. Information: 606-734-3346.

Winchester

Winchester, located near Lexington, has two sites associated with Irish American explorer, soldier, and settler Daniel Boone:

G Fort Boonesborough State Park, on the Kentucky River, 9 miles southwest of Winchester, via KY 627. Daniel Boone's settlement was frequently attacked by Indians. The fort contains craft shops, a museum with many historical items, including Boone memorabilia, and an audio-visual show.

Open daily April-Labor Day; Wednesday-Sunday, rest of year. Fee for museum.

G Old Stone Church, 6 miles south of Winchester via KY 627. Built in the late 1700s, this is the oldest active church west of the Allegheny Mountains. Daniel Boone attended services here.

Louisiana

Crowley

P Named for Patrick Crowley, an Irish railroad worker, Crowley has a population today of 14,000. It owes its success to rice. Over 1/4 of all the rice grown in the country is raised within a 50-mile radius of Crowley. Each October, an International Rice Festival is held. You can visit the rice mills.

Information: 318-788-0177.

New Orleans

℗ **Celtic Cross Monument,** New Basin Canal Park. Between 8,000 and 20,000 workers died as a result of working in the disease ridden Louisiana swamps. These men, many of whom were Irish, sacrificed their lives to build a canal which would connect Lake Pontchartrain with the Howard Avenue section of New Orleans. In recognition of the sacrifice made by many Irish, the Irish Cultural Center of New Orleans erected a Celtic cross.

Ꮐ **Chalmette National Historic Park,** 6 miles from downtown on Rt. 42. The park includes the site of the Battle of New Orleans fought in 1815. New Orleans was saved from the British by forces under the command of Gen. Andrew Jackson. Chalmette National Cemetery is the burial ground for Louisiana veterans. The Beauregard Plantation House, now an information center, has films and exhibits telling the story of the Battle of New Orleans.
Open daily 8 a.m.-5 p.m., except Christmas. Free. Information: 504-589-4428.

ᎻᏆᎪ **Irish Channel,** St. Thomas Street area. This was a lively, boisterous area during the mid-19th century when many Irish immigrants lived here.

ᎻᏆᎪ **Irish Louisiana Museum,** 508 Toulouse Street. The total Irish experience! In the museum you view photos, artifacts, and memorabilia of the Irish immigrants who labored in Louisiana of the 1800s. In the Irish pub downstairs, you satisfy your thirst and social needs. Then you can go into the gift shop and take home a bit of Irish music and reading.
Open daily 10 a.m.-8 p.m. Information: 504-529-1317.

Ꮐ **Jackson Square and Statue.** Dominating the park, in the center of the square, is an equestrian bronze statue of Andrew Jackson, hero of the Battle of New Orleans during the War of 1812. Inscribed on the base of the statue are the words: "The Union Must and Shall Be

Preserved." Lafayette Park, across from the White House in Washington, D.C., and Nashville, Jackson's hometown, have copies cast from the same mold.

Most tours of the French Quarter start out at Jackson Square, in earlier days the site of festive executions. People would gather to watch others being burned at the stake, beheaded, broken on the wheel, and sledgehammered, or on a relatively dull day, simply hanged, branded, or flogged (hardly worth a trip to the square). Today, it is a charming area with the park surrounded by a fence upon which local artists hang their latest, and often quite good, work selling at bargain prices. The flagstone pedestrian mall is the setting for street entertainers. A word of caution, don't feed the pigeons. There are fines. Second word of caution, don't stand under the eaves of the buildings where the pigeons sit. I did.

Park gates are open 8 a.m.-6 p.m., but the mall never closes.

HIA **Margaret Statue,** intersection of Camp and Prytania Streets. Completed in 1884, this is the first statue to a woman ever erected in the United States. It honors Margaret Gaffney Haughery who gave bread and milk from her stores to feed the hungry people of New Orleans.

G **Molly Marine Statue,** Canal Street and Elks Place. Erected in 1943 during World War II, it is the only statue in the country which commemorates the important contribution made by women in the military service. Since the model for this sculpture is unknown, I choose to believe it was inspired by World War II Marine, Irish-American Mildred Malone of Pittsburgh.

G **Musee Conti Wax Museum of Louisiana Legends,** 917 Conti Street. Life-size figures are placed in period scenes set in New Orleans from 1699 to present day. Shown are such diverse characters as Andrew Jackson, Jean Lafitte, Louis Armstrong, and Napoleon. If a little horror will lift your spirits, check out the Haunted Dungeon.

Open daily, except Mardi Gras and Christmas. Fee. Information: 504-525-2605.

G **The Old Absinthe House,** 240 Bourbon Street. Built at the turn of the 19th century, it became a popular tavern in 1826. It remains one today, with only a short break in drinking during the days of prohibition. The absinthe frappe was invented here in 1870. General Andrew Jackson and the notorious pirate Jean Lafitte met here to strategize the defense of New Orleans in 1815. Lafitte had a secret room upstairs to store his lifted loot.

Open daily 11 a.m.-2 a.m. Information: 504-523-3181.

HH, HI **O'Flaherty's Irish Channel,** 508 Toulouse Street. An authentic Irish pub in the heart of the French Quarter offers Irish beer, music, and good cheer. It also has a gift shop and an Irish history museum upstairs.

Open daily noon-3:00 a.m. Information: 504-529-1317.

B **St. Alphonsus Church,** 2030 block of Constance Street. Erected in the mid-19th century in the Irish Channel section of New Orleans, St. Alphonsus was the parish for the new Irish immigrants. Through time the ethnic makeup of the parish changed, and the Baroque-style structure deteriorated and finally closed. But now, following extensive restoration, it has reopened as a social and education center.

Tours by appointment. Fee. Information: 504-522-7420.

S **Tara,** 5705 St. Charles Avenue. When Scarlett vowed to go back to Tara, she was actually returning to a facade on the Hollywood movie set for *Gone With the Wind.* Scarlett would have found the New Orleans Tara familiar, but more comfortable. It is an exact replica built from the plans used for the movie set, except it has four walls and a roof.

Sunset

S **Chretien Point Plantation,** 4 miles from Sunset on Bristol/Bosco Road. The staircase that became famous survives in this magnificent ante-bellum mansion. So enchanted was a photographer by this home that he sent pictures back to Hollywood, and a copy of its staircase was featured in Scarlett O'Hara's Tara. Today, this home provides bed and board to weary travelers.

Open daily 10 a.m.-5 p.m., except Thanksgiving, Christmas, and New Year's. Fee. Information: 318-662-5876, -233-7050.

Maine

Machias

G **Burnham Tavern Museum**, Main and Free Streets. It was here in a 1770 tavern that Capt. Jeremiah O'Brien and his friends developed the strategy which resulted in the first naval encounter of the Revolutionary War. Learning that the British warship *Margaretta* was due to arrive to get lumber, they did their plotting in what is now the oldest building in eastern Maine. They met, they drank, they schemed, and they succeeded in capturing the warship with only 40 untrained men.

Open Monday-Friday mid-June to Labor Day; by appointment, rest of the year. Fee. Children's discount. Information: 207-255-4432.

Machiasport

G **Fort O'Brien**. The first naval operation of the Revolutionary War was led by Capt. Jeremiah O'Brien, whose father emigrated from County Cork. O'Brien and his ill-prepared buddies boarded their little boat *Unity*, sailed out into Machias bay and captured the British warship. The date was June 12, 1775, and the time was right to convince the Revolutionary leaders that a U.S. navy was needed.

After the war officially began, a fort was erected on the hill overlooking the Machias River. The British destroyed it in 1814. Another fort was built at the same spot in 1863. The remains of this structure, Ft. O'Brien, are now a state park.

Open daily, Memorial Day-Labor Day. Free.

G **Gates House,** ME 92. Models of the British *Margaretta* and the *Unity* are displayed in this 1807 Federal-style house. (See above.)

Open Monday-Friday afternoon 12:30-4:30, June to Labor Day; by appointment the rest of the year. Donations. Information: 207-255-8461.

Newcastle

B **St. Patrick's Church,** 2 1/2 miles north of US 1 on ME 215. The oldest remaining Catholic church in New England, it was built in 1808.

Open daily, 9 a.m. to dusk. Donations. Information: 207-563-3240.

Thomaston

G **Montpelier,** High Street, near junction of US 1 and ME 131. Here stands a replica of the 1795 home of Gen. Henry Knox, Revolutionary War hero, and later Secretary of War in George Washington's administration. Knox was the son of an Irish immigrant. An active participant in Irish activities, he held memberships in the Friendly Sons of St. Patrick in Philadelphia and the Charitable Irish Society in Boston. The home, now a state historical museum, contains many of of Knox's original furnishings.

Open Wednesday-Sunday 9 a.m.-5:30 p.m. between Memorial Day and Labor Day. Guided tours. Fee. Discount for children; free for seniors. Information: 207-354-8062.

Waterville

HI **Colby College,** Mayflower Hill. The Miller Library contains work of a number of 19th and 20th century Irish writers.

Information: 207-872-3444.

Maryland

Annapolis

T **Barrister House**, St. John's College, King George Street. Built in 1722, this is the birthplace of Irish American Charles Carroll, author of the Maryland Bill of Rights. It was moved from its original location to St. John's College where it serves as the administration building.

Open, except school holidays. Free. Information: 410-263-2371.

Baltimore

B **Basilica of the Assumption of the Blessed Virgin Mary**, Cathedral & Mulberry Streets. Dedicated in 1806, this is the first Catholic cathedral in the United States. It was begun by the first U.S. bishop, later to become archbishop—John Carroll—a member of a very distinguished Irish-American family. The church was completed in 1821, following the death of Carroll. He and James Cardinal Gibbons are buried beneath the altar. In 1936, Pope Pius XI designated the cathedral a basilica.

Open Monday-Friday 7 a.m.-2:30 p.m. and Saturday-Sunday 7 a.m.-6:30 p.m. Tours 2nd and 4th Sundays of the month or by appointment. Handicapped facilities. Free. Information: 410-727-3564.

P **B & O Railroad Museum**, Pratt and Poppleton Streets. The museum houses the country's first passenger station, the Mount Clare, built in 1851; over 100 train cars; and the original tracks and wooden turntable. The B & O Railroad was founded by Irish-born Alexander Brown.

Open Wednesday-Sunday; closed major holidays. Handicapped facilities. Information: 410-752-2490.

T **Carroll Mansion**, 8090 E. Lombard Street at Front Street. The last home of Charles Carroll. When Carroll died here in 1831, he had been the sole surviving signer of the Declaration of Independence. Period furnishings.

Open daily, except Mondays and holidays. Fee. Information: 410-396-3523.

ᚻᚻ Cat's Eye Pub, 1730 Thames Street, South Point. The Cat's Eye brings in neighborhood professionals and tourists for Guinness and Harp on draught, pub food, and Sunday jazz. It's a small, rustic pub with bar, tables and stage under a ceiling of flags. The friendliness of the patrons suggests that the garrulous bartender may be simply part of the charm. Or perhaps, like us, he found the band's syrupy rendition of "I'll Take You Home Again, Kathleen" a bit jarring in the midst of their jazz concert.

Open daily. Information: 410-276-0866.

ᚻᚻ Dave's Pub, 220 East Lexington Street at Guilford. This is too good a pub to keep it the private oasis of the legals and paralegals who come across the street from the courthouse each evening to wind down. Pointing out different legal types, the bartender said, "There are nights when you could be arrested, prosecuted, defended, and judged and never leave the pub." One of Baltimore's best kept secrets—even some of the other Irish pub habitues claimed not to have heard of it—it has a limited menu, but Irish on tap, and a very happy clientele. It celebrates September 17 (one-half way to St. Paddy's Day), but closes weekends.

Open Monday-Friday, 8 a.m.; closed Saturday-Sunday. Information: 410-752-6433.

S Edgar Allan Poe House, 203 North Amity Street. Built about 1830, Poe lived in this house from 1832-35. While here, Poe wrote "MS Found in a Bottle." At 23, he was on the threshold of fame.

Open Wednesday-Saturday, April-July and September to mid-December; evenings by appointment. Fee. Information: 410-525-1274, -396-7932.

S Edgar Allan Poe Monument and Grave, Burying Ground, Fayette and Greene Streets. Poe, whose grandfather, David, emigrated from (London)Derry, is buried here with his wife, grandfather, mother-in-law and other members of the Poe family. In the darkness of the pre-dawn hours of January 19, the anniversary of Poe's death, three red roses and a bottle of cognac mysteriously appear on his grave each year. The scary question is not who brings the cognac, but who drinks it.

Tours by appointment April-November, 1st and 3rd Friday and Saturday. Fee. Senior discount. Information: 410-328-7228.

S Enoch Pratt Free Library, 400 Cathedral Street. Library contains special collection and exhibit on Edgar Allan Poe and his work.

Open Monday-Thursday 10 a.m.-9 p.m., 9 a.m.-5 p.m. Friday-Saturday. Information: 410-396-5430.

G Fort McHenry National Monument and Historic Shrine, east end of Fort Avenue. Fort McHenry was named for James McHenry, emigrant from County Antrim, who was delegate to the Constitutional Convention and Secretary of War under George Washington and John Adams. Completed in 1803, it has been involved in every American War from the Revolutionary through World War II. Francis Scott Key observed a British attack on the fort which lasted 25 hours. When he saw the flag still waving the next morning, he was inspired to write the words which later served as the lyrics for the national anthem, "The Star-Spangled Banner."

The fort, restored to its pre-Civil War appearance, flies the same flag in the same location today. By presidential proclamation, it flies 24 hours a day. The Visitor Center provides an orientation to the site and a film recalling its history. There are special exhibits for persons with vision and hearing impairment.

Open daily 8 a.m.-8 p.m., June 1 to Labor Day; 8 a.m.-5 p.m. the rest of the year; closed New Year's and Christmas. Fee. Children's discount. Information: 410-962-4299.

HH The Gandy Dancer, 1300 McHenry Street at South Carey. In an old railroad station on the other side of the tracks, with a face which would scare a banshee, stands the Gandy Dancer. Inside, the bar and separate large dining-dance area are only slightly more inviting, but...

Don't pass it by! It's an adventure. What lurks behind this

depression-era look is some of the best Friday night fun in the city of Baltimore. This is where the Irish and Irish Americans celebrate the start of the weekend. Practically empty at 7p.m., when herself and I first stopped by, it's bursting at its beams come 9 p.m. with live Irish music and dancing. Eat before you go. It's one of Baltimore's classic Irish pubs, and my choice in Baltimore for St. Patrick's Day revelers for whom food is a secondary consideration.

Open daily. Information: 410-752-5835.

T **Homewood House**, Charles and 34th Streets. A wedding gift to Charles Carroll from his father, the home can be seen in its original 1801 grandeur. Also a sight to behold behind the mansion is a brick outhouse decorated with a mosaic of graffiti drawn by the boys who resided in Homewood during its reincarnation as a boys' school.

Open Monday-Friday 11 a.m.-3 p.m. and Sunday noon-3 p.m. Fee. Information: 410-338-5589.

T **Johns Hopkins University**, off North Charles Street. Today a small private liberal arts university, world renowned for its medical school, it was once the 140-acre estate of Charles Carroll, Jr., son of the Revolutionary patriot.

HH **McGinn's Irish Pub & Restaurant**, 328 North Charles Street. McGinn's is Baltimore's best known Irish pub and restaurant. Its downtown location, Irish beers, full menu, and Irish entertainment Tuesday, Thursday, Friday, and Saturday nights make it very popular with area business people, tourists, and Irish. It's an attractive grouping of two rooms with a bar and separate dining room. The bar action is overseen by a leprechaun who stands quietly in a corner until, I was assured by one patron, it comes alive on St. Patrick's Day. George McGinn, owner, is a leader in Irish events, and his restaurant is the best choice on St. Patrick's Day for celebrants who put a premium on food.

Open daily. Information: 410-539-7504.

T **Mount Clare Mansion**, Carroll Park at Monroe Street and Washington Boulevard. Built in 1760, the oldest pre-Revolutionary War mansion in Baltimore, it was once the home of Charles Carroll. It contains authentic furnishings and recreated gardens. Guided tours.

Open Tuesday-Friday 10 a.m.-4:30 p.m. and Saturday-Sunday noon to 4:30; closed holidays. Fee. Senior and children's discount. Information: 410-837-3262.

HH P.J. Patrick's, 1371 Andre Street. Sunday nights the newly arrived Irish and the Irish Americans drink their Irish draughts and jam the dance floor. This old, big, rough and rustic spot serves pub grub, but its more likely that it's appeal to the neighborhood working class regulars and Irish patrons is its weekend live Irish entertainment.

Open daily. Information: 410-727-9482.

HH Reilley's Sheeben (Angelina's), 7135 Harford Road. Reilley's is a basement pub with a direct entrance from the street or through the upstairs restaurant, Angelina's. Tables are covered with green checked cloths, and there's a mini-size bar in the rear. Walls hold photos, paintings, and assorted objects; the piano is draped with the Irish flag. The night we visited, a singer-guitarist was accepting requests, most of which were for Irish ballads. "Sheeben," in case you're wondering, means "speakeasy" in Irish, which explains the hole in the front door.

You can mix your nationalities here by accompanying your Irish beer with Italian food from upstairs. The menu carries the following poem. It's enough to make you cry in your beer.

> *Ireland, must we leave you,*
> *Driven by a tyrant's hand*
> *Must we seek a mother's blessing*
> *In a strange and distant land.*

Open daily, except Monday. Information: 410-444-5545.

Bethesda

HH Flanagan's Irish Pub, Inc., 7637 Old Georgetown Road on the corner of Old Georgetown Road and Woodmont Avenue. It's the best bastion of Irish *craic* (fun) in Bethesda. Guinness and Harp on draught, with Happy Hour prices 3 p.m.-7 p.m. Monday-Friday; bargain hors d'oeuvres Monday-Thursday and free on Fridays. Irish specialties include Irish soda bread, shepherd's pie, and an Irish stew which received the award as "1990 best Irish stew among Washington area restaurants." Live Irish music nightly with no cover except for special events. Darts, basketball, televised Irish rugby games, and Monday night football. Flanagan's basement location attracts mainly business/professional patrons week days, mixed group weekends. The authentic Irish pub atmosphere is heightened by the many Irish brogues heard on both sides of the bar. Several dining areas.

Open daily. Information: 301-986-1007.

Ellicott City

Baltimore and Ohio (B & O) Railroad Station Museum, 2711 Maryland Avenue at Main Street. Alexander Brown, who emigrated from Belfast in 1800, became one of the country's foremost business tycoons. He was involved with banking, Irishlinen imports, and cotton exports. He and his son were among the key founders of the Baltimore and Ohio Railroad. The Ellicott B & O railroad station, first terminus of the Baltimore and Ohio Railroad, received America's first steam engine, the *Tom Thumb*, in August 1830. The restored station contains the station master's office, waiting room, and ticket office. The museum exhibits a model railroad and recreates the scenery along the 13 miles of track linking the station to Baltimore.

Open Wednesday-Monday 11 a.m.-5 p.m. from Memorial Day to Labor Day; Friday-Monday the rest of the year. Fee. Senior and children's discount. Information: 410-461-1944.

Emmitsburg

John Hughes Cabin, Mount Saint Mary's College campus, near the National Shrine Grotto of Lourdes. The man who was to become the first Archbishop of New York and the builder of St. Patrick's

Cathedral lived in this small log cabin while working as a gardener in 1820. Hughes, who had emigrated from County Tyrone in 1797, was hired by Father John DuBois, founder of Mount St. Mary's. In return for his services, he received "compensation, board, lodging and private instruction."

The cabin is locked, but the second level can be viewed through windows. Information: 301-447-6122.

℧ **Mount Saint Mary's College and Seminary**, 3 miles south on US 15. Founded in 1808, the Mount is the oldest independent Catholic college in the country. Among the illustrious people who have studied here is John McCloskey, who was to become the first American cardinal. Located on campus is the Hughes log cabin, National Shrine Grotto of Lourdes, and nearby, the Elizabeth Seton Shrine.

Open when classes are in session, other times by appointment. Information: 301-447-6122.

Frederick

𝕋 **Roger Brooke Taney Home**, 123 South Bentz Street. Built in 1799, this house served as the home of Chief Justice of the Supreme Court Taney between 1835 and 1864. Irish American Taney was appointed by Andrew Jackson to succeed John Marshall. He swore in seven presidents, but is best known for his famous Dred Scott Decision. Scott, a slave who had been transported to free territories, claimed that he was now a free man. Taney ruled against him, however, his owner freed him three weeks later. Taney is buried in **St. John's Catholic Church** cemetery, East 3rd and East Streets.

The Francis Scott Key Museum is also located at this site.

Open April-December, Saturday 10 a.m.-4 p.m., Sunday afternoon 1-4. Information: 301-663-8703.

℧ **St. John the Evangelist**, 116 East 2nd Street. America's oldest consecrated Catholic church, St. John the Evangelist was built in 1837 by Irish immigrants who were laboring on the canal. Designed in Greek Revival style, the church was used during the Civil War to house prisoners.

Information: 301-662-8288.

Laurel

HH **Irish Pizza Pub & Castle Lounge**, Montpelier Plaza, Baltimore-Washington Parkway and Rt. 197. Two very large rooms, both with bars, both with game arcades and satellite TV make up this establishment. One room is a family pizza pub and the other an "adults only" lounge (not in the tradition of the pubs in Ireland, which are family gathering spots). The lounge features a gigantic U-shaped bar, tables, and antique organ. Pub walls are covered with murals suggesting castle walls, like most seen in Ireland, that have enjoyed better days. In either room you have your choice of Guinness, Harp, or 27 other beers. During the Happy Hour you get a bargain on 12-ounce draughts and a better one on hors d'oeuvres— they're free. Wide selection of pub grub, but no Irish specialties.

Every Friday evening and Sundays, you can meet one of the little people of Irish fame, billed as "Movie Star Sammy Ross, a real, 3'11" leprechaun." Maybe you saw Ross in John Wayne's "The Conqueror," or maybe you were lucky and missed Wayne at his Tartar worst.

Open daily from 11:00 a.m. Information: 301-490-7777.

Ocean City

HH **Shenanigan's Irish Pub & Seafood House**, 4th and the Boardwalk. Here, they serve not only Guinness and Harp on draught, but their own label. The pub is located a few steps down from the Boardwalk and is a cool escape from the summer sun when you want some pub grub. Very friendly staff.

Open daily during season (call first). Information: 301-289-7181).

Rockville

S F. Scott Fitzgerald Grave, Veirs Mill Road and Rockville Pike. Francis Scott Key Fitzgerald, wife Zelda Sayre, and a number of other relatives are buried in the occasionally tended cemetery of St. Mary's Catholic Church. Fitzgerald, born in 1896, died December 21, 1940, preceding his wife in death by eight years. His stone is inscribed with these final lines from *The Great Gatsby*:

> *So we beat on,*
> *Boats against the current,*
> *Borne back ceaselessly*
> *Into the past.*

HH Hagan's Four Courts, 100 Courthouse Square, second level of the Metro Shopping Center. Hagan's attracts a good share of the legal types from the nearby courthouse for lunch and after work refreshments, which includes their favorite Irish beer on tap. It earns the 4-shamrock award for decor, an unusually attractive, almost regal setting accented in rich wood and greens. Many windows provide a bright and airy feeling. Live Irish entertainment nightly brings in an Irish American crowd. There's talk about tearing down this part of the shopping center, so be sure to call first.

Open daily. Information: 301-738-7172.

Sharpsburg

G Antietam National Battlefield, MD 64/35. The Battle of Antietam or, as the Confederacy called it, the Battle of Sharpsburg, was fought on September 17, 1862. Following prior victories by Confederate General Robert E. Lee, it was here that the military situation was reversed. But at heavy cost to the Irish Brigade, fighting under the command of Irish-born Gen. Thomas Francis Meagher, former Young Irelander.

Visitor Center, 1 mile north of Sharpsburg on MD 65. An audio-tape of points of interest is available for rent; murals and a 26-minute film can be viewed.

Open daily 8 a.m.-6 p.m., June through Labor Day; 8:30 p.m.-5 p.m., the rest of the year; closed New Year's, Thanksgiving, and Christmas. Fee. Senior, children's, and family discount. Information: 301-432-5124.

Silver Spring

B Old St. John the Evangelist Church, 9700 Rosensteel Avenue. A private mission was founded here by Irish-American Jesuit John Carroll in 1774. Today, the church is a reproduction of the original structure, serving a Polish community. It is known to parishioners as Our Lady, Queen of Poland.

Information: 301-681-7663.

Warwick

B St. Francis Xavier and Old Bohemia Mission, Eastern Shore. The church was founded in 1704, one of the earlier Catholic structures in the colonies. The Jesuits opened an academy here in 1745. The distinguished Carroll cousins, Charles, attorney, and only Irish Catholic signer of the Declaration of Independence, and John, first Catholic bishop in the United States, were among its students. Many early parishioners are buried in the adjacent cemetery.

Mass is said at the church the third Sunday in April, May, September, and October. The rectory, containing a museum, is open noon-3 p.m. Sundays, in summer.

Wheaton

HH E.M. McGoo's, 2429 Reedie Drive. McGoo's has a large storage room appearance with a few shamrocks stuck on bare walls. A miniscule corner bar has Guinness and Harp on tap, and you can get a pretty decent sandwich at your table inside or, in summer, out along the sidewalk. It's a newcomer in the area, but it's finding many friends from the neighborhood and the nearby shopping center.

Open daily. Information: 301-946-2777.

Massachusetts

Boston

ℍℍ **The Black Rose**, 160 State Street, is the place most often recommended when you ask about Irish pubs in the Boston area. It's as authentic as the Dingle Peninsula. The appeal comes from the friendliness, good booze, and satisfying grub. You're likely to meet just about anyone in this saloon. I'm told that there's even an occasional visiting Irishman who would welcome a donation to the IRA, but I haven't met one. Guinness and Harp on draught, of course, and a limited menu for lunch and dinner. Live Irish music, often ballads, on weekends.

Open daily 11 a.m.-2 a.m. Information: 617-742-2286.

ⓖ **Boston Athenaeum**, 10 1/2 Beacon Street. The Athenaeum opened at this location in 1847. It is a research library and contains the collections of Gen. Henry Knox and George Washington. Many of Knox's books came from the bookstore he operated on Washington Street in 1771. The Athenaeum has an impressive art collection and holds shows by local artists. It is a private institution, primarily serving its members, but arrangements can be made to use the library for research.

Open Monday-Saturday. Call for hours. Information: 617-227-0270.

ⓖ **Boston Massacre Monument**, The Public Garden. The monument, described by author of the *Blue Guide [to] Boston and Cambridge*, John Freely, as "singularly unattractive," was completed in 1888. On a column it lists the names Patrick Carr and the other four men killed by the British at the Boston Massacre. Quotations from Daniel Webster and John Adams describing the March 5, 1770, tragedy are inscribed.

ⓖ **Boston Massacre Site**, 30 State Street. The site where five colonists were killed is marked by a circle of cobblestones. On March 5, 1770, British soldiers shot into a menacing crowd, killing three men immediately and wounding others fatally. This was the culmination of tensions which had increased when British troops first arrived in Boston. In Boston allegedly to keep order, they were viewed as oppressors. The soldiers were defended by John Adams, and only two were found guilty of manslaughter.

HI **Burns Library**, Bapst Library, Boston College, Chestnut Hill. The Irish Collection includes journals, magazines, and 7,500 books covering Irish history and arts.

Open Monday-Friday, 9 a.m.-5 p.m. Information: 617-552-3282.

B **Cardinal Spellman Philatelic Museum**, 235 Wellesley Street on the campus of Regis College. The museum is named for Francis Cardinal Spellman who served as auxiliary bishop in Boston before being appointed archbishop of New York. It has two galleries of changing stamp exhibits. Cardinal Spellman, a dedicated philatelist, donated his private collection to the college.

Open Tuesday through Thursday, 9 a.m.-4 p.m., Sunday afternoon 1-4, and by appointment. Free. Information: 617-894-6735.

HH **The Claddagh**, 113 Dartmouth. Brought to you by the same management which has the Black Rose and the Purple Shamrock, The Claddagh is an unpretentious, spacious pub within walking distance of Copley Place. Irish beer, of course, and the best in pub grub—even a pretty good salad! As with its siblings, people don't go here for the decor, but they do for the ambience—it has the feel of a real Irish pub.

Open daily. Information: 617-262-9874.

G **Dorchester Heights National Historic Site.** From Aladdin's lamp they came. Two-thousand soldiers and 59 cannon which drove the British out of Boston in 1776. The Red Coats may have credited Aladdin with conjuring up the overwhelming military power, but much of the glory goes to Irish-American general, Henry Knox, with a little help from his friends—2,000 of them. Overnight they had arrived with the cannon that had been dragged by oxen across 300 miles. The same night, the troops crept into Dorchester Heights, bringing with them equipment and ammunition. Appropriately, the Irish general drove the British away on March 17, 1776. This victory is commemorated by a 215-foot-high marble tower.

S **Henry James Home**, 131 Mount Vernon Street. Henry James lived here for a short time in the 1870s. During that period, he completed *Daisy Miller*. This is now a private residence.

S **John Boyle O'Reilly Memorial**, Boylston Street, near the bridge crossing the Back Bay Fens. The memorial, completed in 1896, honors the former owner/editor of the *Boston Pilot*, Fenian revolutionist in Ireland, orator, escapee from an Australian penal colony, poet, and fighter for social justice. A bronze bust of O'Reilly is located in front of other figures, the central one a female representing Ireland with her sons, Poetry and Courage. Unlike many artists, O'Reilly's poetic talents won critical praise during his lifetime. He died in 1890, age 46, one of the most prominent Irish Americans of the late 19th century.

HH **Mr. Dooley's Boston Tavern**, 77 Broad Street, introduces itself as "the pub you've been training for," invites you to "drop in for a stout, you never know who's about," says it's "a great place for a pint and a chat," promises "the mother of all traditional sessions" on Wednesdays, and points out that it has been recognized for the "Best Irish Breakfast" by the "Best of Boston." Well, that about sums it up. A lot of slogans for one place, but it's a place you should try. Even if they're accurate on one of these claims, it's worth a trip.

Open daily with food served 11 a.m.-9 p.m. (617-338-9171).

T **Museum at the John Fitzgerald Kennedy Library**, 5 miles southeast on I-93, off exit 17 on University of Massachusetts Columbia Point campus. The library is considered to be one of the most beautiful contemporary works of architecture in the country. The exhibit hall houses nine sections which encircle a room displaying Kennedy's desk as he used it before leaving for Dallas. The tower contains official papers from Kennedy's administration. In the lower lobby, you can view a film on Kennedy's life and work. Exhibits include a model of PT-109, displays on the Kennedy-Richard Nixon debates, and mementos from childhood and Senate years. A presentation of Robert Kennedy's life, his brother and attorney general, can also be seen. There is a picnic area on the waterfront.

Open daily, except New Year's, Thanksgiving, and Christmas. Handicapped facilities. Fee. Information: 617-929-4552.

Hl Museum of Fine Arts, 465 Huntington Avenue. The Museum contains a wide variety of Irish art, including crystal, paintings, silver, furniture, and ornaments.

Information: 617-267-9377.

S Nichols House Museum, 55 Mt. Vernon Street, Beacon Hill. The four-story brick mansion remains as built in 1804 by Charles Bullfinch. It was the home of Rose Standish Nichols from 1885 until her death in 1960. A most fascinating woman, she was America's first female landscape architect, author of several books, woodcarver, furniture-maker, and founder of a number of organizations, including a pacifist group which included Mrs. Woodrow Wilson and Mrs. Winston Churchill. One of the outstanding attractions of the museum are two art pieces by Augustus Saint-Gaudens, Ms. Nichols' uncle—a statue of "Diana at the Crossroads" and an image of Robert Louis Stevenson.

Call for hours. Information: 617-227-6993.

G Old Granary Burying-Ground, Tremont Street. Opened in 1660, this is considered the most important of Boston's cemeteries because of the number and prominence of the people buried here. Bronze tablets on the gateway identify some of these people, including Patrick Carr and other victims of the Boston Massacre; Paul Revere, John Hancock, Samuel Adams; and early governors, including Irish-American John Sullivan. The "marked" burial site of the men killed in the Boston Massacre is located to the right of the main gate. Since tombstones have been rearranged several times, you can't be certain that a stone actually marks the grave site of the person named.

Open daily 8 a.m.-4:30 p.m.

G **Old South Meeting House**, 310 Washington Street. Irishman Patrick Carr was one of five Americans killed in the 1870 Boston massacre. It was here the colonists met to discuss the massacre. The house, built in 1729 as a Puritan church, was the site of many town meetings concerning events leading up to the Revolutionary War, including the Boston Tea Party. Boston's history is told through a multimedia presentation.

Open daily 9:30 a.m.-5 p.m., April-October; Monday-Friday 10 a.m.-4 p.m. and Saturday-Sunday 10 a.m.-5 p.m., other months; closed major holidays. Fee. Senior and children's discount. Information: 617-482-6439.

HH **Paddy Burke's**, 132 Portland Street, has a special price on Guinness. You can order food daily from a menu of sandwiches, burgers, and steaks and enjoy a full Irish breakfast Saturday-Sunday 10 a.m.-4 p.m. at bargain price. Live Irish entertainment is presented weekly and televised international sports are shown.

Open daily. Information: 617-367-8370.

HH **The Purple Shamrock**, 1 Union, was my first Irish pub experience in Boston, and I remember it well. Not much to look at, it offers the expected Irish friendliness by staff and fellow imbibers. Sometimes dismissed as a tourist spot, I have found it a good place to stop for lunch and a cool one. *The Purple Shamrock* was the title of a Mayor Curley biography.

Open daily. Information: 617-227-2060.

S **Saint-Gaudens' Brooks Statue**, Trinity Church, Copley Square. Within the church stands a statue of Phillips Brooks, designed by Augustus Saint-Gaudens, but finished, following his death, by his assistants.

The current church, the third building to house Trinity, was completed in 1877. It is one of the most impressive churches in the country, described by its chief architect, Henry Hobson Richardson, as a "free rendering of the French Romanesque."

Information: 617-586-6944.

S **Saint-Gaudens' Medallion and Lions**, Boston Public Library, Boyleston Street, Copley Square, across from Trinity Church. Housed within the old library is a medallion portrait, created by Dublin-born Augustus Saint-Gaudens as memorial to Robert C. Billings, a financial supporter of the library. The main staircase in the old library awed Irish-American writer Henry James who described its "splendour of tawny marble." Standing on the landing are two marble lions designed by Louis Saint-Gaudens, the brother of Augustus.

The library, founded in 1852, was moved to this site in 1895. All art was not completed until 1912. In 1964, a new library was built adjacent to the old structure.

Open 9 a.m.-9 p.m. Monday-Thursday and 9 a.m.-5 p.m. Friday-Saturday. Information: 617-536-5400.

S **Saint-Gaudens's Shaw Monument**, Beacon Street, northwest corner of Boston Common. Sculpted by Augustus Saint-Gaudens, it is considered one of the finer public art pieces in the city. The monument is a memorial to Col. Robert Gould Shaw and his 54th Massachusetts Regiment. The Regiment was made up of black enlisted men and white officers, the first African-Americans permitted to serve in the Union forces during the Civil War. The work depicts the Regiment on May 28, 1863, the day they received their colors from the Governor. Shaw and many of the men were killed on July 18, 1863, in a battle at Ft. Wagner, South Carolina. The monument was dedicated on May 13, 1897. Among the honored guests were Sergeant William Carney, whose valor at Ft. Wagner made him the first African-American to receive the Congressional Medal of Honor.

Brookline

T **John F. Kennedy National Historic Site**, 83 Beals Street. The birthplace and early childhood home of the first Catholic president of the United States has been restored to its 1917 condition, the year the president was born. The home includes the original furnishings and family memorabilia. The family moved in 1921. Rose Kennedy, the president's mother, recorded a tour of the home.

Open daily 10 a.m.-4:30 p.m., except New Year's, Thanksgiving, and Christmas. Fee. Senior citizens free. Information: 617-566-7937.

HH O'Leary's, 1010 Beacon Street, is the place to fraternize in an authentic Irish pub. American and traditional Irish food is served daily, and an Irish brunch—including steak and kidney pie—is served Sunday 11 a.m.-4 p.m., followed by an Irish seisiun.

Open daily. Information: 617-734-0049.

Cambridge

HH The Black Rose [Roisin Dubh], 50 Church Street, has live music Wednesday through Sunday, including a traditional seisiun Sunday evening 6-10. Lunch, dinner, and Sunday brunch are served.

Open daily. Information: 617-492-8630.

Cohasset

HIA St. John Memorial, Cohasset Central Cemetery. The bodies of Irish emigrants, drowned off the coast of Cohasset in 1849, are buried here. Fleeing from the Famine, 99 people from counties Galway and Clare died when the *St. John* struck rocks. The Ladies of the Ancient Order of Hibernians erected a 20-foot Celtic cross in 1914.

Lowell

P Lowell was the textile manufacturing center of the country in the early 19th century. Located at the juncture of the Concord and Merrimack rivers, the waterpower potential was recognized by investors. In the early 1820s, textile mills and waterpower canals were built and prosperity came to the city and some of its citizens, but not to the women who worked in the mills. At some mills, more than half of the "girls," as they were called, were Irish immigrants. Textile mill work was the second most popular source of employment for Irish women after domestic service. The life of the textile worker was long and grueling. The Union was unable to improve their lot because of the large influx of Irish and other immigrants who took any job, under any conditions, to earn money for themselves and their families back home. Early in the 20th century, the textile business began to fall off, just as working conditions were improving.

℗ **Lowell Heritage State Park Waterpower Exhibit**, 25 Shattuck Street. A "Working People Exhibit" in a restored 1835 mill boarding house tells the sad story of the effect that mill life had on the Irish and other immigrants and of the contributions made by these groups to the city of Lowell. Hands-on models of waterpower equipment are displayed.

Exhibits and a slide show can be seen in the **Visitor Center**, 246 Market Street. Open daily 8:30 a.m.-5 p.m., except New Year's, Thanksgiving, and Christmas. Information: 508-459-1000.

℗ **Lowell National Historical Park and Heritage State Park**.

The positive and negative effect of immigration on the economy of Lowell is shown through mills, workers' homes, and the canal system.

Free. Seasonal boat, walking, and trolley tours are offered (fee). Admission to the parks is free. Information: 508-459-1000.

Chappaquiddick

Ⅾ Let's take a minute to visualize Chappaquiddick Island. First, it just manages to make it as an island, being a distance from the mainland which can be better measured in feet than miles. When you get off the ferry which takes you from the Edgartown landing to Chappaquiddick, you find yourself on Chappaquiddick Road. Picture a cross. Chappaquiddick Road is the long leg, School Road is the shorter leg. At the point where the two intersect, Chappaquiddick Road gets a new name and a new surface. Chappaquiddick is a 2-lane paved road which abruptly changes to a bumpy, dirt narrow road, called Dike. Chappaquiddick Road, Dike Road and School Road play a part in this tale.

Now, let's take the route which Sen. Edward Kennedy and his ill-fated passenger, Mary Jo Kopechne, took the night of July 19, 1969. Kennedy and Kopechne had been at the Lawrence Party on School Road. They left the party, saying that they were going to take the ferry back to Edgartown. That means they would drive up the 2-lane paved School Road, turn left onto the 2-lane paved Chappaquiddick Road and follow it directly to the ferry landing. However, that did not happen. Kennedy, who was according to most reports, driving, drove up School Road and took a *right* onto the bumpy, narrow, dirt surface Dike Road, and continued a very short distance to Dike Bridge which led over a pond to a deserted beach area. But Kennedy did not cross Dike Bridge, instead he drove off the bridge, flipping his car upside down into the pond.

From this point the story of that night and the next morning becomes confused and contradictory, but either by swimming or getting a boat, Kennedy went back to his hotel in Edgartown and the next morning, some 12 hours later, he and friends went to the police station to report the accident. Kopechne was found dead. Kennedy and his attorneys conferred with the judge, Kennedy pleaded guilty to leaving the scene of an accident, and was freed with a suspended sentence. The other details are very fuzzy, and the tragedy has spawned many books, articles, television shows. But most devastating to the Kennedy clan, the controversy destroyed Ted Kennedy's hope to become president of the United States. But the citizens of Massachusetts continue to elect him to the Senate.

Dike (Dyke) Bridge. On Dike Road, east side of Chappaquiddick Island.

The Lawrence Cottage, School Road. The cottage is a permanent home in a secluded area, completely surrounded by grass, fence, and woods. The cottage was the setting for a party which began at 8:30, the evening of July 18. It was attended by a group of Kennedy's male friends and the six "Boiler Room girls."

Silva House, School Road. The home of John and Dodie Silva is located next door and about 150 yards north of the Lawrence

Cottage. The Silvas considered calling the police about 1:30 a.m. July 19th because of the loud noise coming from the party at the Lawrence cottage.

Edgartown

D **Courthouse.** It is here that Kennedy pleaded guilty to a charge of leaving the scene of an accident on Friday, July 25, one week after the accident. He was given a suspended sentence by Irish-American judge James A. Boyle and was ushered out the back door of the courthouse to avoid the press.

Dr. Donald R. Mills' Office-Home. Dr. Mills examined the body after it was removed from Kennedy's car. He pronounced that death was due to drowning. He did not order an autopsy.

Edgartown Yacht Club. A regatta was conducted earlier in the day of the fatal accident, in which Kennedy, followed by the "Boiler Room Girls" in a chartered boat, participated. He lost, returned to his hotel to change into a bathing suit, and went to the deserted end of Chappaquiddick Island, crossing the Dike Bridge, to meet the "girls" for a swim party.

Police Station/Town Offices. Edgartown Police chief Arena had known Kennedy since the early days when he sometimes chauffeured him as part of his duties as driver at the State House. He met Kennedy at the police station, when he returned from the scene of the accident. Kennedy made several calls from the station and prepared his statement for Arena, which was misplaced.

Shiretown Inn. The lodging where Kennedy and some other members of his group stayed.

Hyannis

T **Hyannis Harbor Tours,** Pier 1 at Ocean Street Dock. The hour tour of Hyannis harbor includes a view of the Kennedy family summer homes in Hyannis Port.

Tours are given 9 a.m.-8 p.m., June 1 to mid-September; 10

a.m.-2:30 p.m., April-May and October. Fee. Information: 508-778-2600.

T John F. Kennedy Memorial Museum, 397 Main Street, Hyannis. Opened the summer of 1992, it closed for expansion the winter of '92, and re-opened spring 1993. The museum features visuals focusing on Kennedy's administration and his relationship to the Hyannis area.

Open Monday-Saturday 10 a.m.-4 p.m., Sunday afternoon 1-4. Fee. Information: 508-775-2201.

T John F. Kennedy Memorial, Ocean Street on Lewis Bay. The memorial comprises a 12-foot high circular stone wall, fountain, and pool. The 35th president grew up in this area and the Kennedy Compound is nearby.

Information: 508-362-3225.

HH Mitchell's Steak & Pub House/Shamrock Lounge, 451 Iyanough Road., Rt. 28, Hyannis. This is the place for award winning chowder—selected #1 on Cape Cod. Lunch specials, candlelight dining, and Irish entertainment make this a popular choice. Sunday brunch is served from 11:30-3:00 p.m.

Open daily. Information: 508-775-6700.

Salem

D Witch Museum, 19 1/2 Washington Square North. The museum recalls the witch trial hysteria which gripped Salem and its citizens in 1692. A multimedia show is presented on the half-hour. One of the victims was "Granny" Anne Glover. She had been taken from her home in Ireland by the British under Cromwell, sold as a slave in Barbados, brought to the United States, and deemed a witch. She spoke an evil language—Gaelic—the "language of the Devil." Anne Glover was hanged.

Open daily 10 a.m.-7 p.m., July and August; 10 a.m.-5 p.m., other months; closed New Year's, Thanksgiving, and Christmas. Fee. Senior and children's discount. Information: 508-744-1692.

D **Witch House**, 310 1/2 Essex Street. Jonathon Corwin, who conducted the infamous Salem witch trials, lived in this 1642 home. There is evidence that some of the accused were examined here.

Open daily. Fee. Discount for seniors and witches (with proof). Information: 508-744-0180.

West Roxbury

S **Brook Farm**, 670 Baker Street. There's not much left to see except one nondescript building, and that may have fallen by the time you read this. But from 1841-47, George and Josephine Riley led a group in a socialist experiment that grew out of the transcendentalist movement. The group included Nathaniel Hawthorne, who set his novel *The Blithedale Romance*, at Brook Farm, and Ralph Waldo Emerson, whose interest in transcendentalism invaded some of his writing.

Worcester

HH **O'Connor's Restaurant & Bar**, 1160 West Boyleston Street. "O'thentic Irish purveyors of famous food, spirits and hospitality," reads their T-shirts, and I'm one of the many satisfied customers who believes the "fame" is well-earned. If you want to avoid a wait, call for reservations. O'Connor's has a large bar with several dining areas. The Irish O'thentic decor is enhanced by the brogues heard at the bar and in the surrounding dining areas.

Open daily. Information: 508-853-0789.

S **John Boyle O'Reilly Tomb**, Holy Rood Cemetery. John Boyle O'Reilly (1844-1890) is buried here. O'Reilly was the owner and editor of the *Boston Pilot*.

Michigan

Ann Arbor

T **Gerald R. Ford Presidential Library**, University of Michigan, North Campus, 1000 Beal Avenue. The library contains documents from Ford's years as congressman, vice-president, and president. Changing exhibits focus on various aspects of these lives.

Open Monday-Friday 8:45 a.m. to 4:45 p.m., except national holidays. Free. Information: 313-741-2218.

Cambridge Junction

HIA **Irish Hills**, 4 miles east of Cambridge Junction on US 12. An Irish immigrant who settled in this area named it Irish Hills because it brought back memories of his homeland.

Dearborn

P **Dearborn Inn and Marriott Hotel**, 20301 Oakwood Boulevard, 1/4 mile from Henry Ford Museum and Greenfield Village. Five colonial homes, an inn and motor house located on 23 acres of landscaped lawns express Henry Ford's idea of what guest accommodations should be. The houses replicate the the homes of Barbara Fritchie, Governor Oliver Wolcott, and Irish Americans Edgar Allen Poe and Patrick Henry.

Information: 313-271-2700; 800-221-7236 (outside Michigan), 800-221-7237 (Michigan).

P **Henry Ford Museum and Greenfield Village**, 1/2 mile south on US 12, 1 1/2 miles west of Southfield Road on Oakwood Boulevard.Ford, whose father emigrated from County Cork, was the founder of Ford Motor Company. Return to America's past through this indoor-outdoor replica of America in the 17th, 18th, and 19th centuries. Dedicated in 1929, more than 1,000,000 visitors a year come from throughout the world.

The museum, covering 12 acres, focuses on transportation, power and machinery, agriculture, lighting, communications, household furnishings, appliances, ceramics, glass, and musical instruments. Included are a hands-on center, special exhibits, tours, and film.

Open daily, except New Year's, Thanskgiving, and Christmas. Fee.

℗ **Greenfield Village** contains 80 buildings from the 17th, 18th, and 19th centuries, moved from throughout the country, and once associated with many famous Americans, such as Irish American McGuffey, Webster, and Carver. Included are the courtroom where Abraham Lincoln practiced, the Wright Brothers' cycle shop, Henry Ford's birthplace, Edison's Menlo Park laboratory, and Harvey Firestone's 19th century farmstead.

Open daily, except New Year's, Thanksgiving, and Christmas. Winter sleigh tours are offered January through mid-March. Fee.

℗ Located on the grounds is the **Suwanee Park**, a turn-of-the-century amusement park, where you can ride in a horse-drawn carriage, steam train, riverboat, or Model T Ford. Fee.

Information: 313-271-1620 or -1976 (recording).

℗ **Henry Ford Estate-Fair Lane**, Evergreen Road on the University of Michigan-Dearborn Campus. Seventy-two acres include the $2 million 56-room mansion, with original furnishings, built by Henry Ford in 1915. It's impressive for its simplicity and the systems of heating, water, electricity and refrigeration, unusual in the early 20th century. The powerhouse and boathouse have been restored.

Open daily May-September; Sundays throughout the year; closed New Year's, Easter, and Christmas. Fee. Senior discount. Information: 313-593-5590.

Information for all Dearborn Henry Ford sites: Dearborn Chamber of Commerce, 15544 Michigan Avenue, 48126 (313-584-6100).

Detroit

ℋ❙ **Detroit Institute of Arts**, 5200 Woodward Avenue. The Institute has one of the country's largest collections of Irish gold jewelry from as early as 2000 B.C.

Open daily, except Monday. Information: 313-833-7900.

Dunleavy'z River Place, 267 Joseph Campau at Franklin. Friendly, but not boisterous. Described in *Craine's Business Review* as "stately elegance," the main dining room has a window wall, exposed brick, and is decorated in dark green and brown. Irish beers and a full menu are provided. The owners use three vans to shuttle customers to and from all downtown sporting and entertainment events. A nice touch!

Open daily. Information: 315-259-0909.

Edsel and Eleanor Ford House, 1100 Lake Shore Road, Grosse Pointe Shores. Edsel, automobile manufacturer and son of Henry Ford, and his wife lived on this 63-acre estate in a stone mansion. The extraordinary home contains an impressive art collection.

Open Wednesday-Sunday afternoons with guided tours on the hour from 1-4. Fee. Senior and children's discount. Information: 313-884-4222.

Old Shillelagh, 349 Monroe, Greektown, starts the St. Patrick's Day season about March 1 with green beer. You can hear folk music every night at 9 and indulge in Shepherd's pie, corned beef, and hamburgers. Shamrocks abound: some on the wall, others hanging from the ceiling. It's a fun place to eat and drink.

Open daily. Information: 315-964-0007.

Grand Rapids

Gerald R. Ford Presidential Museum, 303 Pearl Street, Northwest. Gerald R. Ford, 38th U.S. president, traces his ancestry on his father's side to County Monaghan. According to Debrett's Peerage, as quoted in *Irish America*, Ford's "real last name" is Lynch King, the first and last name of his great-grandfather. The museum, a triangular glass-walled structure, tells the story of Ford's personal and political life as congressman, vice president, and president, through exhibits, films, documents, and slides. There are exibits focusing on his pardon of President Nixon, the bicentennial celebration, and the role of Betty Ford as first lady. Memorabilia, gifts from world leaders, and a replica of the Oval Office during Ford's administration are displayed.

Open Monday-Saturday 9 a.m.-4:45 p.m. and Sunday afternoon noon-4:45, except New Year's, Thanksgiving, and Christmas. Fee. Senior and children's discount. Information: 616-456-2674.

Royal Oak

D **Shrine of the Little Flower,** Woodward Avenue and Twelve Mile Road. A 100-foot crucifixion tower is supported by four crosses. The shrine is composed of limestone, highlighted by blocks representing each of the states. It is incongruous that this godly site was best known as the source of the vituperous rhetoric of its pastor, Father Charles E. Coughlin. In his radio broadcasts of the 1930s, Father Coughlin unleashed attacks against President Roosevelt, communists, and whatever else displeased him. While others honed in on the same targets, few employed the intemperate language and personal assaults characterstic of Father Couglin. At one point, after he had called the president a "liar," he was ordered by his bishop to apologize.

Although he complied, he did not modify his style or vocabulary.

Open Monday-Friday 7 a.m.-3:30 p.m., Saturday 8:30 a.m.-8 p.m., Sunday 7:30 a.m.-3 p.m., and holidays 7:30 a.m.-12 noon. Free. Information: 313-541-4122.

Minnesota

Elk River

P **Oliver H. Kelly Farm,** 15788 Kelly Farm Road. Costumed guides perform chores and invite you to join in plowing behind a team of oxen, cooking molasses, and other activities on this 189-acre living-history farm.

Open daily 10 a.m.-5 p.m., May-September. Interpretive center is open daily 10 a.m.-5 p.m., May-September; Saturday 10 a.m.-4 p.m. and Sunday noon-4:00 p.m., the rest of the year. Fee. Senior and children's discount. Information: 612-441-6896.

Grand Rapids

A city whose economy is supported by iron and paper production, **Grand Rapids** is celebrated for being the hometown of Judy Garland, who used to be Frances Gumm, but will forever be Dorothy. The star of *The Wizard of Oz* is remembered every June with a three day celebration, which includes the permanently installed yellow brick road, films, talent contest, fan club collectors' exchange, and a munchkin or two.

Information: 218-326-9607, 800-472-6366, or write Grand Rapids Area Chamber of Commerce, The Depot, 1 Northwest 3rd Street.

S **Judy Garland Collection,** Central School Heritage and Arts Center, junction of MN 2 and US 169. A yellow brick road leads you to the center, and if you go up to the third floor, you'll find a Judy Garland collection of memorabilia of her life and work. The restored 1895 school now houses the Itasca County Historical Society and museum, shops, and a restaurant. The museum has an exhibit depicting 19th-century Main Street with professional offices, a bank, and store.

Open Monday-Saturday 9 a.m.-5 p.m., Memorial Day-Labor Day; 9:30 a.m.-5 the rest of the year. Fee. Information: 218-326-6431.

Northfield

D **Northfield Historical Society Museum,** 408 Division Street. On the weekend after Labor Day, you can see the James-Younger gang ride into town and try to rob the First National Bank. One of the gang's greatest blunders took place here on September 7, 1876, when eight of them were caught in the act. Jesse and Frank James escaped, but two of the gang were killed, and the rest put away for life in Stillwater State Prison. Three townspeople also perished that day. The town re-enacts this incident annually during the Defeat of Jesse James Days. The celebration includes a parade and a rodeo. The museum was, in its former life, the First National Bank. Its main room and exterior look the same as they did when the outlaws came into town bent on no good. The hands of the clock point to shortly before 2 p.m., the time of the ill-fated crime.

Open 9 a.m.-5 p.m. Monday-Friday, until 9 Thursday evening, 10 a.m.-4 p.m. Saturday, and 1-5 Sunday afternoon. Fee. Information: 507-645-9268, -5604.

Owatonna

S Norwest Bank (National Farmer's Bank), corner Broadway and North Cedar. Designed late in his career by Louis Sullivan and opened in 1908, the structure includes stained glass windows by Louis Millet and four cast iron electric chandeliers weighing 2.5 tons each.

Information: 507-451-5670.

P Old No. 201, intersection of US 14 and I-35. The engine driven by Casey Jones rests peacefully in front of a former depot. But, it's not "Old 382." (See Jackson, Tennessee)

St. Paul

H College of St. Thomas, 2115 Summit Avenue. The Celtic Collection contains 5,000 publications relating to the six Celtic nations, with an emphasis on Irish and Scotch history and literature.

Open Monday-Friday 1 p.m.-4:30 p.m. and every third Saturday 10 a.m.-noon and 1 p.m.-5 p.m. Information: 612- 962-5467.

Tower

T McKinley Monument, Main Street. This is the first monument erected to the memory of William McKinley, 25th president of the

United States. McKinley's paternal ancestors emigrated from County Antrim in 1743.

Mississippi

Biloxi

ℍℍ Mary Mahoney's Old French House Restaurant, 138 Rue Magnolia. Here the Irish and French have collaborated more successfully than they did in their historical joint efforts to defeat the British. This is a very popular place for the locals who can nibble on beignets or po'boys 24 hours a day or dine in Biloxi splendor in the elegant dining room during more restricted hours. Mary Mahoney no longer greets customers, but her spirit remains to add Gaelic charm to the surroundings of aged brick and wood.Customers pay well for their pleasure.

Information: 601-374-0163.

Jackson

𝕊 Mississippi Museum of Art, 201 East Pascagoula Street. Georgia O'Keeffe is among the artists whose work is on permanent display. Others include Picasso and Renoir. A hands-on children's gallery with exhibits and multi-media presentations is located in the Impressions Gallery. The museum houses a research library, art school, and film center.

Open Tuesday-Saturday 10 a.m.-5:00 p.m. and Sunday noon-5; closed major holidays. Fee. Children's discount. Information: 601-960-1515.

Missouri

Independence

𝔻 1859 Marshall's Home and Jail Museum, 217 North Main

Street. Jesse's brother Frank, William Quantrill, and the Younger brothers were among the western outlaws housed at various times in the dungeon cells of this Civil War-era jail. It has been restored to its mid-19th century appearance. The marshall's home contains period furnishings. A one-room school house and a local history museum are located here.

Open Monday-Saturday 10 a.m.-5 p.m., and Sunday afternoon 1-4, March through December; Tuesday-Saturday 10 a.m.-5 p.m., other months; closed holidays. Fee, senior and children's discount. Information: 816-252-1892.

Kansas City

D **Kansas City Massacre**, Union Station parking plaza, Pershing Road and Main Street. As the *Flyer* pulled into Union Station, five gangsters took their positions among the cars in the parking lot. Frank Nash, another bad guy, was a passenger on the train, accompanied by FBI. When Nash, with red wig askew, had been placed safely in a waiting car, the gangsters went into action. A "heavyset" one aimed his machine gun at the officers. One of the policemen shot him in the arm, which set off a heavy barrage of shots from the gangsters. Nash waved his handcuffed arms screaming, "Don't shoot me!" But rather than his saviors, they were his executors. Witnesses claimed the "heavyset" leader of the gang was "Pretty Boy" Floyd.

HH **Ryan's Kerry Patch**, I-29 and Barry Road, is a standout in all categories. It has an impressive group of rooms in a building designed especially to house an Irish pub and restaurant. Large stained glass windows, high ceilings, a gargantuan fireplace, hot and scrumptious leek soup—with big potato chunks—garlic toast, Dagwood-size sandwiches—good service, and cold Harps kept us much later than we planned. The Kerry Patch has three rooms on the first floor—St. Bridget's, St. Patrick's, and the Hibernian. There's another room upstairs and one down, the latter has a second bar. Look for the mural above the door in St. Bridget's room. It displays a primitive painting of many aspects of the Kansas City area, including the Wood characters, Harry Truman, the Kansas City Royals and Chiefs.

My only complaint: When I returned the second time with my family in tow, there was a scribbled note on the door saying they were closed for lunch. Moral: Call first.

Open Monday-Saturday 10 a.m.-11 p.m. Information: 816-776-8309.

Kearney

D **Jesse James Home**, 1 1/2 miles east on MO 92, then 1 1/2 miles north on Jesse James Farm Road. Jesse James was born here in 1847. This is the home in which he and brother Frank grew up.Much of the furniture is original. During the summer, "The Life and Times of Jesse James" is presented at the farm.

In September 1992, a new twist was added to the Jesse James story when a letter was found in the archives of the Library of Congress. The contents suggest that the U.S. Government may have been involved in a bombing of the home. At the time of the incident, Jesse was traveling, but his 8-year-old half-brother was killed, and his mother lost part of an arm.

The people around Kearney, those who loathed Jesse as a killer and those who adored him as a latter day Robin Hood, were enraged by the attack and an investigation was conducted. There were no conclusive results.

When hearing of the new evidence, California Superior Court Judge James R. Ross, Jesse's oldest living descendent, said that the theory that the government was involved in the bombing "is logical." The story goes on.

Open daily 9 a.m.-4 p.m., May 31-October 1; Monday-Friday 9 a.m.-4 p.m. and Saturday-Sunday noon-4 p.m., rest of the year; closed New Year's, Thanksgiving, and Christmas. Fee. Children's discount. Information: 816-635-6065.

Liberty

ᵭ Jesse James Bank and Museum, 15 miles North of Kansas City on the Square. The restored site of an 1866 bank robbery by Jesse and/or Frank James is the first recorded daylight bank robbery. The bank has some of the original furniture and the clock is set at the time of the robbery. There is a question whether James actually took part, since he was ill at the time, however, some of the witnesses reported seeing a man bent over in his saddle.

Open daily, except Sundays, Thanksgiving, and December 20-February 1. Fee. Information: 816-781-4458.

Rolla

ᕼIA University of Missouri at Rolla (UMR), North Pine Street. Engineering students at Rolla have selected St. Patrick as their patron saint. As part of the graduation ritual, students are dubbed knights in the Order of St. Patrick, and the main street is painted green.

Information: 314-341-4111.

St. Joseph

ᵭ St. Joseph holds a Jesse James Festival each June, commemorating the death of Jesse James and the start of the Pony Express system. Information: 816-233-6482.

ᵭ Jesse James Home, 12th and Penn Streets. Jesse James was killed in his home April 3, 1832, by his former outlaw colleague Bob Ford and his brother, Mrs. James's nephews. James had been living quietly in St. Joe under the assumed name of Howard. The one-story house has some of the original furniture, and one wall has a bullet hole made the day of the killing. Tape recordings explain the series of events on the fatal day.

Tours are given of the Jesse James Home Monday-Saturday 10 a.m.-4 p.m. and Sunday afternoon 1-5, May through August; Monday-Saturday 10 a.m.-4 p.m. and Sunday afternoon 1-4, September-April. Fee. Information: 816-233-8206.

D **St. Joseph Museum**, 11th & Charles Streets. The museum contains national, local, and western history exhibits concerned with Jesse James, the Civil War, and Pony Express. There is anAmerican Indian collection.

Open daily, April-September; Monday-Saturday 9 a.m.-5 p.m., Sunday and holiday afternoons 1-5; closed New Year's, Thanksgiving, December 24-25 and 31. Fee. Information: 816-232-8471.

St. Louis

HH **Annie Gunn's**, 16806 Chesterfield Airport Road, Chesterfield. This is a small, nicely decorated pub with long bar and tables decorated in wood, brick, and green. A private snuggery has seating for six. The place is kept busy with friendly regulars who obviously enjoy the food, atmosphere, and conversation as much as the drink. Local critics recommend the Irish style smoked salmon, the trout, and the smoked pork chops. I can vouch for the salmon! Lunch and dinner are served Tuesday-Sunday. The quality, along with moderate prices and the Harp and Guinness, have made Annie Gunn's a success with business people and professionals while still in its infancy.

Open daily (except Monday) 11 a.m.-10 p.m. Tuesday-Thursday;11 a.m.-11 p.m. Friday-Saturday; Sunday 12 p.m.-7:00 p.m. Information: 314-532-7684.

T **Grant's Farm**, Gravois Road at Grant Road. Ulysses S. Grant built a cabin on this site in 1856. Now owned by Anheuser-Busch Co., Inc., you can see the cabin and many other intriguing items on the 281-acre tract: the famous Clydesdale stallion stable and paddock, a trophy room, and miniature zoo with animal shows.

Trackless train tours are given mornings at 9, 10, and 11; afternoons at 1, 2, and 3:30, Tuesday-Sunday, June through August; Thursday-Sunday, mid-April through May, and early September through mid-October. Free. Information and reservations: 314-843-1700.

HH **McGurk's Irish Pub**, 1200 Russell Boulevard, is an authentic neighborhood Irish pub with regulars so regular that their faces appear on the menu and on the walls and across from you at the rectangular bar. When the time is right, they start playing their music. You'll find friendly folk at your elbow, a bartender who tries with modest success not to sneer when he explains that he has Irish beer not green beer, a cheap steak dinner which isn't very good, and a cheaper hamburger which is.

Open daily. Information: 314-776-8309.

HH **Maggie O'Brien's**, 2000 Market Street, has three large rooms, one with green arm chairs at a long bar; tables in other rooms. Decorated in green, wood, and stained glass. The foyer has a display of T-shirts and sweatshirts. Unfortunately, the most interesting ones worn by the staff are not for sale.

The pub is named for owner Harry Belli's two grandmothers, Maggie Belli and Winne O'Brien. Look out for Granny O'Brien hanging near the entrance. Both grandmothers would be pleased to see the crowds of St. Louisans and tourists enjoying Maggie O'Brien's. The Irish stew, while not the best I've tasted—that's in Philly—is the most unusual. It's served inside a loaf of bread! It goes down well with the Irish beer on draught. Entertainment is presented nightly, sometimes Irish.

Open daily until 3 a.m. Information: 314-421-1388.

HH **O'Connell's Pub**, 4652 Shaw at Kingshighway, is your door to the Twilight Zone. An old red brick free standing building with accents of green brick beckons you into a large, semi-dark, high-ceilinged room dominated by a long antique bar. Behind the bar hover two bartenders, each of whom has been with O'Connell's for a quarter of a century. I had the feeling that O'Connell's has been and always will be a legend.

The bar was lined with regulars from the working-class neighborhood which surrounds the pub. They come here not for the music-there isn't any—but to socialize while they consume what is perennially named as St. Louis's best hamburger.

I'll return to O'Connell's because I know it will be there.So will the same bartenders and the same neighbors. But next time I hope they'll have Harp.

Open daily, except Sunday, 11 a.m.-midnight. Information:314-773-6600.

T **Old Courthouse**, 11 North 4th Street. Erected in 1839, the Courthouse is the site of many trials relating to slavery, the most noted, being the Dred Scott case hearing, ultimately tried before Supreme Court Justice and Irish-American Roger B. Taney. Among the features of the Courthouse are its self-supporting cast iron staircases.

Open daily 8 a.m.-4:30 p.m., except New Year's, Thanksgiving, and Christmas. Free. Information: 314-425-4468.

Stanton

D **Jesse James Wax Museum**, I-44 at exit 230. Those of us who are intrigued with stories that the daughter of the last tsar of Russia escaped her executioners will get a kick out of this museum. The staff present the provocative proposition that Jesse James was not, in fact, killed in St. Joseph, Missouri, but lived until a ripe old 102, under the assumed name of Frank Dalton, one of the infamous Dalton brother outlaws. The museum has some Jesse James memorabilia, including affidavits that swear that Jesse lived for many years after the time of his reported death. Wax figures of Irish American outlaws Jesse, Frank James, and Frank Dalton are displayed.

Open daily 8 a.m.-6 p.m., June through August; 9 a.m.-5 p.m., other months. Fee. Children's discount. Information: 314-927-5233.

D **Meramec Caverns**, 3 miles south on County W from exit 230, off I-44. The caverns have seen many strange sights since their discovery in 1716. The five floors of unique formations have served as a storage area for gun powder for the Union forces during the Civil War, an underground station for slaves escaping to the North, and a hideout for Jesse James and his gang. But most bizarre, they were the site of a reunion of nearly forgotten Western outlaws in 1949, chaired by no other than Jesse James at the age of 102, 67 years after his reported killing! Or is it blarney?

There is an exhibit of minerals, crystal, and ultraviolet rock on display at the entrance to the electrically lighted caverns. Guided tours are given.

Open daily 9 a.m.-5 p.m., March through December; extended summer hours; closed Thanksgiving and Christmas. Fee. Information: 314-468-3166.

Montana

Butte

℘ In 1900, 25 per cent of the population of **Butte** was Irish. Although most of the Irish emigrating to the States settled in the eastern cities, they went where the work was, and in the late 19th and early 20th centuries that included Butte with its copper, gold, and silver mining. You can see how they and their fellow miners worked and lived and contrast it with how the mine owners and their families lived.

℘ **Copper King Mansion**, 219 West Granite Street. For contrast with how the Irish workers lived, visit the 1884, 32-room estate of Senator W. A. Clark, "copper king." Restored and furnished according to the period style, it has hand-carved fireplaces, frescoed ceilings, and a pipe organ.

Guided tours daily 9 a.m.-5 p.m., except Christmas. Fee. Senior and children's discount. Information: 406-782-7580.

℘ **World Museum of Mining and Hell Roarin' Gulch**, West Park Street, 1 mile west at Orphan Girl Mine. Hell Roarin' Gulch is a 19th century mining camp. The museum contains equipment, memorabilia, and exhibits of early mining activity. Gift shop and picnic area available.

Open daily 9 a.m.-9 p.m. mid-June to Labor Day; Tuesday-

Sunday 10 a.m.-5 p.m. April 1 to mid-June and after Labor Day to mid-November. Free. Information: 406-723-7211.

Deer Lodge

℗ **Towe Ford Museum,** 1106 Main Street. The museum contains one of the world's largest collections of Fords and Lincolns, covering the spectrum from 1903 through the 1960s. Among the over 100 vehicles exhibited is Henry Ford's personal Lincoln camper.

Open daily 8 a.m.-9 p.m., June through August; call for times during other months. Fee. Children's discount. Information: 406-846-3111.

Helena

☾ **Thomas Francis Meagher Equestrian Statue** at the state Capitol. Born in Waterford, Ireland in 1823, Meagher led a life that movies are based on. Unfortunately, none has been. After being arrested by the British for his efforts with the Young Ireland movement to achieve Irish independence, he was banished to Tasmania, Britain's Siberia. He escaped to the States, where in 1861 he formed a unit which became a part of the 69th New York State Militia. A brigadier general by 1862, he led the Irish Brigade to glory. Following the Civil War, Meagher was appointed acting governor of the territory of Montana. He died mysteriously when he fell from a steamboat near Fort Benton, Montana, and drowned. He may have been attempting to elude former Confederate soldiers whom he believed were trying to kill him.

Nebraska

Lincoln

Sheldon Memorial Art Gallery and Sculpture Garden, 12th and R Streets. Georgia O'Keeffe is among the painters featured in this collection, focusing on the work of American 20th-century artists.

Others include Eakins, Hopper, Hoffman, and Sargent. American sculptors represented include Hunt, Lipchitz, Smith and Tucker. The museum offers 20 changing exhibits each year. On the grounds is a 5-acre sculpture garden.

Open daily Monday-Saturday 10 a.m.-5 p.m., Thursday and Saturday evenings 7-9, and Sunday 2 p.m.-9 p.m.; closed major holidays. Free. Information: 402-472-2461.

North Platte

G **Buffalo Bill Ranch State Historical Park**, 1 mile north of North Platte, Buffalo Bill Cody's hometown, on Buffalo Bill Avenue. The ranch contains an 18-room house and barn. Films and exhibits can be viewed.

Open daily, Memorial Day-Labor Day. Free. Buffalo stew cookouts Wednesday-Friday at 6 p.m., July 1 to early August. Information: 308-535-8035.

P **Union Pacific Historical Museum**, 1416 Dodge Street in Union Pacific Headquarters Building. The museum contains a collection of items relating to the history of the railroad, built with the help of many Irish Americans. It also contains an Abraham Lincoln display with a miniature of his funeral train.

Open Monday-Friday 9 a.m.-3 p.m., Saturday 9 a.m.-noon; closed Sundays and holidays. Free. Handicapped facilities. Information: 402-271-5457.

Omaha

B **Boys Town**, 10 miles west of Omaha on Dodge Street (US 6). The community was founded in 1917 by Father Edward J. Flanagan, from County Roscommon, as a home for troubled and abandoned children. Boys Town became world famous when it was filmed in 1938 by Irish-American John W. Considine, with Irish American actor Spencer Tracy and Mickey Rooney. It was followed by the sequel *Men of Boys Town* with the same stars. Today, located on a 1400-acre site, it is a national diagnostic, treatment, and research institute for children with hearing, speech, language, and learning disorders, with satellite programs in other states. Be sure to see Father Flanagan's Historical House and Shrine, the Boys Town Farm, the Hall of History, and the Memorial Chapel.

Tours daily, except New Year's, Good Friday afternoon, Thanksgiving, and Christmas. Handicapped facilities. Free. Visitor Center open daily 8 a.m.-5:30 p.m., Memorial Day-Labor Day,and 8 a.m.-4:30 p.m., the rest of the year; closed holidays. Information: 402-498-1140.

O'Neill

G O'Neill, a town of 4,000 people, is the "Irish capital of Nebraska." It was founded by General John J. O'Neill as an Irish colony in 1874. O'Neill's military skills were demonstrated in the Civil War, when he led a Black force of men against the Confederacy and, less successfully, in the ill-conceived Fenian invasion of Canada.

Information: 402-336-2355, or write Chamber of Commerce, 312 East Douglas.

Nevada

Carson City

S State capital **Carson City** was founded in 1848, under the name of Eagle Ranch. It was renamed for Kit Carson, pioneer and Indian fighter. During the silver rush of the late 19th century, Carson became notorious as a center of social activity for the great wild Westerners. It was also known as the site of the heavyweight championship match between Irish "Gentleman Jim" Corbett and English "Ruby Robert" Bob Fitzsimmons.

Corbett had won the championship in a fight with another famed Irishman, John L. Sullivan, in 1892. It had been the first match to be fought under the Marquis of Queensberry Rules. Corbett retired, but came out of retirement to meet Fitzsimmons on St. Patrick's Day

1897. This was the first legitimate fight to be filmed, and it was one of the great fights in boxing history! The boxers were out for blood, and so were the 4,000 spectators, watched over by Irish American Marshall Bat Masterson.

The odds were 10-6 in favor of Corbett when the fighters entered the ring shortly after noon on a hot Vegas day. Fitzsimmons greeted Corbett with a rage of punches. Corbett easily avoided them while landing his own in Fitzsimmons's face. In the sixth round, under a ferocious barrage of blows, Fitzsimmons fell to his knees. It was the beginning of the end. But when it finally came, it was Corbett who went down from a powerhouse blow to the solar plexus. Fitz was the new heavyweight champion of the world. Corbett, not at his most "gentleman-ly," crossed the ring and struck out at the new champ. Corbett was dragged from the ring shouting his demand for a rematch.

Self-guided tours of Carson City are available. Information: 702-882-1565, or write the Carson City Chamber of Commerce, 1900 South Carson Street.

Reno

HH **Molly Malone's Irish Pub,** 125 West Third Street, provides shuffle board, pool tables, darts, and progressive poker along with the Irish beer, pub grub, and green beer on St. Patrick's Day and September 17th (the half-way point).

Open daily. Information: 702-329-1987.

Shelby

S **Marias Museum of History and Art,** 206 12th Avenue. The Museum presents some unusual exhibits, including one on the 1923 Dempsey-Gibbons boxing match. Others are barbed wire and fossils.

Open Monday-Friday afternoon 1-5, evenings 7-9, and Saturday afternoon 1-4 from Memorial Day-Labor Day; Tuesday noon-4 p.m., other months; or by appointment; closed major holidays. Free. Information: 406-434-2551 or -434-7127.

Virginia City

℘ With a population of nearly 30,000 people in the 1870s, **Virgina City** was one of the most (in)famous cities of the Old West and Western literature. It was also one of the richest, thanks to the Comstock Lode, which produced more than $1 trillion in gold and silver. At its height of success, Virginia City had four banks, an opera house, numerous theaters, one church for every 5,000 people, and 1 saloon for every 275.

Many Irish Americans worked the mines; some Irish Americans made their fortunes here, including the Hearsts.

Today, Virginia City, set on the side of Mt. Davidson, has a population of 695. It's a calmer, but still interesting city to visit. You can tour some of the old mansions and mines, ride on the V&T railroad, see the diagonal slit in the mountain that marks the Comstock Lode, breathe the cool, clear air, and thrill to the beauty of the countryside.

New Hampshire

Derry

ℍℐ𝔸 **Derry**, 8 miles southeast of Manchester on US 93. Built with the help of skilled Irish immigrants and waterpower, Derry had a strong economy based on linen manufacturing. This combination supported Derry, today with a population of 12,000, from the early 19th century into the 20th.

Dublin

ℍℐ𝔸 **Dublin**, 16 miles east of Keene on NH 101. Dublin was named in recognition of the Irish, the first group of people who tried in 1753 to establish a settlement here. They were unsuccessful. The heavily wooded area was located too far from water to interest industry. However, it was incorporated in 1771, and in the early 19th century, it was recognized as an ideal refuge for summer vacationers. Today, with 1,500 citizens, it remains a popular vacation spot.

Durham

G **Durham** was the home of Gen. John Sullivan, hero of the Revolution and governor of New Hampshire. It was here, in a meeting house, that Sullivan and his comrades hid the gunpowder stolen from Fort William and Mary. (See below.) A tablet marks the spot.

New Castle

G **Fort Constitution,** in a small park east of the square. Formerly the British Fort William and Mary, it was seized on December 14, 1774 by John Sullivan and a band of New Hampshire militia who stole the gun powder. Paul Revere, better known for his midnight ride, is credited with having alerted the colonists to the opportunity. The gun powder was returned to the British four months later when the colonists fired on them at the Battle of Bunker Hill. The attack on Fort William and Mary was the first open act of aggression against the British. Sullivan was made a major general in the Continental Army. Remnants of the fort can still be seen.

Peterborough

S **MacDowell Colony.** In 1907, Edward MacDowell, Irish American composer and pianist, invited other artists to share the quality of life he enjoyed at his retreat in the Peterborough area. Although he died a year later, the colony has survived and provides a quiet and inspirational setting for painters, musicians, film makers, poets, and composers. Colony Hall, the library, and MacDowell's grave can be visited.

Peterborough was the inspiration for for Thornton Wilder's "Our Town."

Open Monday-Friday afternoons 1-4. Information: Colony Hall, High Street.

Plainfield

S Saint-Gaudens National Historic Site, 15 miles south of Hanover on NH 12A in Cornish. Dublin-born sculptor Auguste Saint-Gaudens lived in this early 19th-century home from 1848-1907. The studio contains about 100 of his works, including the famous "Adam's Memorial" and "Shaw Memorial." This is the site of summer concerts and exhibits by contemporary painters and sculptors, including a "sculptor-in-residence" program.

Open daily, mid-May through October. Fee. Information: 603-675-2175, or write Superintendent, RR 2, Box 73, Cornish.

Portsmouth

HH Molly Malone's Restaurant and Pub, 177 State, prides itself on being an Irish steak house, but it has a wide variety of offerings. Irish coffee is a specialty. Entertainment is presented nightly in the pub and at a Sunday jazz brunch.

Open daily. Information: 603-433-7233.

HH The Press Room, 77 Daniel Street. When it comes to going Irish, it's tough sledding in New Hampshire. But, try the Press Room on a Friday night and you might get lucky. Occasionally, around 9, you can catch a live group playing what the management bills as pre-1850 Celtic music. A pianist or guitarist warms up the crowd starting at 5 p.m. You might want to call first, but on the other hand you don't have a lot to lose. If it's Celtic night, great. If it isn't, you can still hang out in a popular spot. So put on something casual and come join the media folk who flock to this 3-story brick nightspot from far and near. A cover fee is sometimes charged.

Information: 603-431-5186.

New Jersey

Bridgewater

HH **Jack O'Connor's**, 1288 Rt. 22E, brings a large, loyal, local following to this 1929 mammoth green building. They may come for the socializing in the pub, where they can choose Guinness, Harp, or 14 other beers on draught. Or they may come for the corned beef and all day salad bar with 80 hot and cold foods, including sandwiches, steak, and lobster. Or they could be coming for Irish music.

Open Monday-Thursday 11 a.m.-12:30 a.m.; Friday-Saturday 11 a.m.-12 midnight; Sunday, 12 noon-11:30 p.m. Information: 201-723-1500.

Camden

B Irish Quakers founded **Camden** in 1851. They named their settlement Pine Tree Hill, but the name was changed in 1768 to recognize the services that Lord Camden had made to the American colonies.

Cedar Knolls

HH **Durkin's Irish Cafe**, 235 Ridgedall Avenue at Morris County Mall, is a large, attractive bar and restaurant in green and wood. Its shopping center location brings in a cross-section of customers intent on enjoying the Guinness or Harp on draught and the lunch or dinner with fish and steak specials. They have a variety of games to play while you wait for your meal. It's a good choice if you're in the area.

Open daily. Information: 201-540-0264.

Long Branch

T Long Branch was the preferred summer home of seven U.S. presidents: Hayes, Garfield, and Irish Americans Grant, Arthur, Benjamin Harrison, McKinley, and Wilson. Seven President's Park is named in their honor. Long Branch, founded in the late 1700s, was one of the earliest seashore resorts. It earned its reputation as the guardian of the morality of its guests by requiring that women be escorted to the beach by gentlemen. In later years, Long Branch relaxed its rules and became a lively refuge for colorful personalities like Irish American Diamond Jim Brady and Lily Langtry. Gambling and other adult pleasures attracted many of the famous and infamous. Seven President's Park has ocean front picnic areas.

Morristown

ℍℍ Dublin Pub, 4 Pine Street, has a U-shaped bar, two restaurant areas, and a good blend of blue and white collar patrons. Guinness and Harp are on tap, and there's a limited menu featuring Irish stew and Dublin steak. Along with its sibling, Molly Malone's (see Whippany), it sponsors a spring golf trip to Ireland (something a number of Irish pubs are doing). This is a good pub with cheerful staff and happy customers. The best choice in the area.

Open daily, 11 a.m.-1:30 a.m. Information: 201-538-1999.

Paterson

ℙ Botto House and the American Labor Museum, 83 Norwood Street, Haledon. Irish American Elizabeth Gurley Flynn was one of the leading labor leaders who spoke to Irish and other textile workers from the balcony of this national landmark. In 1913, textile workers walked out of the Paterson silk mills, demanding decent working conditions and an end to child labor. The Botto House was used as a meeting place for the strikers. Today, it contains a museum in which the history of the labor movement is shown through exhibits, period rooms, and gardens.

Open Wednesday-Sunday, except major holidays. Fee. Information: 201-595-7953.

𝕊 Paterson Museum, Thomas Rogers Building, 2 Market Street. The museum contains the shell of the submarine invented and built by John P. Holland in 1878 in Elizabeth, New Jersey, and his second submarine built in 1881. Holland was born in 1841 in Liscannor, County Clare. He emigrated to the United States in 1873.

Closed Monday and holidays. Fee. Information: 201-881-3874.

Princeton

T Woodrow Wilson School of Public and International Affairs, Princeton University. Named in honor of 28th President of the United States and the former president of Princeton University. Reflecting pool and "Fountain of Freedom" were designed by James Fitzgerald.

Information: 609-452-3603.

South Orange

HI The McManus Collection, McLaughlin Library, Seton Hall University, 405 South Orange Avenue. The Collection includes letters, autographs, and about 4,000 volumes of Irish history.

Open Sunday 1 p.m.-11 p.m., Monday-Thursday 8 a.m.-11 p.m., Friday 8 a.m.-5 p.m., Saturday 9 a.m.-5 p.m. Information: 201-761-9431.

Trenton

HH Tir Na Nog, 1324 Hamilton Avenue. And now for something different: An Irish pub that lists no phone number, and depends for business on word of mouth! That's confidence. When we stopped there early Friday afternoon, the long bar was packed with regulars from the neighborhood. An earlier phone conversation with Irish Billy Briggs, owner, helped me to discover the secret of Tir Na Nog's success. Billy Briggs! He's witty and charming, the kid of guy you'd enjoy bending an elbow with regularly. But Billy was busy other places the day Herself and I stopped by. He was in New York recording an album with colleagues from other Irish pubs. The guy on the next bar stool told me that Billy had just signed to appear in an off-Broadway show.

Tir Na Nog is located in half a row house, a bit cramped. So far,

Billy has been unable to persuade his neighbor to sell him the rest of the building. You can hear music every night except Monday and Thursday, and there are dart boards handy. No food, but snacks to go with the Harp and Guinness on draught. Do note the sign on the door. Tir Na Nog is "cigar friendly" and the smoke hangs over the bar like clouds over Dingle on a soft day.

Open daily. You should have no trouble remembering the address. It represents 1 country, 32 counties, and 4 provinces.

Westmont

ﷲﷲ **Katie O'Brien's**, 427 Crystal Lake Avenue, Westmont, Haddon Township. A large, free standing palatial structure contains a light, airy bar and two dining rooms with fireplace and large Irish flag. All rooms are attractively decorated in greens with light woods. It was quiet on Saturday afternoon, except for a few dedicated dart throwers enjoying their game along with the large screen TV and a few pints of Guinness. The menu includes Irish stew, burgers, chili, pizza, finger foods, and a large salad bar at low to moderate prices. Live Irish music weekends. This establishment is worth the drive from Philadelphia and surrounding areas.

Open daily, 11 a.m.-2 a.m., bar open 1 p.m.-2 a.m. Information: 609-858-2253.

Whippany

ﷲﷲ **Molly Malone's Pub**, 325 Rt. 10, occupies a small, free-standing Tudor-look house with rectangular bar and separate dining area. Irish ambience is enhanced by the stained glass scene over the bar and Irish maps on the wall. Although lacking the authentic character of its Morristown sibling, Dublin Pub, it's a pleasant setting to sip a pint and grab a bite to eat, especially on Friday and Saturday when you can enjoy live Irish music.

Open daily, except Sunday. Information: 201-887-5070.

New Mexico

Farmington

ᕼᕼ **Clancy's Pub**, 20th and Hutton, is home away from home to a wide variety of people who enjoy Irish beer and a large TV screen for sports watching. Anyone who gets hungry can have Irish stew or choose from a number of items on the lunch or dinner menu. Anyone who is thirsty can drink Harp, Guinness, or Guinness Gold. And when it's St. Patrick's Day, here's the place to get green beer. There aren't many places in New Mexico which can say the same thing!

Open 11 a.m.-2 a.m. Monday-Saturday; noon.-midnight Sunday. Information: 505-325-8176.

Lincoln

Ð **Lincoln**, with a population today of about 70, is best known as the center of the Lincoln County War and the life and death of Billy the Kid, also known as William Bonney and Henry McCarty.

Ð **Lincoln State Monument**, 30 miles east of Ruidoso on US 70, then 10 miles west on US 380. Lincoln County was the location of a notorious war involving a number of Irish Americans, the most famous of whom is Billy the Kid (Henry McCarty). Other participants carried the Irish names of Murphy, Dolan, and Riley. These noble names were pitted against Tunstall, an Englishman; McSween, a Scot; and John Chisum, nationality unknown. The English group built a store across the street from the Murphy Store. Not appreciated! Dolan showed his displeasure by assuring Tunstall that he was going to kill him. The Murphy group ran the local grift, and they didn't need anyone to share the profits. A Murphy posse, appointed by a Murphy judge, met Tunstall on the road and saved everyone a lot of time by killing him. But unbeknownst to all, watching this dastardly deed was a teenage friend of Tunstall's—Billy the Kid!

Who was Billy the Kid, and why was he in Lincoln? Billy, son of Irish emigrants, lost his father when he was a mere tot and his mother when he was 14. At 17, he had a disagreement with a blacksmith in

Arizona, and the blacksmith lost. Using the name William Bonney, he had escaped a lynch mob, gone into New Mexico, and taken a job with Tunstall.

Billy, enraged to see his friend killed, threatened revenge on "every son of a bitch who helped kill John." He and his buddies, including such names as O'Keefe, O'Folliard, and McCloskey, killed the entire Murphy posse and began a five-day-war. McSween was killed. Billy was later tried in the Lincoln County courthouse, convicted, and sentenced to die on the gallows. But, Billy killed his guards and escaped to die another day (actually, another night). Details vary, but the most romantic story finds Billy on his way to safety in Mexico, when he stops for a liaison with a young woman. "Quien Es?" calls out Billy as he enters the señorita's darkened bedroom. He is answered by a barrage of bullets shot from the gun of Sheriff Pat Garrett.

The events leading to the escape of Billy from the courthouse are re-enacted annually on the first weekend in August. The monument memorializes the five-day war.

Ð Lincoln National Historic Landmark. A tour of the area includes five restored buildings along a two-block section of Lincoln. Among the buildings you should visit are the Lincoln County Courthouse, a church, grocery store, the Greek Revival home of Dr. Earl Woods, physician and wine maker, and the mercantile store of L. G. Murphy & Co. Murphy's is now a museum displaying Indian and pioneer relics.

Open daily 9 a.m.-6 p.m., March 1 to mid-November; varied hours the rest of the year; closed state holidays. Fee. Under 15 years, free. Information: 505-653-4372.

Santa Rosa

Ð Billy the Kid Museum, 1601 East Sumner Avenue, 44 miles southeast of Santa Rosa via US 84. The museum houses 60,000 items, including relics associated with Billy the Kid, the Old West, and Old Fort Sumner.

Open daily mid-May to mid-September; daily, except Sunday, the rest of the year; closed Thanksgiving and Christmas. Handicapped facilities. Fee. Information: 505-355-2380.

D **Billy the Kid's Grave**, Fort Sumner State Monument, 3 miles east of Santa Rosa on US 54/66, 32 miles south on US 84. "Billy the Kid, boy bandit king. He died as he lived." So reads the inscription on the tombstone. Billy the Kid was killed here and buried outside the fort, near the front gate.

Visitor center for the fort has military, Indian, farming, and archaeological exhibits. Open Thursday-Monday, except state holidays. Donation. Information: 505-355-2573.

Taos

G **Taos** is a cosmopolitan blend of Indians, Spanish-American farmers, writers, artists, and tourists. Founded in 1615 by Spanish colonists, it was once the home of Kit Carson, Irish-American trapper, Indian fighter, explorer, and soldier. Many historical sites are supported by the Kit Carson Memorial Foundation, including:

G **Kit Carson Home and Museum**. Memorabilia of Kit Carson can be seen in this restored 1825 home, along with relics of the Spanish Colonial period and artifacts of the mountain men. The mountain men developed many trails, as they searched the Rockies for furs. Carson lived here from 1843-1848. The rooms are decorated with period furniture.

A Penitente chapel is located here. Penitente is a religious order found predominantly in Spanish-American communities, especially in New Mexico. It is noted for its severe practices, including self-flagellation.

Open daily 8 a.m.-6 p.m., June through October, and 9 a.m.-5 p.m., November through May; closed New Year's, Thanksgiving, and Christmas. Fee. Information: 505-758-4741.

G **Kit Carson Memorial State Park**, 2 blocks north of the plaza. The park includes the cemetery where Kit Carson and other historical Western figures are buried.

New York

Albany

℣ **Cathedral of the Immaculate Conception**, Eagle Street and Madison Avenue. The 1852 Gothic Revival cathedral was one of several churches built by John McCloskey, including the completion of St. Patrick's Cathedral in New York City. McCloskey, whose parents emigrated from County Derry, became archbishop of New York in 1864, and in 1875 the first American cardinal. The cathedral has a carved pulpit and contains many items of historical interest.

Open Monday-Friday 6 a.m.-4 p.m., Saturday morning 8-11, and Sunday 8 a.m.-6 p.m. Free. Information: 518-463-4447.

Buffalo

℣ **The Great Fenian Raid.** The day the Irish invaded Canada was not one of the prouder moments in the noble history of Irish warriors. A group of Fenians, unhappy with Britain's unilateral decision to enshroud Ireland in union, came up with the imaginative and incredible decision to invade Canada, then exchange it for Ireland's freedom. Many tales are told, but it's agreed that half of the troops expected to participate never got to Canada because of an insufficient number of boats to carry them across the St. Lawrence River. The men who did arrive succeeded in capturing a fort which had been abandoned. But instead of following up their victory and moving further into Canada, they decided to... what else? Celebrate their victory, then celebrate some more. Meanwhile, the Canadians, not amused by the presence of the Fenians in their country, marched on the fort and drove them back into the United States where they were imprisoned briefly.

For a different perspective, see Malone, N.Y.

℣ **Naval and Servicemen's Park**, One Naval Park Cove. Five Irish-American brothers, the Sullivans, were lost in the Pacific during World War II, when their ship was sunk. Here, in the largest inland naval park in the country, you can board several ships, including a guided missile cruiser, World War II submarine, and a destroyer *The Sullivans.*

Open daily 10 a.m.-dusk, April-October; Saturday-Sunday 10 a.m.-dusk in November. Fee. Senior and children's discount. Information: 716-847-1773.

T **Theodore Roosevelt Inaugural National Historic Site.** 641 Delaware Avenue. Theodore Roosevelt, who traced his lineage to Counties Meath and Donegal, was sworn in at Wilcox Mansion as 26th president of the United States in 1901. He became presidentwhen another Irish American, President McKinley, was assassinated. The 1838 Greek Revival site contains many Roosevelt memorabilia and items relating to McKinley's assassination. A slide show and art exhibits can be viewed.

Open Monday-Friday 9 a.m.-5 p.m. and Saturday-Sunday noon-5 p.m., April-December; Monday-Friday 10 a.m.-5 p.m. and Sunday noon-5, the rest of the year, except holidays. Fee. Information: 716-884-0095.

Canastota

P The town of **Canastota** provides a vivid reminder of the work done by the early Irish immigrants. Eleven of the early 19th century buildings still stand along the Erie Canal which runs through the city.

P **The Erie Canal**, built between 1817 and 1825, remains an important inland waterway linking New York City to Lake Erie at Buffalo. Although freight traffic has declined through the decades, the number of vessels using it in recent years has increased. Its continued existence is a tribute to the work of Irish immigrants who constructed the canal and to the wisdom of New York Gov. DeWitt Clinton, himself a descendant of an Irish immigrant. Clinton insisted on its development over the objections of then president Jefferson.

P **Canal Town Museum**, 122 Canal Street. Exhibits show the development of the canal and its effect on the surrounding region.

Open Monday-Friday. Free. Information: 315-697-3451.

𝓅 **Old Erie Canal State Park**, NY 5 & 46 or I-90, exits 33, 34. Much of the old canal can be seen here including aqueducts, change bridges, and towpath. You can boat, fish, snowmobile, and iceskate. Information: 315-627-7821.

Cooperstown

𝓢 **Casey at the Bat**

> *And somewhere men are laughing,*
> *And somewhere children shout,*
> *But there is no joy in Mudville—*
> *Mighty Casey has struck out.*

Ernest L. Thayer wrote this poem in 1881 and it has inspired many sequels and satires by other writers. It has a special place in the Baseball Hall of Fame in Cooperstown where an opera, "Mighty Casey," was performed. It even stimulated various baseball players to claim to be the "Mighty Casey." But finally in 1935, Thayer identified his inspiration—Daniel Henry Casey, a classmate in high school. Thayer and Casey had had a rough time when the "big Irishman" took umbrage at a remark Thayer made about him in the school newspaper. Daniel never became a ball player, but he did become principal of Grafton Junior School in Worcester, where he was working at the time of his death.

𝓢 **National Baseball Hall of Fame and Museum**, Main Street. Along with boxing, baseball is one of the major sports in which Irish Americans have historically excelled. The Hall of Fame room features plaques honoring baseball's most outstanding participants. Displays focus on world series games, ball parks, All-Star games, and history of baseball. Gift shop.

Open daily, except New Year's, Thanksgiving, and Christmas. Fee. Handicapped facilities. Information: 607-547-9988.

East Durham

HIA **East Durham** or, as it prefers to be known, "Ireland's 33rd county," the "Irish Catskills," or the "Irish Alps," has attracted generations of Irish Americans to its resort spots and festivals each summer. "Take a drive to Ireland," invites the East Durham Vacationland Association, to "the Irish Music Capital of America." Amazingly, these slogans don't represent too much hype. There are an astonishing number of Irish-oriented pubs, motels, and activities. Look at these names: Gavin's Golden Hill House, The Shamrock House, Rose Motel, Mullan's Mountain Spring Hotel, Carmody's, Erin's Melody, McGrath's Motel, The O'Neill House, Fitzsimons, Furlong's, Keogh's, Killarney's...

East Durham promotes itself as the home of the National Shrine of Our Lady of Knock, the East Durham Irish Cultural and Sports Centre, the Irish American Heritage Museum, and the John E. Lawe Memorial Sports Stadium. Here's an idea of what a summer is like in East Durham: Irish American Golf Open, Gaelic football and hurling, dog shows, sheep dog trials, and top names in Irish music.

Information: 518-634-7100 (weekends) or write East Durham Vacationland Association, Box 67-IV, 12423.

Erie

℗ **Erie Canal**, 6 miles west of Erie on NY 5S at Fort Hunter. The last remains of the original canal built in 1822 largely by "Paddys." From this site, you can see the three stages in the development of the canal.

Information: 518-829-7516.

Horseheads

G When the first white settlers arrived here in 1789, they were greeted by the site of bleached skulls glistening in the sun. These were the remains of several hundred horses used by Gen. John Sullivan (emigrant from Limerick) in his war against the Iroquois Nations. When the horses collapsed on his way back to Pennsylvania, Sullivan destroyed them. This grizzly sight gave name to a now thriving city of nearly 7,000 people.

Lake George Village

G **Fort William Henry Museum**, Canada Street (US 9). The museum, rebuilt from the original 1755 plans for the fort, contains artifacts from the French and Indian Wars. On March 17, 1757, the French interrupted a St. Patrick's Day celebration, expecting that the soldiers, many of whom were Irish, would not be prepared for the attack. But they were. The French sustained heavy losses before they retreated. The fort featured prominently in James Fenimore Cooper's *The Last of the Mohicans.*

Open daily 9 a.m.-8 p.m., July-August; 10 a.m.-5 p.m., May-June and September-October. Fee. Senior and children's discount. Information: 518-668-5471.

Loudonville

HH **Eamonn's Loudonhouse**, 151 Menands Road, two miles northeast of Albany. Just opened at the time of this writing, Eamonn's will be featuring "plenty of cabaret" and "top class food and service." With plenty of space, it has facilities to handle receptions and banquets. This is another venture by Irish radio star, host/comedian Eamonn McGirr, who has an Irish pub and family restaurant in Dennisport, Cape Cod. You'll want to catch Eamonn's imitation of Sinead O'Connor. He broadcasts on WVCR 88.3 FM, Sunday noon-3 p.m. from Sienna College.

Open daily. Information: 518-463-7440.

Malone

HIA **Franklin County Fairgrounds**, Main Street. Malone was the site of preparations for the 1866 and 1870 Fenian invasions of Canada. More than 2,000 Irish Americans bivouacked at the fairgrounds, awaiting arms coming in from many parts of the country. The Fenians planned to invade Canada in order to force England to relinquish control over Ireland. The goal was honorable; the plan naive; the strategy a tragi-comedy of errors.

The Fenians, founded by exiled Irish patriot John O'Mahoney, had support from Irish Americans and many others who had no love for the British. The Irish, survivors of the recent battles of the Civil War, were confident that they would achieve their objective. Then, on the eve of their planned action, Irish American president Andrew Johnson ordered Irish American General Meade to stop the invasion. Meade seized the weapons from the storehouses and jailed 11 of the Fenian leaders. That ended the incursion from Malone. The Fenians dispersed and with the help of private donations and government support, they went home.

In 1870, they returned and set up headquarters in the Flanagan Hotel.

H1A **Flanagan Hotel**, Main and Elm Streets. The Flanagan Hotel is rated 2-star by Mobile Travel Guide. This rating must be based on reports from the Irish who spent most of their nights sleeping on the fairgrounds. When we visited in the summer of 1993, the Flanagan looked as if it hadn't been renovated since the Fenians left.

As the Fenians planned in their headquarters in the Flanagan, the Canadians also prepared, and so did President Grant, who issued a command that no invasion of Canada was to take place. According to the Plattsburgh, NY, *Press-Republican*, General Meade arrived too late to stop the invasion, but in time to prevent the 1,300 reinforcements from leaving Malone. The Fenians who crossed the border were quickly dispatched by the Canadians. When they arrived back in the States, they found no sympathy from the American government, and more important, no money to get home. Boss Tweed of Tammany Hall, who counted on Irish Americans for much of his political strength in New York City, came through, and most of the men went home. A few went to jail for short periods of time and were fined $10 each. The fines were paid by supporters.

New York City

T Alfred E. Smith Boyhood Home, 25 Oliver Street. Born around the corner at 174 South Street, Al Smith spent his boyhood years at this site. He attended school across the street at St. James. Governor of New York from 1819 to 1929, he was nominated by the Democratic Party to run against Herbert Hoover in the 1928 presidential race. As the first Irish Catholic to be nominated by a major party for the highest office in the land, he was subjected to an onslaught of attacks. Some of these attacks were repeated when John F. Kennedy ran for president 32 years later.

HIA American Irish Historical Society, 991 5th Avenue. Some 7,500 books and manuscripts about individuals, organizations, Irish and Irish-American history can be found here. The staff is very helpful. Call 24 hours ahead for an appointment with an historian, or just stop in to review the material.

Information: 212-228-2263.

HIA Annie Moore Statue, Ellis Island. Annie, a 15-year-old girl from County Cork, was the first immigrant processed at Ellis Island. She came through January 1, 1892, and was followed by nearly 5 million of her countrymen and women through the same golden door. Annie's statue was erected in 1992 in conjunction with Ellis Island's centennial celebration. It was supported by the Irish American Cultural Institute and is displayed in the Immigrant Museum. A twin was placed in Queenstown in Cobb, County Cork, the port from which Annie sailed. Her statue was unveiled by Irish president, Mary Robinson.

Ellis Island operated as a point of entry for immigrants between 1892 and 1924. See the American Immigrant Wall of Honor and the copper panels engraved with the names of 200,000 immigrants. Perhaps, you'll find an ancestor's name.

The museum is open daily 9 a.m.-5:30 p.m., except Christmas. Free. Catch a ferry at Battery Park in lower Manhattan sailing every half hour between Memorial Day and Labor Day and every 45 minutes the rest of the year. Ferry service also offered from Liberty Park in Jersey City.

Information: 212-264-8711.

B **Cardinal Hayes Place,** lower Manhattan, near St. Andrew's Place, Pearl and Duane Streets. Named for Patrick Joseph Cardinal Hayes (died 1938), archbishop of New York, who was born in this area. Hayes served as an altar boy at the original St. Andrews Church, which stood on the spot adjacent to Cardinal Hayes Place. The new **St. Andrews** was erected 1n 1939 in the same location by Maggins and Walsh, Robert J. Reiley firm.

HIA **Castle Clinton National Monument,** Battery Park, Manhattan. This was the entry point for seven million Irish and other immigrants between 1855 and to 1890 when Ellis Island was opened (1892). Castle Clinton, formerly a fort, then an entertainment center, was a major improvement over the earlier immigration center. Its high walls enabled authorities to keep out the rush of "runners" and others who were intent on getting their hands on the few possessions the Irish had brought with them. Today, Castle Clinton is a visitor center and point of departure for the Statue of Liberty and Ellis Island.

Free. Information: 212-344-7220, or write Superintendent, Manhattan Sites, 26 Wall Street, 10005.

S **CBS Tower,** 51 W. 52nd Street. One of the architectural skyscraper wonders created by Dublin-born Kevin Roche. Roche is the 1982 recipient of the coveted Pritzker Architecture Prize.

HIA **Chelsea,** west of Fifth Avenue, 14th-30th Street. Always a neighborhood of mixed ancestry, a large number of Irish settled here. Today, the area is attracting the upwardly mobile young who can better afford the rents than the blue collar worker.

T **Chester A. Arthur Statue,** Madison Square Park, 23rd Street and Broadway. The statue of the 21st U.S. president was sculpted in 1898.

T, S **City Hall.** Broadway and Park Row. Dedicated in 1812, City Hall was built at the instigation of the mayor, DeWitt Clinton, whose grandfather was born in Ireland. Recognized today as an architectural masterpiece, it was neglected for many years. John Francois Mangin and John McComb, who traced his ancestry to County Antrim, designed the building in the Federal style. Clinton later became a New York legislator, governor, and U.S. senator. He is, perhaps, best known for his advocacy for the construction of the Erie Canal, but his greatest achievement may be the establishment of the New York Public School system.

S **Cohan Statue**, Duffy Square, 46th Street and Broadway. Famed Irish composer and musical comedy star, George M. Cohan, is immortalized with a bronze statue at this corner. How appropriate that his statue is located in the same square as TKTS, where you can buy theater tickets and get them for half-price the day of the performance. The statue was moved from Cohan's hometown of Providence, which has no memorial to one of their most famous sons.

HH **Davy Byrnes Bar and Restaurant**, 538 Willet Avenue, Port Chester. One of Westchester's newest Irish pub-restaurants, it offers a full Irish menu daily, including Irish breakfast and a Sunday brunch noon-4 p.m. Entertainment includes live Irish music Sunday evenings at 7 and Irish sports videos Monday nights.

Open daily. Information: 914-937-2106.

T **Duane Park and Duane Street.** The park, a miniature space, is located at the juncture of Duane and Hudson Streets. James Duane, whose father emigrated from Galway, was the first post-American Revolution mayor of New York City.

B **Duffy Statue and Duffy Square**, 43rd Street and Broadway. Here stands a statue of Canadian-born, Irish American Reverend Francis Duffy, chaplain of the Fighting Sixty-ninth. The Irish regiment gained respect for its valor during World War I. At the time of his death, Father Duffy was serving as pastor of **Holy Cross Church**, 333 West 42nd Street. Father Duffy's statue was dedicated in the

Times Square area in 1937. Two years later the area around the statue was named Duffy Square.

ℋℋ **Eagle Tavern**, 355 West 14th Street at 9th Avenue. This is an authentic Irish pub, in the meat packing district, where you can enjoy traditional Irish music Monday, Friday, and Saturday; rock and bluegrass other evenings. Noise can get very loud, but people stay calm.

Open evenings 8 p.m.-4 a.m. Information: 212-924-0275.

ℋℋ **Eamonn Doran**, 998 Second Avenue, between 52nd & 53rd Streets, is an authentic Irish pub in a long narrow room with bar and tables, plus separate dining area. An Irish-American flag on the wall has orange stripes and green shamrocks in place of stars. It's a very lively place with a friendly bartender and customers comprised of neighbors, tourists, Irish, and people from the United Nations. It's a good choice to wind down after work or wind up for the evening. A full menu includes corned beef and cabbage, Gaelic steak made with Irish whiskey, steak and kidney pie, and boiled bacon and cabbage. Guinness and Harp are on tap and, if you're the designated driver, Ballygowan Spring Water can be ordered.

Open daily noon-4 a.m. Information: 212-752-8088 or -753-9191.

ℋℐ𝒜 **Elizabeth Seton College**, 1061 North Broadway, Yonkers. A collection of Irish books, including two volumes of sheet music, can be viewed, but not checked out.

Open Saturday-Thursday 8:30 a.m.-10 p.m., Friday 8:30 a.m.-5 p.m. Information: 914-969-4000.

ℬ **Father Duffy Tombstone**, St. Raymond's Cemetery, Bronxdale and Tremont Streets, the Bronx. A Celtic cross, in the country's oldest Roman Catholic cemetery, marks the resting place of Father Francis Duffy, chaplain of the Fighting 69th.

ℋℋ **Fitzers Restaurant**, 687 Lexington Avenue, Fitzpatrick Manhattan Hotel. Fitzers serves Irish specialties, including salmon and lamb, for lunch (Monday-Friday) and dinner. The management promotes their food fare by pointing out that the menu is created specially by Sean Dempsey, chef at Fitzpatrick's Castle Hotel in Dublin. Sunday jazz lunch.

Open daily. Information: 212-355-0100.

ℋℐA/D **Five Points**, Baxter-, Park-, and Worth Streets, Lower Manhattan. Located in the area of a former pond and marshlands and invaded by tanneries and a brewery, it was once a foul, crime ridden slum—home to many Irish who could afford nothing else in the early and mid-1800s. With the increased immigration occurring between 1845 and 1860, stemming from the Famine in Ireland, the Irish and the slums spread into the Lower East Side. Today, the county courthouse stands where the Brewery once spewed forth its stench.

Five Points was also the home of the Kerryonians, an exclusive group of County-Kerry born criminals. Active in 1825, it was one of America's earliest organized group of outlaws. They gathered at a grocery store on Worth Street (then Center)and spent their time mugging Englishmen.

𝒯 **Foley Square**, Duane, Centre, Pearl, and Lafayette Streets. Thomas F. Foley, saloon keeper and string-puller, was recognized as giving support to Irish American political hopefuls. He is credited in some circles with gaining the governorship of New York for Al Smith. His greatest political satisfaction came from dashing the U.S. senatorial dreams of newspaper publisher William Randolph Hearst, who had attacked Foley in his newspapers. Foley Square is the setting for the U.S. Courthouse. Designed by Cass Gilbert, it's a 32-story office building with 50-foot columns, topped by a pyramid of gold.

𝒮 **Ford Foundation Building**, 320 East 43rd Street. Designed by Dublin-born architect, Kevin Roche, it is appropriately impressive for a foundation which gives millions to arts and science. A massive 1967 cube-shaped building of granite and glass surrounds a garden setting. Roche is recognized as one of America's leading architects.

𝒮 **Gaelic Park**, 240th Street and Broadway. The center was used for many Irish activities for a number of years. Hurling and Gaelic football (soccer to Americans) drew crowds of fiercely loyal fans. The social gathering that followed the Rockland games was used as an opportunity to find jobs and apartments, especially by newcomers. But that was yesterday, before a dispute between the New York Gaelic Athletic Association and Manhattan College, the present owner of the park.

At the time of this writing, games are being played at Rockland County State Park, while negotiations are underway to buy land and buildings presently owned and occupied by the King's College in Briarcliff.

T, G **General Grant National Memorial**, Riverside Drive and 122nd Street, Manhattan. Ulysses S. Grant died from throat cancer at Mount McGregor, New York, on July 23, 1885. He and his wife are buried at this site.

Open Wednesday-Sunday 9 a.m.-5 p.m., except holidays. Free. Information: 212-666-1640.

HIA **Greenwich Village**, 14th Street south to Houston Street and Washington Square west to the Hudson River. In earlier days, this area was the estate of Sir Peter Warren, who emigrated from Ireland and became a wealthy New York businessman. Today, it is known as a haven for artists and lovers of books, food and coffee houses.

S **Hamilton Grange**, 287 Convent Avenue, between 141st and 142nd Streets, in the Hamilton Heights Historic District. Designed by famed Irish American architect John McComb, Jr., Hamilton Grange is the last home of Alexander Hamilton, George Washington's secretary of the Treasury. It was built as a summer home in 1801, 300 feet from its present location. Hamilton lived here until killed in a duel with Aaron Burr in 1804.

Open Wednesday-Friday 9 a.m.-5 p.m. Not wheelchair accessible. Fee. Information: 212-283-5154.

S **High Bridge**, Aqueduct Bridge crossing the Harlem River at West 174th Street. Built in 1842, the High Bridge was designed by

Reverend Thomas Levins, from Drogheda, architect and pastor of old St. Patrick's Cathedral. Early in its life, the bridge attracted many sightseers who enjoyed strolling on the promenade which stretched across the top the bridge. Regrettably, this charming activity came to an end when it attracted criminals.

HIA Hunter College, 68th Street and Park Avenue. The college is named in honor of Thomas Hunter, teacher from County Down, who served as the first president of the former teacher training college, today a university with more than 20,000 students.
Information: 212-772-4000.

HIA Ireland House, 1-A Fifth Avenue, Greenwhich Village. Dedicated April 26, 1993, by Ireland's taoiseach Albert Reynolds, New York University's Ireland House is a renovated town house which serves as a center for Irish and Irish American culture, historical and current.
Information: 212-998-4636 (New York University).

HI Irish Arts Center, 553 West 51st Street. The center opened in 1975 with the goal of carrying on Celtic culture. Today, it offers a variety of classes, including drama, music, dance, and Irish lessons. Sessions are open to members at nominal fees. Most teachers receive no compensation for their services.
Information: 212-757-3318.

HH Irish Circle Pub, 102nd Street & Rockaway Beach Boulevard, Rockaway. The pub is operated by four New York City firemen who run what is described by Joe Murphy (*Irish Voice*) as "among the few Irish pubs left from the good olde days of Rockaway Beach." A full menu and live Irish music is part of the appeal.
Open daily. Information: 718-474-0060.

B John Street Methodist Church, John Street between William and Nassau Streets. The first Methodist church in America was erected on this site in 1768 by Irish Methodists, headed by Philip Embury, from County Limerick, and his cousin, Barbara Heck. Reportedly, the original church was born out of a poker game when Mrs. Heck returned home to find her husband and cousin engrossed in their cards. Shocked, she persuaded her cousin to return to the ministry. An interesting side note is that one of the early sextons was Peter Williams, an African American, who later became a successful businessman and founded the first Black Methodist church in New York, the Mother Zion Church.

HH J.P. Clare's, 100 West 82nd Street, wins high praise from Sidney Zion, *New York Observer*, who says, "Nothing brightens up the world like a great new saloon, and this is the best since Toots Shor died and the developers wiped out Manuche's and The Absinthe House." Dinner is served daily.

Open daily. Information: 212-362-6060.

S Judson Memorial church, 55 Washington Square and Thompson Street. Augustus Saint-Gaudens sculpted the statuary.

HH Kinsale Tavern, 1672 3rd Avenue, says Jane Freiman in *New York Magazine*, is a "Classic Irish pub...[with] an outstanding sirloin steak...big crusty burgers...huge salad plate..." Everything about this tavern is authentic including the staff and many of the customers. Add to this good Irish beer and you have a winner.

Open daily 10:30 a.m.-4:30 a.m. Information: 212-348-4370.

S *Long Day's Journey into Night* House, 21 Trel Street, was featured in the film based on Eugene O'Neill's play.

G Margaret Corbin Commemorative Tablet, 183rd Street and Fort Washington Avenue. Irish American Margaret Corbin's husband was a gunner at Fort Tryon. When he was killed during a British attack, Margaret carried on in his place until captured by the British.

P Mike Quill Corner, southeast corner at intersection of Broadway and West 240th Street. Dedicated in November 1992, this memorial recognizes the contributions made by Michael J. Quill, founder and president of the International Transport Workers Union and New York councilman for more than a decade. Quill was born in Kilgarvan, County Kerry, in 1905, and molded on the Irish streets of New York City.

HIA **New York Public Library,** 5th Avenue and 42nd Street. The New York Public Library maintains a research collection with over 5,000,000 volumes, including a large number of Irish and Irish-American materials.

Main room open Tuesday-Wednesday 11 p.m.-7:30 p.m. and Thursday-Saturday 10 a.m.-6 p.m., except legal holidays. Free. Information: 212-930-0800.

HH **O'Flannagan's Bar & Restaurant,** 1215 First Avenue at 65th Street, is known as a great Irish singles bar. It brings them in with dancing and Irish music nightly. While the other singles may be the main attraction, the patrons appreciate the Irish lamb stew and steak that complements the Irish beer. Irish sports are shown on giant TV screens, and when it's not too noisy, you can hear them.

Open 11 a.m.-4 a.m. Information: 212-439-0660.

B **Old St. Patrick's Cathedral,** between Mott and Mulberry Streets. The cathedral was dedicated in 1815, shortly after the end of the War of 1812. In 1817, Old St. Patrick's opened St. Patrick's Free School, the first in the city. A fire in 1886 severely altered the appearance of the cathedral. It remained as the cathedral church of the See of New York City until the completion of the new St. Patrick's Cathedral on Fifth Avenue in 1879.

HH **The Old Stand,** 914 Third Avenue, is a neighborhood pub named after a Dublin bar. It gathers a big after-work crowd to enjoy the Irish beer and the free buffet provided Monday-Friday evenings from 5 to 7. Lunch and dinner are served daily, and an Irish brunch Saturday-Sunday. Tables are very close, but separated from the bar by a partial partition. Only the juke box to interfere with conversation.

Open daily. Information: 212-759-4836.

S **Poe Cottage,** Grand Concourse and East Kingsbridge Road, Bronx. Edgar Allan Poe lived in this early 19th century cottage from

1846 until his death in 1849. These years saw the birth of some of his most famous works, including "Annabel Lee" and "The Bells." The home, dwarfed by surrounding high rises, contains period furniture, some personal belongings, and an exhibit of Poe and his wife, and films.

Open Wednesday-Friday 9 a.m.-5 p.m., Saturday 10 a.m.-4 p.m., and Sunday afternoon 1-5. Guided tours are available. Fee. Children's discount. Information: 212-881-8900.

P **Police Academy Museum,** 235 East 20th Street. The Irish were law enforcement for many decades in New York and other eastern cities. John McManus headed the New York police in 1815, and during the mid-19th century, the New York City police were nearly all Irish or Irish American. In 1918, Ellen O'Grady became the first female deputy commissioner. Currently, you find few Irish-born policemen walking the beat in New York, because New York police must be American citizens.

Relive the history of law enforcement in New York City through the displays of police equipment, uniforms, Al Capone's machine gun, and counterfeit money.

Open Monday-Friday 9 a.m.-3 p.m., except holidays. Free. Proof of identification required. Information: 212-475-9467.

T **Prospect Park,** between Prospect Park West and Prospect Park Southwest, Flatbush and Parkside Avenues, Brooklyn. Located at the north entrance is the Grand Army Plaza with a memorial to John F. Kennedy and an arch commemorating Civil War heroes. The park has many historic buildings, a Quaker graveyard, trails, and boating facilities.

Open daily dawn to dusk. Information: 718-788-0055.

B **Rectory of the Shrine of the Blessed Elizabeth Bayley Seton,** 7 State Street. Designed by John McComb, Jr., at the turn of the 19th century, it was occupied by Union forces during the Civil War. Following the war, Charlotte Grace O'Brien, an Irish immigrant, purchased the home and operated it as the Mission of our Lady of the Rosary, housing Irish immigrant girls. Today, it is a shrine to the first American-born saint.

Open daily.

G **Robert Murray Estate Plaque**, 16 Park Avenue (35th Street),Murray Hill. This area was once the farm of Irish-born Robert Murray. When General Howe arrived in New York on September 15, 1776, in pursuit of the American army, Mrs. Murray delayed the General by entertaining him in her home, an offer no officer and gentleman could refuse. A plaque marks the center of the farm.

HH **Rosie O'Grady's**, 800 7th Avenue, is a deservedly popular pub and dining room. The square bar near the entrance fills quickly with upscale workers from the area who enjoy the opportunity for good conversation with their Harp and Guinness on tap. The modest menu includes several Irish dishes at reasonable prices. Upstairs is the Manhattan Club, under the same ownership, where you can hear live Irish music. A number of visits confirm thisas one of my favorite Irish pubs in New York.

Open daily. Information: 212-582-2975.

S **Roundabout Theater Company** 100 East 17th Street. Works by George Bernard Shaw are frequentlly performed by established actors.

Information: 212-420-1360.

S **Saint-Gaudens' Farragut Monument**, Madison Square Park, 23rd Street and Broadway. The statue of Admiral Farragut, by Dublin-born sculptor Augustus Saint-Gaudens, was unveiled in 1881 by the sailor who had bound Farragut to the mast during the Civil War Battle of Mobile. Saint-Gaudens depicts the wind blown Farragut with two female figures representing Loyalty and Courage. This was Saint-Gaudens' first major success. The base, actually an extension of the statue, was designed by architect Stanford White. White figured in one of the most sensational crimes of the century, when he was shot and killed by the deceived husband of actress Evelyn Nesbit—the "girl in the red velvet swing."

℧ **St. James Church**, 23 Oliver Street. St. James Parish, established in the mid-1820s by a Cuban priest, Felix Varela, has an enviable Irish heritage. The first church, purchased by Father Varela from another denomination, was destroyed by fire. The parish built another church nearby, and named it St. James. Originally, the parishioners were Irish from the slums of Five Points. The Ancient Order of Hibernians in America (AOH) was founded here in 1836. A plaque on the door of St. James School, across the street, announces that Al Smith had his formal education here. Smith was the first Irish Catholic nominated for president by a major political party. Today, the parish is primarily Hispanic.

Information: 212-233-0161.

℧ **St. Malachy's**, 239 w. 49th Street. The "actor's chapel" was named St. Malachy O'More (1095-1148) who is thought to have been born in County Down. Services are scheduled around theater performances.

Information: 212-489-1340.

℧ **St. Paul's Chapel**, Broadway and Fulton Streets. Dedicated in 1766, this Episcopalian chapel is noted for memorials to celebrated Irish Americans, including Thomas Addis, Robert Emmet, W.J. MacNeven, and Richard Montgomery. It is the oldest church and the oldest public building in continuous use in Manhattan. New York Governor George Clinton, brother of New York governor DeWitt Clinton, had a pew here, as did George Washington. It is the only colonial church remaining.

Open daily 8 a.m.-4 p.m. Donations. Information: 212-602-0800.

℧ **St. Patrick's Cathedral**, 5th Avenue and 50th Street. Named for Ireland's and New York's patron saint, the cathedral is a monument to God and a tribute to the dedication, determination, and sacrifice of Irish Americans who were the primary force in the development of the quintessential cathdral. Begun in 1850 by Archibishop John Hughes, at a time when to be Irish and Catholic was to be doubly despised in New York, the Cathedral was known as "Hughes Folly."

It was built far from the city center with initial funding from contributions by the wealthier members of the diocese. It was consecrated in 1879, a massive white marble Gothic Revival structure, covering a city block with its three aisles 300 feet long, several chapels, and seating for 2,500 worshipers.

Hughes and other Irish-American archbishops are buried there: John McCloskey, Michael Corrigan, John Farley, Patrick Joseph Hayes, Francis Cardinal Spellman, Terence Cooke; and the writer and television personality Archbishop Fulton J. Sheen.

Today, the world's largest St. Patrick's Day parade passes for review in front of St. Patrick's Cathedral and, in recent years, John Cardinal O'Connor, Archbishop of New York.

St. Patrick's is no longer a parish church serving an Irish neighborhood. Among the hundreds that visit daily are representatives from all religions and ethic groups. But despite its ecumenical appeal, this splendid structure will always be identified as an Irish church.

Open daily 6:30 a.m.-8:45 p.m. Information: 212-753-2261.

D **St. Raymond's Cemetery**, Bronxdale and Tremond Avenues. Not all New York Irish were priests, politicians and police officers, some were bad guys.County Kildare-born Vincent "Mad Dog" "Baby Killer" Coll and his brother in crime, Owney "the Killer" Madden, were among the more notorious on the dark side. Coll got his name when he fired into a crowd killing a five-year-old child instead of his intended victim, another gangster. Owney, who headed an Irish gang named the Gophers, returned the favor. He arranged for Coll to be gunned down while talking with him on the phone. Coll is buried in St. Raymond's with his sister and his brother in life and crime, Peter. The large tombstone was erected by Coll when his brother was slain. Victor died at 23, his brother at 24. In between killings, Owney kept busy with another of his enterprises, the **Cotton Club**, famed Harlem night spot, which was located at Lenox Avenue and 143rd Street.

T **Tammany Hall**, Union Square, Southeast corner of 17th Street. The once respected, later notorious, political organization, Tammany Society was headquartered at this site. It was founded in 1789 and grew rapidly in power through succeeding decades. It experienced a great boost in power with the influx of the Irish during the mid-1800s. Tammany helped the immigrants get settled in their new homeland, arranged jobs, and loaned money. In return, the Irish helped Tammany win elections. Despite their numbers, the Irish did not take control of the organization until "Boss" Tweed was ousted in the 1870s. He was followed in time by John Kelly, Richard Croker, and Charles Murphy. With the Irish ascendancy, the corruption which had evolved under Tweed continued. In the early 1900s, Murphy tried to clean up the Tammany image. But by the 30s, Fiorello La Guardia was able to become mayor, in part, by opposing Tammany Hall. It finally dissolved in the 50s.

T **Theodore Roosevelt Birthplace National Historic Site,** 28 East 20th Street. Roosevelt, born October 27, 1858, lived here until 1873. The reconstructed home contains four floors of original and period furniture. A stuffed lion and big game heads are among the memorabilia from Roosevelt's personal life. You can visit the master bedroom, library, parlor, dining room, and nursery.

Open Wednesday-Sunday 9 a.m.-5 p.m., except government holidays. Fee. Senior and children's discount. Information: 212-260-1616.

T **Theodore Roosevelt Memorial, Bird Sanctuary, & Trailside Museum,** Cove Road. Eleven acres owned by the National Audubon Society includes a memorial to the 26th U.S. president focusing on his contributions to conservation. On the property are bird exhibits and nature trails.

Open Monday-Thursday 9 a.m.-4:30 p.m. and Friday 9 a.m.-2 p.m. Call for weekend hours. Closed New Year's, Thanksgiving, and Christmas. Donations. Information: 516-922-3200.

HH **Tommy Makem's Irish Pavilion,** 130 East 57th Street. The triad logo, copied from the tomb at Newgrange, means "wine for support, food for the body, and music for the soul." The attractive room features a copper topped long bar, Guinness and Harp on tap, friendly Irish bartender, and live music Thursday-Saturday. The menu features Irish specialties. The crowd is mixed middle to upper income with a fair share of bankers and enough Irish to add to the authenticity of the pub. Tommy Makem, as you must know, is the noted Irish singer.

Open Monday-Saturday noon-10 p.m. Information: 212-759-9040.

S **Trinity Church**, Broadway at Wall Street. The present church is a Gothic brownstone built in 1846. It is the burial place of Robert Fulton, Pennsylvania-born Irish-American inventor and artist.

Best known, erroneously, for inventing the steam boat, he did demonstrate that the steam boat was practical when he designed and built the *Clermont.* Alexander Hamilton is also buried here.

Open Monday-Friday 8 a.m.-6 p.m., Saturday and Sunday until 4 p.m.; museum open Monday-Friday 9 a.m.-11:45 a.m. and 1 p.m.-3:45 p.m., Saturday 10 a.m.-3:45 p.m., and Sunday afternoon 1-3:45. Free. Information: 212-602-0800.

S **Victor Herbert Statue**, Central Park near 72nd Street and Bandstand. The statue honors Dublin-born Victor Herbert, creator of such celebrated musicals as "The Red Mill," "Naughty Marietta," and "Babes in Toyland."

S **Woodlawn Cemetery**, 233rd Street and Webster Avenue. Among the noted people buried at Woodlawn are Irish-Americans George M. Cohan and Victor Herbert. Woodlawn, one of the country's most beautiful cemeteries, presents Sunday concerts throughout the year. (Sunday concerts in a cemetery?) They often include Cohan's lively compositions.

Oyster Bay

T **Sagamore Hill National Historic Site**, 3 miles east via East Main Street and Cove Neck Road. Theodore Roosevelt lived here until his death in 1919. It served as the summer White House during his terms as president. The home contains original furnishings and memorabilia. An audio-tape by his first daughter Alice can be rented. On the grounds is the Old Orchard Museum containing exhibits and a film of Roosevelt's personal and professional life.

Open daily 9:30 a.m.-5 p.m., except New Year's, Thanksgiving, and Christmas. Fee. Seniors and children free. Information: 516-922-4447.

Rome

P **Erie Canal Village**, 2 1/2 miles west of Rome on NY 49. View a restored section of the canal by a 1900 steam train or 1840 horse-drawn packetboat. The 1840s canal village includes settler's cabin and barn, hotel, train station, blacksmith shop, ladies shop, Victorian manor home, visitor's center, snack bar, and picnic area.

Open daily 10 a.m.-5 p.m. mid-May through October. Fee. Information: 315-336-6000, ext. 247, or weekends 1-315-337-3999.

Saratoga Springs

HH **The Parting Glass**, 40 Lake Avenue, has a long history in Saratoga, known for the quality of its Irish music, as well as country and blues. Tommy Makem is one of the entertainers who has appeared several times in recent years. The food is good, especially the Sunday Irish breakfast—the quality is reflected in the price, however. The bar is dark and classic Irish; dart competitions are held regularly.

Open daily. Information: 518-583-1916.

Syracuse

P **Canal Center**, Lyndon Road, 4 miles east of Syracuse at junction of NY 5 and 92, in Erie Canal State Park. Exhibits depict the massive canal structures located nearby.

Open daily Memorial Day-Labor Day and daily except Mondays remainder of year. Free. Information: 315-471-8593.

₪₪ Coleman's Irish Pub, 100 South Lowell Avenue. The pub with two front doors. One for most of us; a tiny one for the Little People. Whichever door you enter, you'll find what you like behind it: a square bar, two dining areas, gift shop, and rooms upstairs for special occasions. Priority seating for leprechauns is located on both floors. Some believe that it's the special consideration shown to the Little People that accounts for the lasting success of this authentic Irish Pub, but more likely it's the excellent food, Irish beer, reasonable prices and the gregarious host.

Once a "spit on the floor pub," Coleman's was expanded and redecorated in a manner which raised it several notches on the quality scale, but it's still a neighborhood pub. Only now the neighborhood has expanded beyond Tipperary Hills to encompass greater Syracuse. Coleman's is a 4-shamrock pub.

Open daily. Information: 315-476-1933.

₱ Erie Canal Museum, Weighlock Building, 318 Erie Boulevard. Exhibits depict the development and operation of the Canal. The museum contains a research library.

Open daily, except Mondays and holidays. Free. Information: 315-471-0593.

₪IΛ Green Light, corner of Burnett Park and Thompkins Street. On this corner hangs the only stoplight in the country (world?) where the green light—not the red light—is on top. This is the result of efforts made a generation ago by residents of the neighborhood of Tipperary Hills. That's one explanation. Another is that it happened one St. Patrick's Day when some of the celebrants leaving Coleman's Irish Pub turned the light upside down. When you think about it, both stories might be true! You can buy a T-shirt or post card at Coleman's or the Irish shop across the street (also a Coleman enterprise) that pictures this unique Irish-American phenomenon.

North Carolina

Boone

G **Boone,** a town of 12,000, located at the top of the Blue Ridge Mountains, was named for former resident Daniel Boone who lived here in the 1760s.

G **Boone Monument,** Appalachian State University campus. A monument to Daniel Boone is created of stones from the fireplace of the cabin he owned in this area.

G **Daniel Boone Native Gardens and Daniel Boone Theater.** Horn in the West Drive, east of Boone off US 421. The complex is named for the famed Irish-American Indian fighter and pioneer who lived here in a cabin in the 1760s. The **Squire Boone Museum,** named for Daniel's brother, is also located here.

Open daily May-October.

G **Horn in the West** is a musical drama, based on Daniel Boone's adventures in the Appalachian Highlands. It is presented in the outdoor amphitheater Tuesday-Sunday evenings June to mid-August. A museum is open during the same period from 1 p.m.-8:30. Fee. Senior and children's discount. Information: 704-264-2120.

Greenville

G **Guilford Courthouse National Military Park,** off US 220. One of the last battles of the Revolutionary War was fought between Gen. Nathaniel Greene's forces and the army of Lord Cornwallis. The British won the battle, but suffered great losses, leading to Cornwallis's surrender at Yorktown. One of the more colorful men fighting under Greene was American Charles Lynch, who headed a volunteer regiment. Lynch was from the town of Lynchburg, Virginia, founded by his Irish ancestors. He became notorious as a judge who dealt out severe extralegal sentences to those unfortunates who came before his court. Flogging was his most usual punishment, but hanging would be forever linked to his name.

Exhibits are set up throughout the battlefield. At the visitor center, you can view films and obtain a 2 1/2 mile auto tour handout. The visitor center is open daily 8:30 a.m.-5 p.m., with extended hours in the summer. Information: 919-288-1776.

Kenansville

G **Kenansville**, population 1,000, was founded about 1735 by Irish, German, and Swiss immigrants. They first named their town Golden Grove. In 1785, Grove Academy was established here. In 1818, Golden Grove was renamed in honor of Gen. James Kenan, who had emigrated from Ireland in 1730. Kenan fought in the Revolutionary War and was involved in the development of the Bill of Rights. Kenansville has several ante-bellum churches and a number of restored homes.

Information: 919-296-0369, or write Town Hall, Courthouse Square.

G **Liberty Hall**, NC 11, 24, 50. Built in the early 19th century by Thomas Kenan II, son of General Kenan, the 11-room Greek Revival house remained in the family until 1964, when the General's great-great grandchildren restored it as a memorial to their ancestors. Most of the decor is authentic, and much of the furniture is original. There are other buildings on the grounds, including the smokehouse, carriage house, and necessary house (outhouse).

Open Tuesday-Saturday and most holidays 10 a.m.-4 p.m.; Sunday 2 p.m.-4 p.m.; closed New Year's, Thanksgiving, and Christmas. Fee. Children's discount. Information: 919-296-0522.

Pineville

T **Andrew Johnson's Birthplace**, Mordecai Historic Park, Mimosa Street. This is the house in which Andrew Johnson, 17th U.S. president and descendant of Ulster ancestors, was born in 1826. The park is also the site of a furnished 1785 house with many of the original furnishings, an early Raleigh post office, and other 18th- and 19th-century buildings.

Open Tuesday-Thursday and Saturday-Sunday, March-December, except major holidays. Free. Information: 704-834-4844.

T **James K. Polk Memorial State Historical Site,** 12 miles south of Charlotte (1/2 mile south of Pineville) on US 521. The birthplace of the 11th president of the United States includes a replica of a log cabin, outbuildings, and visitor center with exhibits and 25-minute film. Polk traced his ancestry back to Ulster through both parents.

Open Monday-Saturday 9 a.m.-5 p.m. and Sunday afternoon 1 p.m.-5 p.m., April-October; Tuesday-Saturday 10 a.m.-4 p.m. and Sunday afternoon 1-4 other months. Free. Information: 704-889-7145.

Raleigh

S **North Carolina Museum of Art,** off I-40, Wade Avenue exit; follow signs to 2110 Blue Ridge Boulevard. The museum contains art by Georgia O'Keeffe, whose father was born in Ireland. O'Keeffe was an early model for the working woman, and her art reflected her own great individuality and strength. She also served as a model for her husband, photographer Alfred Stieglitz, whose photographs of O'Keeffe are considered among his best work. In later years, she moved to New Mexico where she died in 1986, at the age of 99. Work by other painters displayed by the museum includes Thomas Hart Benton, Botticelli, Winslow Homer, Raphael, and Van Dyke.The artwork in arranged in eight major collections. Films and concerts are presented in the educational wing.

Open Tuesday-Saturday 9 a.m.-5 p.m., Friday 9 a.m.-9 p.m., Sunday afternoon noon-5; closed New Year's, Fourth of July, Thanksgiving, and Christmas. Free. Information: 919-833-1935.

Waxhaw

T **Andrew Jackson Birthplace.** The birthplace of the 7th president of the United States has long been in dispute. While it is agreed that he was born in the Old Waxhaw Settlement, a few miles south of Waxhaw, the debate is to whether it was on the South Carolina or North Carolina side. Despite considerable effort, the remains of the cabin have never been found. Jackson, himself, claimed his birthplace was in South Carolina. Waxhaw, however, is the site of an annual June drama, "Listen and Remember," presented in an outside theater. The drama retells the story of the Jackson family and the early history of the settlement.

North Dakota

Medora

T **Theodore Roosevelt National Park.** The park was named in honor of Theodore Roosevelt, 26th U.S. president, in recognition of his early efforts to conserve America's natural resources. The park comprises nearly 75,000 acres in North Dakota's Badlands. Roosevelt came to the area in 1883 on a hunting trip. He invested in two ranches and became an active member of the community, serving as president of the Little Missouri River Stockmen's Association. References to his life during this period show up in some of his publications. Among the attractions of the park are the herds of American bison, pronghorn antelope, elk, deer, and smaller animals. The park is colored by scoria, a red cinder-like substance created when sand and clay is set ablaze by lightning and grass fires. Picnic areas, trail rides, and campsites are available.

Open all year round. Fee for vehicles from May through September. Camping fees mid-April through October. Information: 701-623-4466, or write Superintendent, Theodore Roosevelt National Park.

Ohio

Canton

T **William McKinley**, 25th president of the United States, opened a law practice in Canton in 1867. It is here, in 1896, where he conducted his famous and successful "front porch" campaign for his second presidential term. *The Repository*, founded by Mrs. McKinley's grandfather, is still published.

T **McKinley Museum of History, Science and Industry**, 800 McKinley Monument Drive, N.W. Built in 1963, the museum contains McKinley memorabilia, Historical Hall, hands-on Science Hall, and a Street of Shops. It was during McKinley's administration that Hawaii was annexed and the Spanish-American War was fought.

Open daily. Planetarium shows, Saturday-Sunday; closed New Year's, Easter, Labor Day, Thanksgiving, and Christmas. Handicapped facilities. Fee. Senior citizen discount. Information: 216-455-7043.

T **McKinley National Memorial**, McKinley Monument Drive, N.W. The Memorial includes the tomb and statue of William McKinley, 25th president of the United States. McKinley was shot by an anarchist on September 6, 1901, and died nine days later.

Information: 216-455-7043.

Cleveland

B **John Carroll University**, Warrensville Center and Fairmount Boulevard in University Heights. A Jesuit university, located on a 60-acre campus of 21 Gothic-style buildings, it was named for John Carroll, first Roman Catholic bishop in the United States. On campus are a fine arts gallery, seismological observatory, and collection of G. K. Chesterton works.

Information: 216-267-1187.

Columbus

𝕋 **McKinley Memorial**, west entrance to state capitol grounds. The statue portrays the 25th president, William McKinley, delivering his last presidential address before his assassination.

Information: 614-221-6623.

Oxford

𝕊 **McGuffey Museum**, Spring and Oak Streets. Restored home of Irish American William Holmes McGuffey, best known as compiler and editor of the *McGuffey Eclectic Readers*, published during his tenure as professor at Miami University. More than 122 million copies of the *Readers* were sold and used in the elementary schools during the 19th century. The stories blend moral messages into stories and poems. In later years, McGuffey was president of the Cincinnati College (now University) and Ohio University. He ended his teaching career as professor of moral philosophy at the University of Virginia at the time of his death in 1873. The museum contains his books.

Call for hours. Free. Information: 513-529-1809.

Put-in-Bay

𝔾 The village of Put-in-Bay, population 146, was settled in 1811. A year-round resort reached by ferry, it has two sites associated with Commodore Oliver Hazard Perry, whose mother emigrated from County Down:

𝔾 **Perry's Cave**, Catawba Avenue. The cave has lived two lives. It is alleged to have held ammunition used by Perry in the Battle of Lake Erie and later housed prisoners. The cave is 208 feet by 165 feet, 52 feet below the surface. A temperature of 42 degrees Fahrenheit—10 degrees above freezing—made it a good place to store ammunition, but not so good for the prisoners.

Open daily, Memorial Day-Labor Day; weekends May, September, October; by appointment other times. Fee. Information: 419-285-2405 or -3045.

G **Perry's Victory and International Peace Memorial.** In 1813, during the War of 1812, Commodore Perry defeated the British in the Battle of Lake Erie, fought near Put-in-Bay. The victory gave control of the Lake Erie region to the United States making feasible, if not wise, an invasion of Canada. The memorial to Perry is a granite column of Greek Doric design. It contains an observation tower providing views of Canada and the islands.

Hourly lectures daily; evening programs. Fee. Information: 419-285-2184, -3512, or write Superintendent, PO Box 549.

Warren

H **Warren,** population 56,600, founded in 1799, may have provided inspiration for two of Stephen Foster's most famous compositions. "Jeannie with the Light Brown Hair" is thought to have been written at one of its stagecoach inns, the Austin House, and a walk along the Mahoning River may have stimulated the idea for "My Old Kentucky Home." (See My Old Kentucky State Park, Bardstown, KY, for a different version of Foster's inspiration.)

Oklahoma

Enid

P **Homesteader's Sod House,** 30 miles west of Enid on US 60 and 5 1/2 miles north of Cleo Springs on OK 8. Built by Irish American Marshall McCully (maternal grandmother's name was O'Banion) in 1894 and restored by the Oklahoma Historical Society, it is a 2-room sod house of the type built by homesteaders in the late 19th century. It is believed to be the only one in the country still standing. Authentic furnishings and farm equipment are displayed.

Open 9 a.m.-5 p.m. Tuesday-Friday, afternoons Saturday-Sunday; closed Mondays, New Years, Thanksgiving, and Christmas. Handicapped facilities. Free. Information: 405-463-2441.

Oklahoma City

G **National Cowboy Hall of Fame and Western Heritage Center,** 1700 Northeast 63rd Street, 1/2 mile west of I-35 on I-44. Among the major attention getters of this 32-acre memorial to pioneers of the Old West is a 32-foot statue of Irish American Buffalo Bill Cody. But the most impressive is the $50 million Western art collection, including work by Frederick Remington and Charles Russell.

Take time to visit the West of Yesterday, where you can live the life of many Irish Americans of the 1880s. Visit a gold mine or a saloon or one of the other replicas of old West buildings. The Western Performers Hall of Fame features portraits of Irish American actor John Wayne, Walter Brennan—remember TV's "The Real McCoys"?—and those immortal stars of the Saturday matinees—Tom Mix, Gene Autry, Roy Rogers, and Dale Evans.

Open daily 8 a.m.-6 p.m., late May through early September; 9 a.m.-5 p.m., the rest of the year. Closed New Year's, Thanksgiving, and Christmas. Fee. Seniors and children's discount. Information: 405-478-2250.

Shamrock

HIA **Shamrock,** Highway 13, northeast of Oklahoma City about half way to Tulsa. Oklahoma was not a top choice as a new home by the Irish immigrants. It wasn't even in the running. But some of the new Americans brought with them from Ireland the lust for land, and Oklahoma was able to satisfy their desires. Between 1912 and 1915, Edwin L. Dunn, a Tulsa realtor, founded the town of Shamrock, painted many of the buildings green, and named its streets Cork, Dublin, Killarney, Tipperary, and in case anyone missed the point, Ireland. The *Blarney* and the *Brogue* printed the news of and for the more than 10,000 townsfolk.

Today, Shamrock's population is about 200, but its Irish identity lingers on in the names of its streets, its combination gas station-grocery store painted green, and in the spirit of one of its foremost citizens, Mrs. Jones, who in her 80s serves as Grand Marshall of the annual St. Patrick's Day parade.

Pauls Valley

℗ **Murray-Lindsay Mansion,** 21 miles west of Pauls Valley on OK 19, 2 miles south on OK 76 in Lindsay. The 3-story Classic Revival mansion was built in 1880 by Frank Murray, an Irish immigrant, who wed a Choctaw woman. Murray ultimately amassed an estate covering 20,000 acres within the Chickasaw Nation. The home contains the original furnishings.

Open daily, except Mondays and major holidays. Handicapped facilities. Free. Information: 405-756-3826.

Oregon

Oregon City

℗ **McLoughlin House National Historic Site,** McLoughlin Park, 7th and Center Streets. Dr. John McLoughlin, known as the "father of Oregon," built his home in 1845. McLoughlin's father was born in Donegal, Ireland. In spite of his early training, McLoughlin spent little of his life as a medical man, preferring instead the world of commerce. From 1825 to 1845, he served as "chief factor" of Hudson Bay Company, and in this position reigned over an immense territory now made up of Oregon, Washington, Northern California, part of Wyoming, Nevada, British Columbia, and Alberta. He was noted for his kindness to settlers.

McLoughlin and his Irish American wife, Marguerite McKay, had four children. The eldest, John, who was in charge of a Hudson Bay post in Russian-controlled territory, was killed by his own men, in what the follow-up investigation deemed to be "justifiable homicide." McLoughlin had proof to the contrary. The continuing controversy led to his resignation from the company and his subsequent building of the Oregon City home, where he lived until his death on September 3, 1957.

After his death, his home was purchased, expanded, and re-opened as the Hotel Phoenix. With time and industrialization of the neighborhood, the home entered into a new phase in its life. It added a corps of entertainers, and the bedrooms were rented by the hour.

When a move was finally made to preserve the home, some citizens believed that its sinful recent history would doom it to oblivion. Wiser minds prevailed, and the home was moved to a site which McLoughlin had earlier identified as the setting for a park. Today the home contains many of its original furnishings, including McLoughlin's desk and four-poster, hand-carved bed.

Open Tuesday-Saturday 10 a.m.-4 p.m. and Sunday afternoon 1-4, February-December; closed January and holidays. Fee. Senior and children's discount. Information: 503-656-5146.

Pennsylvania

Allentown

T **George Taylor House and Park**, 4 miles north off US 22 at Lehigh and Poplar Streets, Catasaqua. Built in 1768, it is the restored home of George Taylor, one of the three Irish-born signers of the Declaration of Independence. Museum and garden.

Open Saturday and Sunday, June-October and by appointment. Free. Information: 215-435-4664.

Ashland

P **Museum of Anthracite Mining**, Pine & 17th Streets. The technology of mining anthracite coal is demonstrated.

Open daily, May-October; closed Mondays, November-April, and holidays. Handicapped facilities. Fee. Information: 717-875-4708.

P **Pioneer Tunnel Coal Mine and Steam Lokie**, 4 blocks off PA 61. Two tours are offered. An electrically powered mine car will take you down where miners will explain the operation. It gets chilly down there, so take a sweater. The other tour takes you by mine car around the mountain to an abandoned strip mine and a bootleg coal hole.

Open daily 10 a.m.-6 p.m., Memorial Day-Labor Day. Call for times during other months. Information: 717-875-3850 or -3301.

Bally

HH **Jim Finegan's Bally Hotel**, 660 Main Street, Rte. 100. A delightful, informal pub, located in a 150-year-old hotel, lives on in a Pennsylvania Dutch country village. The small bar has Guinness and Harp on tap, and you can order from the kitchen 11 a.m.-9 p.m. Sunday brunch is served 10:30 a.m.- 2 p.m. Live entertainment Friday and Saturday nights brings in a mixture of white and blue collar neighbors. Ask Jim, the owner, about Finnegans Wake at the Bally Hotel. Better yet, join them for the holiday the weekend before St. Patrick's Day!

Open daily. Information: 215-845-2440.

Bryn Mawr

T **Harriton House**, 1 1/4 miles north of US 30 on Morris Avenue, 1/2 mile west on Old Gulph Road, north on Harriton Road. The restored 1704 two-story stone house was the home of Charles Thomson, secretary of the Continental Congress. Thomson was born in Derry, Ireland, and came to the States as a child. Some original furnishings are displayed. Picnicking is permitted on the 16 acre estate.

Open Wednesday-Saturday, 10 a.m.-4 p.m. and by appointment; closed holidays. Guided tours by prior arrangement. Fee. Senior discount; students free. Information: 215-525-0201.

Carnegie

ⵌⵌ **The Pour House**, 215 East Main Street, lives and breathes Irish. It has one room of modest size, with long bar and tables. Loaded with Irish articles, it displays flags, mugs, leprechauns, poems, photos, mini-green lights, bar lamps made from Jameson bottles, framed T-shirts from Pittsburgh's past 14 St. Patrick Day parades, and a variety of Irish-American newspapers on the bar. Located on a brick street in restored downtown Carnegie, it has the feel of a pub which is comfortable with itself and its regulars; strangers are treated with tolerance and, maybe, a little suspicion, like you find in some of the pubs in the villages of Donegal. A video of Pittsburgh's most recent St. Patrick's Day parade was being shown during our visit.

Guinness, on draught, is served with the Irish measure of a 20-ounce pint at a nice price. Harp's available in bottles. The kitchen was closed when we visited, and the bartender wasn't sure just when it might open again. Entertainment comes from a big screen TV and, on Tuesdays and most Saturday nights, live Irish music.

Open daily, except Sunday, from 4 p.m. Information: 412-279-0770).

Coudersport

ⵌ1Ⴑ **Coudersport** is located in north central Pennsylvania, not far from the New York border. It was founded by John Keating, an Irish adventurer, who managed a land company owning most of Potter county. Keating enticed people to the area by offering 50 acres of land to the first 50 families to settle there. He named the village for a Dutch banker.

Today, Coudersport has 2,800 people and an economy based on light manufacturing.

Easton

Ⴁ,Ⴑ Easton played an integral role in the Revolutionary War. The Declaration of Independence, signed by at least eight Irish Americans was read for the first time in public from the steps of the Northamp-

223

ton County Courthouse in Centre Square. The courthouse was built in 1765 on land deeded by the William Penn family for the price of one red rose annually. Today, the Soldiers and Sailors Monument stands on this site. George Easton, one of the eight Irish Americans signing the Declaration of Independence, lived here.

A self-guided walking tour can be obtained form Historic Easton, Inc., P.O. Box 994, 18044. Information: 215-258-1612, or Two Rivers Visitors Center, YWCA, North Third Street.

𝕋 **Parsons-Taylor House**, 4th and Ferry Streets. Built in 1757, the stone house was the home of George Taylor, one of the three Irish-born signers of the Declaration of Independence. Open by appointment. Free. Information: 215-253-1222.

Erie

𝔾 **Oliver Perry Monument**, Presque Isle State Park, 5 miles north of Erie, west off Peninsula Drive (PA 832). A monument in honor of Commodore Oliver Hazard Perry was erected in commemoration of his victory over the British in the Battle of Lake Erie. The Isle, a wild life refuge, has many miles of beaches.

Open daily 5 a.m. to dusk, Memorial Day-Labor Day. Visitors in vehicles permitted until 11 p.m. Handicapped facilities. Information: 814-871-4251.

H **Flagship *Niagara*,** 164 East Front Street. "We have me the enemy and they are ours," reported Captain Oliver Hazard Perry. The year was 1813, and the Americans had just won a victory over the British on Lake Erie.

Open April-October. Call for hours. Fee. Information: 814-452-2744.

Etna

HH **Blarney Stone Restaurant**, 30 Grant Avenue, is a pleasant pub-restaurant with a bar, dining area, separate dining room, a room upstairs for private parties, and a small gift shop. Guinness and Harp

are on draught and a full menu is available for lunch or dinner, 11
a.m.-10 p.m. You can hear Irish music only on special occasions, one
of which is the celebration of Bloomsday in June, and naturally St.
Patrick's Day. The Blarney Stone houses a dinner theater where
Nunsense has been running for many months. The Blarney Stone is
popular with neighbors and even out-of-town guests who, owner
Tom O'Donohugh says, are bussed in for special events. One reason
that I'd go back is the friendliness of the bartender and waitress—a
sign of an authentic Irish pub.

Open Tuesday-Sunday, 11 a.m.-2 a.m. Information: 412-781-
1666.

Gettysburg

G **Gettysburg National Military Park.** The Battle of Gettysburg
(July 1-3, 1863) was the turning point of the Civil War. It was the
last major invasion of the North made by the Confederacy. Southern
forces were under the command of Gen. Robert E. Lee, while the
Northern troops were led by Gen. George Gordon Meade, a descendant of a County Kerry emigrant, Andrew Meade. Irish Americans
fought on both sides, but predominantly on the side of the Union.
The remnants of the illustrious Irish Brigade, which had sustained
heavy casualties at Fredericksburg and Chancellorsville, was destroyed at Gettysburg, as it fought under its emerald green flag. The
Irish are honored by a number of monuments in the park.

G **Gen. George G. Meade Equestrian Statue,** Hancock Avenue.
Created by sculptor Henry K. Bush-Brown after two years of research, the bronze statue recognizes the military expertise of the man
who not only won the critical battle of Gettysburg, but continued to
lead the army for the next two years of the war.

G **Irish Brigade Monument,** Sickles Avenue, the Loop. More than
forty federal units during the Civil War were made up primarily of
Irish, but the most famous was the Irish Brigade. It was organized
and commanded for most of the war by Thomas Francis Meagher.
The brigade was initially made up by the 63rd, 69th, and 88th New

York Infantry Regiments. Later it was expanded to include the 116th Pennsylvania Infantry, predominantly Philadelphia Irishmen, and finally, another Irish regiment, the 28th Massachusetts.

Throughout its short life, the Brigade was always at the forefront of the battles, which resulted in disproportionate numbers of Irish fatalities. They earned their reputation for heroism at Bull Run, the Peninsula, Antietam, Fredricksburg, Chancellorsville, and Gettysburg. The Irish Brigade ended its illustrious history in 1864.

The Irish Brigade Monument, designed by William Rudolph O'Donovan, was dedicated on July 2, 1888. It honors the three New York regiments (63rd, 69th, and 88th) which combined to finance the project. Made of granite and bronze, it is one of the most striking and dramatic monuments in the park with its shaft formed in the shape of the Celtic cross; five medallions representing the three regiments, New York State, and the seal of Ireland; and a mournful Irish wolfhound lying at its base. A bronze plaque recognizes the 14th New York Independent Battery commanded by Capt. James Rorty, who served with the Brigade at Gettysburg on temporary assignment.

G **28th Massachusetts Infantry**, Sickles Avenue at the Loop. An Irish harp identifies the heritage of the members of the largest unit of the Irish Brigade, as does the phrase "Faugh A Ballaugh," a rallying cry of the Irish meaning "Clear the Way." The monument, dedicated July 2, 1886, is topped with a granite eagle.

G **116th Pennsylvania Infantry**, Sickles Avenue at the Loop. Commanded by Major St. Clair A. Mulholland, this unit of the Irish Brigade has an unusual monument. J. H. Kelly sculpted a scene in granite which does not honor victory, but reminds one of the horror of war. It depicts a young soldier lying dead near the remains of a farmer's fence. It is a scene which Mulholland had witnessed and foreshadowed the devastation experienced by his unit. The monument was dedicated September 11, 1889.

G **Father William Corby Portrait Statue**, South Hancock Avenue. Father Corby was chaplain to the Irish Brigade's 88th New York Infantry. Immediately prior to the unit entering battle, Father Corby stepped up on a rock and, with the sounds of battle raging in the background, he granted general absolution to the men. The statue, dedicated in 1910, depicts Fr. Corby in this act; some say the base is formed by the rock upon which he had stood. Following the war, Corby served as president of the University of Notre Dame, where an identical statue was erected in 1911.

G **66th New York Infantry**, Sickles Avenue, the Loop. Many Irish belonged to the 66th, but not in sufficient numbers to be identified as an Irish regiment. Sculpted by Byron M. Pickett from granite and bronze, it incorporates a shamrock over the unusual representation of a Union and Confederate soldier shaking hands. The monument was dedicated in 1889.

G **The Civil War Library and Museum**, 18045 Pine Street. This Civil War collection includes uniforms worn by Irish American generals Ulysses S. Grant and George Meade, life masks of Abraham Lincoln, over 12,000 volumes, and other memorabilia.

Open Monday-Saturday 10 a.m.-4 p.m. Information: 215-735-8196.

G **James Wadsworth Portrait Statue**, North Reynolds Avenue. The Wadsworth statue is a tribute to a soldier and a humanitarian. As a soldier, he led the first Union infantry division at Gettysburg. As a humanitarian, he struck up an unusual relationship with Patrick McCracken, a farmer and suspected Confederate spy. McCracken was arrested and jailed without a trial. When Wadsworth heard his story, he believed the farmer, set him free and, from his own pocket, gave him money to return to his home in Virginia.

Three years later, in 1864, Wadsworth was wounded in battle. He was left in the field behind the Southern lines, where he was found and carried to a Confederate hospital. His wound was diagnosed as fatal. McCracken, who lived nearby, was bringing food to the wounded, when he recognized his benefactor. He managed surreptitiously to get milk to his friend, but when he returned with food that afternoon, the general was dead. He obtained permission from the Confederate surgeon to take the body back to his farm. He contacted Mrs. Wadsworth, who had the body sent to New York. Patrick McCracken had returned the favor to his friend.

G **The Smith Civil War Memorial**, North Concourse Drive, West Fairmount Park. General George Meade is memorialized in bronze. The memorial was erected at the turn of the 20th-century to honor Pennsylvania Civil War heroes.

G **Grant Statue**, Kelly Drive. The statue represents Gen. Ulysses S. Grant astride his horse.

Information on all Gettysburg sites: 217-334-6274, or write Gettysburg Travel Council, Inc., 35 Carlisle Street.

Greensburg

HH **Callaghan's**, 534 South Main Street, is a small, charming pub with separate dining area. Distinctive for its simplicity, eating there is like having a beer and sandwich in the home of an Irish neighbor.

And it doesn't cost much more. Guinness and Harp are on draught. Callaghan's has a loyal following among neighbors and business people.

Open daily. Infromation: 412-832-3339.

Gwynedd Valley

HI, HIA **The Irish American Cultural Institute Library**, Sumneytown Pike and Route 202, Gwynedd Mercy College. Located in the Lourdes Library, the Institute holds about 700 books on Irish history and Irish Americans, which can not be checked out. See one of the few $15,000 reproductions of the *Book of Kells.*

Open during academic sessions, Monday-Thursday 8 a.m.-4:20 p.m.; Saturday noon-3:30 p.m.; Sunday 3 p.m.-10 p.m. Summer hours vary. Information: 215-646-7300.

Harrisburg

HH **Coakley's**, 305 Bridge Street, New Cumberland, is a popular neighborhood bar attracting all ages, classes, and cultures. It salutes the Irish, some in name only, with 16 drinks, including the Black Rose, Banshee, Barry Fitzgerald, Bill Bailey, and Pearl Bailey. Guinness and Harp are on tap as well as green beer on St. Patrick's Day. Enjoy Irish music or darts. Lunch and dinner (served daily) feature specialties like O'Malley's corned beef and cabbage and country Irish stew. We had the stew and a club sandwich. Try the stew, skip the club sandwich.

Open daily. Information; 717-749-7853.

Hazleton

P **Eckley Miner's Village**, 10 miles northeast of Hazleton off PA 940. One of hundreds of company-owned mining villages or "patches" built in the anthracite coal region during the 1800s. At one time Eckley was home to more than 1,000 people, with churches, school, store, social club, and homes ranging from duplexes to large homes belonging to the mine owners. *The Molly Maguires*, with Sean Connery and Richard Harris, was filmed here in 1970. Paramount Studios didn't think the village looked authentic, so they replaced some structures and modified others.

Today Eckley is a living museum where some twenty miners and their families still live. A number of buildings are still being restored or constructed. Many which are standing are not open to the public, but Eckley is well worth visiting. A stroll down the single road will give you a feel for the life of the Irish families who lived here in the mid to late 1800s.

Open Monday-Saturday 9 a.m.-5 p.m.; Sunday noon-5 p.m.; closed major holidays. Limited access to buildings is available with a guide Memorial Day to Labor Day and weekends in September and October. Fee. Information: 717-636-2070.

Lancaster

S **Robert Fulton Birthplace**, 14 miles south of Lancaster on PA 222. Robert Fulton, artist and inventor, was born in this recently refurbished, little stone house. Fulton demonstrated the feasibility of the steamboat when he sailed up the Hudson River in 1807.

Open Memorial Day-Labor Day, Saturdays and Sundays. Handicapped facilities. Fee. Information: 717-548-2679.

T **Wheatland,** 1120 Marietta Avenue, 1 1/2 miles west of Lancaster on PA 23. The 1828 restored Federal mansion was home to James Buchanan, 15th president of the United States, from 1848-1868. Buchanan's father was born in Ramelton, County Donegal. Like William McKinley, Buchanan conducted his second campaign from his home. Like McKinley, he was successful.

Tours daily April-November, except Thanksgiving and Christmas. Candlelight tours early December. Fee. Senior and student discount. Information: 717-392-8721.

Limeport

HH **Ye Olde Limeport Hotel,** Limeport Pike, has a pleasant restaurant separated from a most unpretentious pub by a short hall and a couple of dangling shamrocks. The best time to visit is in March for Finnegans Wake. Split your time between Limeport and Bally (down the road a piece), and you'll have a holiday to remember—if you can. A full menu and Guinness, Harp, and Guinness Gold.

Open daily, except Mondays. Information: 215-967-1810.

Philadelphia

HIA **The Balch Institute for Ethnic Studies,** 18 South 7th Street. The research library contains material relating to Irish and 69 other ethnic groups. The Institute displays the richness of America's heritage through exhibits of photographs, clothing, and artifacts representing the various nationalities which have shaped the country. A permanent exhibit is devoted to ports of entry other than Ellis Island.

Museum open Monday-Saturday 10 a.m.-4 p.m.; library open 9 a.m.-5 p.m. Donation. Information: 215-925-8090.

HH **Downey's,** South and Front Streets, across from the Delaware

River. This is one of the country's better Irish pubs, home of Downey's Irish Whiskey cakes (other flavors too) shipped around the country. It mixes traditional pub informality with lace curtain quality. You can sit at the magnificent bar or in one of the two dining rooms and pass the time looking at the artifacts on the walls and ceiling. They reflect either the Irish heritage of the owner, Jack Downey, or his years in broadcasting. Don't miss the old leprechaun above the seafood bar. (According to legend, if you catch a leprechaun, you may find his pot of gold.)

Guinness and Harp are on tap, and the kitchen prepares a full list of edibles for lunch and dinner, including an Irish breakfast, seafood pie, potato soup (thick with potato and rich with cream), Irish stew (lamb), and Dublin Bay lobster bisque. Sunday brunch is offered. Neighbors, tourists, locals, and Irish gather at Downey's.

If you haven't been keeping track, a September 17th celebration will remind you that you're half-way to St. Patrick's Day. And as a further aide, the sign behind the bar will let you know exactly how many more days before the Big Day.

Open daily until 2 a.m. Information: 215-625-9500.

D **Edgar Allan Poe National Historic Site,** 532 North 7th at Spring Garden Street. When he lived here in 1843-44, Poe wrote some of his most terrifying horror stories, including "The Telltale Heart," "The Black Cat," and "The Gold Bug." Walk by the home at midnight on Halloween and chill to the shadow of a raven which appears on the house. It may simply be a shadow from a statue in the garden, but on the other hand... "his eyes have all the seeming of a Demon that is dreaming."

Open daily 9 a.m.-5 p.m., except New Year's and Christmas. Free. Information: 215-597-8780.

HIA **Historical Society of Pennsylvania,** 1300 Locust Street. The Society maintains a large collection of family records and passenger lists of Irish and other immigrants.

Open Tuesday, Thursday, Friday, Saturday 10 a.m.-5 p.m., Wednesday from 10 a.m.-9 p.m. Information: 215-732-6201.

G, T Independence Hall, Chestnut Street, between 5th and 6th Streets on Independence Square, Independence National Historical Park. In this 1732 brick building, the Declaration of Independence and the Constitution were signed. The inkstand used for signing the Declaration is in the Assembly Room, which has been restored to its appearance during the period. Among the signers of the Declaration of Independence were Irish Americans Charles Carroll, whose grandfather, also Charles Carroll, was attorney general of Maryland; Thomas Lynch, Thomas McKean; George Read; Edward Rutledge; and emigrants from Ireland, James Smith, George Taylor, and Matthew Thornton. Charles Carroll was the only Irish Catholic to sign the Declaration. Charles Thompson, who emigrated from Ireland as an indentured servant, read the Declaration to Congress in his capacity as secretary of the Congress. A **statue of Commodore John Barry** stands in Independence Square, located behind Independence Hall.

Open daily, 9 a.m.-4 p.m., with extended hours in the summer. Free. Information: 215-597-8974.

HH Irish Pub, 1123 Walnut, has a friendly red-haired bartender who loves his work, his customers, and his pub. "What's the best Irish pub in Philadelphia...other than this one," I asked. He finally convinced me—at least for the time it took to sample the wares—that his is. But the Friday night after work crowd was across the street at Moriarty's.

This is a good, traditional Irish pub with a long bar and small dining area in the rear under a huge boxing mural, reminding one of the era when the Irish dominated the boxing world. Guinness and Harp are on draught, and pub grub is on the menu, including Irish stew. You can catch Irish entertainment here occasionally. Dick Burke, who has another pub up the street, and one in Atlantic City, has a good place here. A lot of older Philadelphians seem to know it, but it seems to be a secret with the TGIF crowd.

Open daily. Information: 215-925-3311.

HH Irish Pub, 2007 Walnut Street, serves the best Irish stew I've ever eaten in a pub. It was a cold, cold December day, when we scurried down Walnut Street to visit the Irish Pub for the first time, little knowing the treat that lay ahead. When the waitress placed the stew on the table before us, we knew from the splendiferous aroma that this was something very special. It was, and it's worth a trip to the Irish Pub just to taste it. But, while you're there, you'll want to sample the Guinness or Harp they have on draught.

And take some time to look at the Irish paraphernalia that cover the walls. This is one of the three successful Irish pubs owned by Dick Burke (see above and Atlantic City.)

We sat in one of the dining rooms, but the circular bar situated in a high-ceilinged room which was once a bank, is a popular place for the after work crowd to gather. The bartender said they get a young crowd, and I guess that explains the DJ they have some evenings. But the folks I saw in the afternoon covered a broad age range.

Open Sunday-Wednesday 11 a.m.-12 p.m.; Thursday-Saturday 11 a.m.-1 p.m. Information: 215-568-5603.

HJA **The Library Company of Philadelphia.** Established in 1731, it served as the unofficial Library of Congress in the late 18th-century. Ten signers of the Declaration of Independence, including Thomas McKean, were library patrons. The library contains more than 400,000 books, half of which are rare. Walt Whitman's *Leaves of Grass* and Melville's *Moby Dick* are among its first editions.

Open weekdays 9 a.m.-4:45 p.m. Free. Information: 215-546-3181.

B **Old St. Joseph's Church**, 321 Willings Alley, established in 1733. Commodore John Barry, Irish American and "Father of the American Navy," was a member of the parish.

Open Monday-Friday 10:30 a.m.-1:30 p.m. with Mass at noon; Saturday, 10:30 a.m.-6:30 p.m., Mass at 5:30 p.m.; Sunday 7 a.m.-4 p.m. Information: 215-923-1733.

HJA **Penn's Landing**, between Market and Lombard Streets, on the Delaware River. William Penn, founder of Pennsylvania, and his secretary, James Logan of County Armagh, landed at this point in 1682. The 37-acre site has a museum, sculpture garden, and several historic ships. Festivals, concerts, and special exhibits are held throughout the year.

Information: 215-923-8181.

Hl **Rosenbach Museum and Library,** 2010 Delancey. Dublin-born novelist and poet James Joyce (1882-1941) is best known for his novel *Ulysses,* based on Homer's *Odyssey,* and *Finnegans Wake,* his last work. Manuscripts by Joyce are on display in the library, along with those of Charles Dickens and Geoffrey Chaucer. Tours are available.

Open Tuesday-Sunday 11 a.m.-4 p.m., September-July; closed December 22-25 and major holidays. Fee. Senior and children's discount. Information: 215-732-1600.

B **St. Mary's Church,** 252 South 4th Street. St. Mary's graveyard is the burial place for a number of early Irish American parishioners, including Commodore John Barry; Thomas Fitzsimmons, the only Catholic to sign the Constitution; Gen. Stephen Moylan, Revolutionary War aide to George Washington, who was born in Cork; and Matthew Carey, Dublin newspaper editor and prominent Philadelphia publisher and bookseller. St. Mary's is Philadelphia's first Catholic cathedral.

Guided tours Sunday 11:30 a.m.-4 p.m., Easter to October 31,; Mass Saturday afternoon at 5 and Sunday morning 9 and 10:30. Information: 215-923-7930.

T **Stenton,** 18th Street between Courtland Street and Windrim Avenue. When William Penn, founder of Pennsylvania, emigrated from Ireland, he was accompanied by his secretary, James Logan, a native of Armagh. Logan later became mayor of Philadelphia, acting governor, and chief justice of Pennsylvania. He built his Pennsylvania colonial mansion in the early 18th century. George Washington really did sleep here, and it served as headquarters for Gen. William Howe during the Battle of Germantown. The home is furnished with 18th and 19th century pieces.

Open Tuesday-Saturday, except holidays and January. Fee. Information: 215-329-7312.

Pittsburgh

HH Gallagher's Pub, 2 South Market Place, has two lives—as a luncheon spot and after work hangout for workers from the nearby office buildings, and a sing-a-long club for an older group in the evenings. Whatever the time of day, I've found it a lively place. Guinness and Harp are on tap, and you'll find Irish stew on the pub grub menu.

Open daily, except Sunday. Information: 412-261-5551.

HIA Irish Center of Pittsburgh, 6886 Forward Avenue. A full menu of entertainment and educational opportunities are offered at this 4-acre site. Irish dance, and Irish knitting are taught, and concerts, speakers, swimming, dancing, and special events are offered.

Information: 412-521-9712.

HH Mick McGuire's, Market Place, is located across from Gallagher's, in the heart of Pittsburgh's downtown business district. Students, office workers, and Irish nationals find their way here. If you're a college student, you'll think Sundays pretty dull. If you're not a college student, you should know that Saturday nights belong to the young and the courageous who crowd the bar and dining area—the music is loud, the students louder. Guinness and Harp are on tap, and a full menu is offered. Irish music only on special occasions.

Open daily. Information: 412-642-7526.

HH Mullaney's Harp & Fiddle, Penn Avenue and 24th Street, on the Strip. Another authentic Irish pub done in the popular wood and green. But this is one of the better ones. It's a brightly lighted room, with bar set up a few steps, partially set off by a half wall. Guinness and Harp on draught are complemented by Guinness Gold and beers from Scotland, England, Australia, Holland, Czechoslovakia, and two non-alcoholic beverages, Keene's and O'Doul's. The menu includes such Irish treats as lamb stew, smoked salmon, Monk's Supper (leek soup, black bread, cheddar cheese), and Tinker's Plate (sampler of salmon, potato skins, cheddar cheese, soup, and sour dough bread). There are pretzel sticks on the bar for those who just want to nibble while they enjoy live Irish music Wednesday-Saturday.

Brian Mullaney with sister Anne and friend Sean Patrick Murphy (the latter two practicing attorneys in Pittsburgh) have created one of the better Irish pubs, not only in the Middle Atlantic, but in the country. They have attracted a large, happy following in the short time they've been open. This one's worth going out of your way to visit. But, be prepared, it can get very loud with its fun-loving crowd of upscale post-college patrons.

Open daily except Monday. Information: 412-642-6622).

S Stephen Foster Memorial, University of Pittsburgh campus, Bigelow Boulevard, 5th Avenue, Bellevue Avenue, and Forbes Avenue. Pittsburgh's Stephen Foster is memorialized by a majestic memorial which houses a theater and collection of the composer's music and memorabilia.

Library and museum are open Monday-Friday 9 a.m.-4 p.m., Saturday-Sunday afternoons 1-4; closed university holidays. Fee for guided tours. Senior and children's discount. Information: 412-624-4100.

HI University of Pittsburgh, 5th Avenue and Bigelow Boulevard. The Gothic structure thrusts 42 stories upwards, encompassing a 3-story Commons Room surrounded by 23 nationality rooms. The Irish Room, contributed by the Republic of Ireland, is made of stone. Each of the rooms reflects the culture of the ethnic group which created, funded, and furnished it. Saturday and Sunday are the best days to visit, since these are classrooms. During the last three weeks of December, the nationality rooms are decorated with the holiday traditions of the countries they represent.

Open Monday-Saturday 9 a.m.-3 p.m., Sunday 11 a.m.-3 p.m.

Fee April-August, December, and Saturday-Sunday; senior and children's discount. Free other months. Handicapped facilities. Closed New Year's, December 24, 25, 31. Information: 412-624-6000.

Reading

G **Daniel Boone Homestead,** 7 miles east on US 422 to Baumstown, then north on Boone Road. Daniel Boone was born here in 1734. The site encompasses 579 acres with house, barn, blacksmith shop, sawmill, camping, picnic area, and trails.

Open daily, except Mondays and major holidays. Fee. Senior citizen rate. Information: 215-582-4900.

Scranton

P **Scranton** is located in the anthracite coal region of eastern Pennsylvania, where many Irish labored in the mines and mills. This is the area where the Molly Maguires were organized to combat the brutal treatment by mine owners. Scranton was founded on the site of a Monsey Indian village and named for George and Seldom Scranton, who built five iron furnaces using anthracite coal instead of charcoal. Scranton had a major iron and steel industry until 1901, when mills moved closer to Lake Erie. In the late 40s, Scranton faced the loss of the anthracite coal mines which had been depleted. Today, Scranton, with its population of nearly 100,000 is an example of a city which has revived its economy through diversification.

P **Lackawanna Coal Mine Tour.** Descend 250 feet into the earth where you walk to two coal veins. The dark, damp, slippery, cold-conditions are very unpleasant, but superior to what the early Irish miners endured.

Open Wednesday-Sunday, May-October. Fee. Senior citizen discount. Information: 717-963-6463.

P **Pennsylvania Anthracite Heritage Museum.** The museum depicts the history and culture of the anthracite region.

Open daily, except some major holidays. Handicapped facilities. Fee. Senior citizen discount. Information: 1-717-963-4804.

℣ **Scranton Iron Furnaces,** 291 Cedar Avenue. Four of the original five iron furnaces employing Irish immigrants, built in the mid-19th century and used until 1901, have been partially restored. Visitor center and exhibits.

Open daily. Free. Information: 717-963-3208.

Swissvale

ℍℍ **Murphy's Taproom,** 1106 S. Braddock Avenue, stands out. The Pittsburgh area is blessed with some great Irish pubs; Murphy's Taproom isn't one of them. This may be the only time you'll wish the owner would charge more for the beer and spend the extra money to fix up the place. But then the Taproom might lose some of the unforgettable characters who populate the place, one of whom was standing on two bar stools screaming. He may have been trying to get the attention of the bartender or other patrons, but if so he failed. No one gave him more than a passing glance as they sipped their Guinness. On the other hand, perhaps one of the darts which sail perilously close to the bar had found a sensitive mark.

In the off chance you may care—and it is an adventure—the Taproom includes four brightly lit rooms: a rectangular bar, billiard room, and a dining room separated from a second sometimes-used bar by the dance floor. The Irish decor is a string of shamrock lights lopsidedly gracing the door leading from the front bar to the dining area. Live Irish music is played Sundays and Wednesdays.

Open daily. Information: 412-241-9462.

Tarentum

℣ **Tour-Ed Mine & Museum,** Exit 14 off PA 28, 1/4 mile north on Bull Creek Road. Take a trip many Allegheny County Irish American men and pre-teenage boys took in the 19th and early 20th centuries 250 feet down towards the center of the earth in old coal mine cars where you'll see mining equipment still in operating condition. A museum contains a company store, a miner's cabin, and souvenir shop.

Open daily 1 p.m.-4 p.m. Memorial Day-Labor Day. Fee. Children's discount. Information: 412-224-4720.

Villanova

ℍℐ𝔸 **Villanova University.** The Irish Studies Program of Villanova is embarking on an extensive study of the effect of the Irish Famine on America. Villanova was founded in 1843 by Augustinian priests. Their contribution in helping the Famine refugees and the Philadelphia Quakers will also be studied. The Falvey Memorial Library holds the Joseph McGarrity correspondence concerning American support for Irish independence during the years 1920-1948.

Rhode Island

Newport

℗ **The Elms,** Bellevue Avenue. Modeled after the 18th century Chateau d'Asnieres, near Paris, this mansion was built in 1901 for Pennsylvania coal tycoon Edward J. Berwind. This estate is interesting for various reasons. First, it houses many magnificent period pieces, some original furnishings; second, bronze and marble statuary, fountains, and gazebos decorate the landscaped grounds; and third, it makes a powerful statement when contrasted to the shanty towns and miners'cabins of the Irish Americans, whose men and children slaved in the Pennsylvania mines 12 hours a day to dig the coal that paid for this opulent life style.

Open daily 10 a.m.-5 p.m., April-October; Saturday-Sunday 10 a.m.- 4 p.m., other months. Fee. Children's discount. Information: 401-847-1000.

𝕋 **Hammersmith Farm,** Ocean Drive. Dating back to 1640, Hammersmith earned its greatest fame as a summer retreat for the president during the Kennedy administration. (A generation before, an

Irish Catholic would have been welcome at Newport only to clean-houses or care for children.) The 28-room mansion was built in 1887 by John Auchincloss, whose son, Hugh, married Janet Lee Bouvier, mother of Jacqueline Bouvier Kennedy Onassis. The reception following the wedding of Jacqueline to John F. Kennedy, future president of the United States, was held here. A gift shop is located in the former children's playhouse.

Guided tours daily mid-March to mid-November and early December. Fee. Information: 401-846-0420.

HH Irish-American Athletic Club, 624 Thames Street, challenges athletic skills with basketball. But the night we visited, weight lifting was the more popular exercise—raising and lowering pints of Guinness. Don't be put off by the "Club" designation. You can join the exclusive gathering in minutes. One buck bought us membership for a year to this good, solid, working class Irish-American pub.

Open daily. Information: 401-849-5190.

P Irish Servant Plaque, at the beginning of the Cliff Walk, 5 minutes from downtown, at the end of Memorial Boulevard. During the late 19th and early 20th century, the Irish servants met along the ocean side to celebrate the end of another 12-hour day working in the Newport mansions. A plaque marks the area. After viewing this spot, visit Rosecliff.

P Rosecliff, Bellevue Avenue. This 1902 mansion was inspired by Marie Antoinette's Grand Trianon at Versailles. Among its 70 rooms are a 40' x 80' ballroom, the largest ballroom in Newport, and Louis XV and Louis XVI antique furnishings. The grounds have garden sculptures, including the Court of Love, designed by Dublin-born artist Augustus Saint-Gaudens. Rosecliff gives you an opportunity to compare how the living quarters of employers and servants.

Open daily 9 a.m.-5 p.m., April-October. Fee. Children's discount. Information: 401-847-1000.

B Whitehall Museum House, Berkeley Avenue, 3 miles north of Newport, between Route 138 and Green End Avenue. Anglican bishop George Berkeley, born in Dublin in 1685, lived here from 1729 to 1731. A respected philosopher who contributed to the formation of today's metaphysical thought, he also had unusual ideas about architecture. During his short stay here, he created a false double-front door and a cruciform hall with stairway. Berkeley donated the house to Yale University and, through subsequent reincarnations, it has served as a tearoom, tavern, and living quarters for British soldiers during the Revolution.

Open daily 10 a.m.-5 p.m. July and August and by appointment during June and September. Fee. Information: 401-846-3116, July-August; 401-846-3790, September-June.

Saunderstown

P **Silas Casey Farm**, Boston Neck Road. Home to the Caseys since the 1700s, the 360-acre farm still functions much as it did centuries ago. The Casey family was prominent in military and political arenas. The farmhouse contains original furnishings, paintings, military and political memorabilia. The grounds, which were the site of military action during the Revolutionary War, are fenced in by miles of stone walls.

Open Sunday-Tuesday-Thursday afternoons 1-5, June-October. Fee. Information: 401-294-9182.

Providence

S **Sarah Helen Whitman Home** (The John Reynold's House), 88 Benefit Street.

> *Helen, thy beauty is to me*
> *Like those Nicean barks of yore,*
> *That gently, o'er a perfumed sea,*
> *The weary, wayworn wanderer bore*
> *To his own native shore.*

"To Helen," one of Poe's most admired poems, was written for Helen Whitman, a woman who had won Edgar's heart. Ms. Whitman kept the poem, but returned his heart. Poe and Helen were romantically entwined in the 1840s, but Helen lived here 1803-1878. The home is privately owned and not open to the public.

However, just down the street at 251 Benefit is the **Providence Athenaeum**, a magnificent Greek style library built of granite. In the deep, dark stacks of books, you may sense the ghosts of Edgar and Helen who were reported to have "courted" there. The Anthenaeum is open to the public.

Information: 401-831-7440.

South Carolina

Camden

HIA **Camden** was founded by Irish Quakers in the mid-18th century. First named Pine Tree Hill by the settlers, it was later changed to honor Lord Camden. The area was the site of many battles during the Revolutionary War. You can learn about the history of Camden byvisiting the **Camden Archives and Museum**, 1314 N. Broad Street. The museum displays artifacts, documents, and memorabilia recalling earlier days of Camden.

The museum is open Monday-Friday 9 a.m.-4:30 p.m.; closed holidays. Free. Information: 803-432-3242.HIA **Historic Camden**, 1 mile south on South Broad Street.This is the 92-acre archaeological site of the original Irish Quaker settlement with restored 18th- and 19th-century dwellings.

Open Tuesday-Saturday 10 a.m.-5 p.m., Sunday afternoon 1-5, June 1-Labor Day; closed Mondays and one hour earlier weekdays the rest of the year, except holidays. Fee. Student and children's discount. Information: 803-432-9841.

HIA **Quaker Cemetery**, Campbell Street, Southwest. The burial site was used as early as the 1700s.

Charleston

T **Calhoun Mansion**, 16 Meeting Street. Elaborate and opulent, this 1876 Victorian mansion was the home of Patrick Calhoun, grandson of Irish-American U.S. vice president John C. Calhoun. Cherry and oak woodwork, ornate plaster, and an entryway with 75-foot domed ceiling created one of the more elegant homes of old Charleston.

Open Wednesday-Sunday 10 a.m.-4 p.m., except major holidays. Fee. Information: 803-722-8205.

HIA **Hibernian Hall**, 105 Meeting Street. The Hibernian Society was founded in 1799 by eight Irishmen who wanted to help Irish emigres South Carolina following the unsuccessful rebellion against England of 1798. Through the years, the Society has alternated its leadership between Catholic and Protestant in order to maintain the focus of the organization on charitable, not theological, goals. The Hall, an example of Greek Revival style, is the setting for an annual St. Patrick's Day celebration.

T **John C. Calhoun Monument**, Marion Square, Calhoun Street between King and Meeting Streets. The Square contains a monument to John C. Calhoun, native South Carolinian, who served as vice president in 1924 under John Quincy Adams and again in 1928 with Andrew Jackson. Calhoun and Jackson were both Irish Americans. Calhoun resigned the vice presidency in order to serve as senator from South Carolina.

HH **Tommy Condon's**, 160 Church Street, management says, "Scarlett was Irish, so don't be surprised to find an authentic Irish Pub in Charleston." Guinness and Harp are on draught and Irish specialties include fresh seafood. The crowd at Condon's joins cheerfully in the sing-a-long entertainment weekends.

Open daily. Information: 803-577-3818.

Clemson

T **Clemson University**, US 76, 11 miles west of I-85 exit 19B.

Clemson University was established in 1889 on the former 1400-acre estate of U.S. Vice President and South Carolina Senator John C. Calhoun. The university was named for Thomas G. Clemson, Calhoun's son-in-law, who bequeathed the land for the purpose of establishing a "scientific college." On the campus is Fort Hill, a mansion set on 1,100 acres purchased by Calhoun during his first term as vice-president. It contains many original furnishings belonging to Calhoun and Clemson. Other buildings on the campus include a library, art gallery, and Hanover House, built in 1716 and moved to the campus in 1941.

Fort Hill is open Monday-Saturday morning from 10 a.m.-5 p.m. and Sunday afternoon 2-5; closed holidays. Donations.Information: 803-656-4789.

Columbia

T **Woodrow Wilson Boyhood Home**, 1705 Hampton Street. Built by his father, this house was where Wilson lived during his late teens. The Victorian home contains period furniture and memorabilia of Wilson's family and his career.

Closed Mondays, New Year's, Thanksgiving, and last two weeks in December. Fee. Information: 803-352-1770.

Sullivan's Island

HIA **Sullivan's Island** is named for Capt. Florence O'Sullivan of the *Carolina*, the first English ship to bring settlers here in 1670. It is the setting for Edgar Allan Poe's gory story "The Gold Bug." Sullivan's Island is where American forces won their first battle with the British during the Revolutionary War.

South Dakota

Deadwood

P **Deadwood** lives! With a population of around 2,000, it's lost something since the days when 25,000 prospectors poured in to get their share of the gold discovered in 1876. And it's not as wild as it was when Wild Bill Hickok was killed in a poker game. But Deadwood is alive with memories that haunt the Gulch and fascinate visitors. Gambling is still legal in Deadwood, but it's generally limited to a maximum bet of $5.

℗ **Broken Boot Gold Mine**, 1 mile west on US 14A. Broken Boot operated from 1878 until 1904. Guided underground tours provide an insight to the working life of Irish American and other gold miners.

Open daily 8 a.m.-6 p.m., May-August; 8 a.m.-4 p.m., September. Fee. Children's discount. Information: 605-578-9997.

𝕋 **Theodore Roosevelt Monument**, 4 1/2 miles west, off US 85, on Mount Roosevelt.

Keystone

𝕋 **Mount Rushmore National Memorial**, 2 miles southwest of Keystone via US 16A and 244. Heads of Theodore Roosevelt, Thomas Jefferson, George Washington, and Abraham Lincoln are carved into granite at the top of the mountain. Each face is 60-feet high. Each president represents a specific achievement. Roosevelt symbolizes the expansion of the country and the need for conservation; Washington, the founding of the nation; Jefferson, the Declaration of Independence and the Louisiana Purchase; and Lincoln, the preservation of a house undivided. The memorial can be viewed from the visitors center 1,400 feet below or from various observation areas for closer inspection. Visit the sculptor's studio to see the tools and models he used. Campsites and picnic areas are located in nearby parks and forests.

A strange story regarding the site was recently reported in the *Star*. A Japanese businessman offered to buy Mt. Rushmore for $18 million. He wanted to move it to his country. This probably should be filed with the Elvis Presley sightings.

The studio is open daily 9 a.m.-8 p.m., mid-May to mid-September; the memorial and visitors center are open daily from 8 a.m.-l0 p.m., mid-May to mid-September and 8 a.m.-5 p.m., the rest of the year. Free. Information: 605-574-2523.

Lead

℗ **Homestake Gold Mine.** George Hearst, father of newspaper publisher William Randolph Hearst, made the family fortune by buying an interest in this mine. (See San Simeon, California, to learn about the toys his money bought for his son.) Opened in 1876, the mine remains one of the most productive gold mines in the Western Hemisphere. Guided surface tours are available. (See Deadwood for an underground tour.)

Open Monday-Saturday 8 a.m.-5 p.m. and Sunday 10 a.m.-3 p.m., June-August; Monday-Friday 8:00 a.m.-4 p.m., May and September; closed major holidays. Fee. Senior and student discount. Information: 605-584-3110.

Wall

𝔇 **Wild West Historical Wax Museum**, Main Street. The museum contains life-size figures of Jesse James, Wild Bill Hickok, Wyatt Earp, Doc Holiday, and John Wayne.

Open daily 8 a.m.-9 p.m., May-October. Fee. Family and children's discount. Information: 605-279-2915.

Even if you're not into wax and Wayne, you'll find a visit to Wall, population 800, a trip back in time. Here you can still see many buildings built during the 19th century and find ruts made by the wagons which carried Irish prospectors westward on their quest for gold from the Black Hills.

Tennessee

Columbia

𝕋 **James K. Polk Ancestral Home**, 2 blocks off the square on US

43. The home contains memorabilia of the Polk family and original furnishings from the White House. Next door is Polk's sister's home which displays the First Lady's jewelry and exibits relating to Polk's political and Mexican War experiences.

Open Monday-Saturday 9 a.m.-5 p.m. and Sunday afternoon 1-5, April-October; closes one hour earlier weekdays, November-March; closed December 24-25. Fee. Senior and children's discount. Information: 615-388-2354.

Dover

G **Fort Donelson National Battlefield and Cemetery**, 1 mile west of Dover, US 79. "Truce?" suggested Confederate General Simon B. Buckner. "Unconditional and immediate surrender!" responded Gen. Ulysses S. Grant. That is what he received, and with it "unconditional surrender" Grant was able to pierce the heart of the Confederacy. Today, you'll find many well marked remains of the fort. The Dover Hotel, where Buckner surrendered to Grant is on the grounds.

The visitor center, museum, and hotel are open daily, except Christmas. Free. Information: 615-232-5706.

Greeneville

T **Andrew Johnson National Historic Site**, College and Depot Streets. The site includes the Andrew Johnson Homestead, the home where he lived from 1830-1851, the cemetery where he is buried, and a museum containing his tailor shop. The home is not open to the public.

Open daily 9 a.m.-5 p.m.; closed Christmas. Homestead fee; children free. Information: 615-638-3551.

G **Davy Crockett Birthplace Park**, 10 miles east of Greeneville off US 11E. The 62-acre park features a limestone slab marking Davy Crockett's birthplace and a replica of the log cabin in which he was born in 1786. You can camp (fee) and picnic. Free.

Information: 615-257-2061, or write Box 103-A, Limestone, 37681.

Jackson

> *Casey Jones, mounted to the cabin,*
> *Casey Jones, with his orders in his hand,*
> *Casey Jones, mounted to the cabin,*
> *And he took his farewell trip to the promised land.*

℗ **Casey Jones Home and Railroad Museum**, Junction I-40 and US 45, bypass exit 80A. Irish American Jones is reputed to have inspired the "Ballad of Casey Jones," in which Casey heroically stays at his engine in an effort to avoid a collision with another train. The epic is based on a true incident which occurred in April 1906. The museum contains an engine similar to the legendary "Old 382" of the poem. (See Owatonna, Minnesota)

Open Monday-Saturday 8 a.m.-8 p.m. and Sunday afternoon 1-5, June-September; Monday-Saturday 9 a.m.-5 p.m. and Sunday afternoon 1-5, October through May; closed Easter, Thanksgiving, and Christmas. Fee. Senior and children's discount. Information: 901-668-1222.

Knoxville

☙ In 1791, **Knoxville**, current population of 165,000, was named in honor of then Secretary of the Treasury Henry Knox.

Lawrenceburg

☙ **David Crockett State Park**, west of Lawrenceburg on US 64, is a 1,000-acre park located on the banks of Shoal Creek, where Crockett operated a gristmill. The museum is housed in the gristmill. The park has a pool, bathhouse, fishing, boating and rentals, trails, tennis, picnic area, playground, restaurant, and summer theater.

Fee. information: 615-762-9408

Maryville

☙ **Sam Houston Schoolhouse and Visitor Center**, 5 miles northeast of Maryville, off US 411. Sam Houston moved to Maryville in 1807 and taught in this log schoolhouse in 1812. Built in 1794, four years after the founding of Maryville, it has been restored to its original condition. The visitors center contains a museum of Sam Houston memorabilia.

Closed New Year's and Christmas. Free. Information: 615-983-15500, or contact Blount County Chamber of Commerce, 309 South Washington Street.

Morristown

G **Crockett Tavern and Museum**, 2002 Morningside. This is the six-room boyhood home of "King of the Wild Frontier" Davy Crockett, descendant of immigrants from County Donegal. The tavern is reproduced and furnished in authentic furniture of the 1790s, when Crockett's father operated the tavern, shrewdly located on the trail west.

Daily, mid-March to mid-November; closed Easter. Fee. Information: 615-587-9900.

Nashville

T **The Hermitage**, 12 miles east of Nashville off I-40 to Old Hickory exit. Seated on 625-acre homesite, Andrew Jackson's Hermitage was built in 1819, then rebuilt after a fire in 1834. An unusually beautiful home, all furniture is original. Jackson and his wife, Rachel, returned here after he left the presidency. They are buried on the grounds. The Andrew Jackson Center is a 28,000-square feet museum and visitor center. Opened in 1989, it contains many Jackson memorabilia. You can also see the film "Old Hickory."

Included in the price of admission is the Tulip Grove across the street, created by Mrs. Jackson's nephew, and the Hermitage Church, known locally as "Rachel's Church."

Open daily 9 a.m.-5 p.m., except 3rd week in January and major holidays. Fee. Senior and children's discount. Handicapped facilities, including wheelchairs. Information: 615-889-2941.

T **James K. Polk Tomb**, State Capitol, Charlotte Avenue. James K. Polk, 11th U.S. president, and Mrs. Polk are buried on the grounds of the state capitol building near the equestrian statue of Andrew Jackson, the 7th U.S. president. (Identical statues are located in Lafayette Park, Washington, D.C., and Jackson Square, New Orleans.) The State Capitol, work of William Strickland, so enchanted the architect that he obtained permission to be buried within its walls. The capitol is located next to the James K. Polk office building which houses the Tennessee State Museum.

Open weekdays 9 a.m.-4 p.m., Saturday 10 a.m.-5 p.m., and Sunday afternoon 1-5; closed major holidays. Free. Information: 615-741-2692.

T **Tennessee State Museum**, 505 Deadrick Street, in Tennessee Performing Arts Center. The museum contains a number of articles associated with Irish Americans, including: Andrew Jackson's inaugural top hat, Sam Houston's guitar, and Davy Crockett's gun. An operating gristmill is on the premises, along with many exhibits of Tennessee's history.

Information: 615-741-2692.

T **Tennessee Performing Arts Center**, 505 Deadrick Street, James K. Polk Office Building. The center contains three theaters named after Irish American presidents: the Andrew Jackson Hall used for concerts; the James K. Polk Theater for dramas, musicals, and dance; and the Andrew Johnson Theater, a theater-in-the-round.

Information: 615-741-2787.

Rutherford

G **Davy Crockett Cabin**, off Highway 45. "The King of the Wild Frontier" built a cabin on the nearby Obion River. Many of the logs from the original cabin were used to reconstruct it on the grounds of the Rutherford Elementary School. Among the artifacts in the cabin is a rocking chair built by Crockett. Crockett's mother is buried at the site.

Texas

Borger

G **Hutchinson County Museum**, 618 North Main Street, 37 miles north of Borger. In 1864, Kit Carson, 200 soldiers, and 75 scouts engaged 3,000 Southern Plains Indians in the biggest Plains Indian battle to occur in Texas. Ten years later, another battle occurred in this area when 28 buffalo hunters stood off 300 Comanches. The effect these encounters had on Borger were minimal when compared to the population boom in 1926, climbing from 15 to 35,000 in three months when oil was discovered. Today's population is nearly 16,000. The museum traces the lively history of the area.

Open Monday-Friday 9 a.m.-5 p.m., Saturday 11 a.m.-4:30 p.m., and Sunday afternoon 2-5; closed holidays. Free. Information: 806-273-6121.

Brackettville

G **Alamo Village Movie Location**, 7 miles north of Brackettville on FM 674. Although the movie, financed by Irish American star John Wayne, failed at the box office, the Alamo still stands, not just in San Antonio, but in Brackettville. The movie set for the 1959 disaster consists of a replica of the Alamo, a Western town, museums, and a cantina.

Open daily 9 a.m., varying closing times; closed December 21-26. Fee. Children's discount. Information: 512-563-2580.

Hillsboro

G **Confederate Research Center and Audie Murphy Gun Museum**, Hill College History complex. Audie Murphy was born in 1924 to a Irish sharecropping family in Texas. Between the ages of 18 and 21, he became the most highly decorated serviceman in the United States military. He received the Congressional Medal of Honor for single-handedly holding off a German force consisting of

250 men and 6 tanks. After the service, he went into films, where he starred in "To Hell and Back," based on an autobiography he wrote of his war experiences. He later played leading roles in a number of B-grade Westerns, married movie star Wanda Hendrix, and died in a small plane crash in 1971.

The museum contains Audie Murphy's uniform and guns. It also has a large number of Civil War weapons and documents. Seminars are held on U.S. history.

Open Monday-Friday, 8 a.m.-noon and 1 p.m.-4 p.m.; closed college holidays. Free. Information: 817-582-2555.

Dallas

T **John F, Kennedy Memorial Plaza**, Main, Commerce & Market Streets. A 30-foot monument to John F. Kennedy marks the area where Kennedy was assassinated, November 22, 1963. The president was killed while riding with his wife in an open car. Assassin Harvey Oswald was killed later that day by Jack Ruby. Considerable controversy continues to surround the events leading up to theassassination.

Open daily. Free.

T **The Sixth Floor**, 411 Elm Street. The bullets which killed President John F. Kennedy were shot from the sixth floor of the former Texas School Book Depository. Today, this floor is a memorial with displays relating to the life and death of Kennedy. Portable audiotapes may be rented to explain the exhibits.

Open Sunday-Friday and holidays 10 a.m.-5 p.m., Saturday 10 a.m.-6 p.m.; closed Christmas. Fee. Senior and children's discount. Information: 214-653-6666.

Galveston

S **The Ashbel Smith Building**, University of Texas Medical Center. The beginning of what now constitutes a medicalcomplex, the Ashbel Smith Building was designed by Irish-born architect Nicholas J. Clayton and built in the early 1890s.

Information: 409-772-2618.

ß Bishop's Palace, 1402 Broadway. Built in 1886, the former residence of Bishop Byrne is ornately embellished with marble, mosaics, stained glass, hand carvings, touches of gold, and objects d'art. It was designed by Irish-born architect Nicholas J. Clayton. It's an architectural masterpiece and/or overly indulgent, depending upon one's point of view, but not to be missed.

Open daily Memorial Day-Labor Day, and daily, except Tuesdays and major holidays, rest of year. Guided tours. Fee. Information: 409-762-2475.

Houston

ℍ Birraporetti's, Center on Gray, turns up about as often as Malone in the Irish pub world. And each of the multiplying Birraporettis has a "great Irish kitchen" to accompany "a heck of an Irish pub." Owned by Michael Horan, this combination reflects his heritage—Italian mother, Irish father. The pub at River Oaks Center is classic Irish, a spacious room dominated by a square bar in the center, surrounded by booths. Guinness is on draught, and it goes down nicely with Italian food, lunch or dinner.

I'm a bit biased, because I spent my best St. Patrick's Day to date in this pub. But success speaks for itself. In the last twenty years, Birraporetti's has opened five other establishments in Houston and spread to Dallas.

Birraporetti's is open seven days a week, but if you choose to go on St. Patrick's Day, go early. It's not unusual for an Irish pub to fill up quickly on the Day, but by 9:00 a.m.?

Information: 713-529-9191.
Other Houston locations:
500 Louisiana (713-224-9494).
8600 Westheimer (713-784-9990).
Greens Road (713-876-2000).
W. Oaks Mall (713-531-9797).
939 Katy Freeway (713-461-8555).

G Dick Dowling Memorial, Hermann Park. A group of Irish-

American Houstonians, with a minimum of men and ammunition, scored a Confederate victory during the Civil War—the Battle of Sabine Pass. When three Union gunboats off Port Arthur moved towards shore, the 42 men, mostly Galway-born, put the boats out of action. The fleet sailed away. Under the command of 25-year-old Lt. Richard W. Dowling, the men had accomplished their mission in 15 minutes with one cannon and a few shots.

Information: 713-523-5050, or write Greater Houston Convention and Visitors Council, 3300 Main Street.

HH **Griff's Shillelagh Inn** has several great things going for it. It's authentic Irish, it's sports oriented, and it's wild on St.Patrick's Day. Being Irish means it's informal, friendly, and fun. With its emphasis on sports, it attracts the professional athletes as well as the wannabes—ingredients for a lively crowd when the time is right. One of those times is St. Patrick's Day, and I remember vividly several of them spent in front of the pub, where a keg was set up; behind the pub, where another keg was set up; and inside, where people managed to dance, despite the crowds. Even more amazing was that my first year, one celebrated athlete streaked the place!

Open daily. Information: 713-528-9912.

Huntsville

G **Sam Houston Memorial Museum Complex**, 1836 Sam Houston Avenue. A 15-acre complex contains an exhibit hall, law office,and a museum with memorabilia of the life of Sam Houston. Also, on the grounds are two of Sam Houston's homes—Woodland, built in 1847, and the 1848 Steamboat House, where he was living at the time of his death in 1863 at the age of 70. Houston's ancestors emigrated from Ulster.

Open Tuesday-Sunday 9 a.m.-5 p.m., except New Year's, Thanksgiving, and December 24-25. Free. Information: 409-295-7824.

G **Sam Houston's Grave**, 3 blocks north of Huntsville Courthouse in Oakwood Cemetery. Sam Houston's large stone monument is inscribed with a testimonial from Andrew Jackson who served as his commander at one time: "The world will take care of Houston's fame."

Open daily, dawn until dusk.

Jefferson

HI, T **Excelsior House**, 211 Austin Street. Jefferson was a thriving, bustling city following the Civil War, in the days of river travel to St. Louis and New Orleans. But when the river travel declined in the 1870s, so did Jefferson. Texas's one time largest city has a population today of about 2,200. Among the many historical sites to be enjoyed is the Excelsior House, which hosted such historical giants as Irish Oscar Wilde, Irish American and future president Ulysses S. Grant, future president Rutherford B. Hayes, and Jay Gould, financier. Original furniture, hotel registry, and other documents are displayed. The hotel, still in operation, has been restored to its 1858 appearance.

Tours afternoons at 1 and 2. Fee. Information: 903-665-2513.

La Grange

B **Father Miguel Muldoon Monument**, on Highway 77, south of LaGrange. Father Muldoon was the son of an Irishman who emigrated to Spain and married a Spanish woman. Muldoon came to the new world where he was assigned to Stephen F. Austin's colony, located in what is now Texas. Many of Austin's colonists were Protestants who professed Catholicism in order to win land grants from the Mexican government. This gave birth to the expression "Muldoon Catholic," referring to skin-deep Catholics. Muldoon helped the colonists by acting as an intermediary with the Mexican government, at one point offering himself as a hostage to the Mexicans to avoid bloodshed. He supported Texas independence.

Nacogdoches

P **Old Stone Fort Museum**, Stephen F. Austin State University, Clark and Griffith Boulevards. Erected in 1779 and rebuilt in 1938,

The museum has exhibits and artifacts from early Texas, including the first newspaper typeset in Texas.

Open daily, except Monday; closed university holidays. Handicapped facilities. Free. Information: 713-569-2408.

San Antonio

Ⓖ **The Alamo**, east side of Alamo Plaza. The Alamo, built in 1718, is one of the most famous sites in American history. Defended by 189 soldiers, it withstood a 2-week siege by General Santa Ana and his 5,000 Mexican troops. On March 6, 1836, the Alamo fell, following the deaths of 1,600 Mexicans and all of the defenders. The only remains of the Alamo mission are the church and the Long Barrack Museum. Names and representations of the heroes of the Alamo can be seen on the Plaza. Children familiar with the Davy Crockett story will particularly enjoy the Alamo, since he was one of the many Irish American defenders.

Open Monday-Saturday 9-5:30 p.m., Sunday and holidays 10 a.m.-5:30 p.m.; closed New Year's and December 24-25. Free. Information: 512-225-1391.

ℋℋ **Durty Nellie's**, on the Riverwalk, in the Hilton Hotel. This pub should waft you back to Shannon on wings of nostalgia. A photo of Shannon's Durty Nellie's hangs on a wall, and we're told this pub was inspired by it. Having visited the original version almost as often as San Antonio's, I don't see much similarity. But, who cares, both can be great fun. In Texas you can enjoy your favorite Irish beer on draught, eat peanuts and drop them on the floor, and sing along with the piano player. It's always crowded evenings, and it's the place—the only place—in San Antonio to go on New Year's Eve if you want to welcome in the New Year with "It's a Great Day for the Irish."

Open daily. (210-222-1400).

Ⓖ **Fort Sam Houston**, between I-35 and Harry Wurzbach Highway. Building 123 houses the Fort Sam Houston Museum with personal memorabilia, weapons, and other exhibits and artifacts. The

3,300- acre fort was established in 1876 and houses Fifth Army headquarters and Brooke Army Medical Center.

Open Wednesday-Sunday 10 a.m.-4 p.m. Self-guided tour information available in the quadrangle daily from 8 a.m.-dusk. Information: 512-221-4232.

HIA Institute of Texas Cultures, 801 South Bowie Street. The Institute serves as a tribute to the Irish and 25 other identified ethnic groups which contributed to the development of Texas. One exhibit focuses on the history of the Irish in Texas. A multi-screen audio-video presentation is shown.

Open Tuesday-Sunday 9 a.m.-5 p.m.; closed Thanksgiving and Christmas. Donations. Information: 512-226-7651.

San Patricio

HIA San Patricio, 12 miles northeast of Corpus Christi at US 37 and 77. Being Catholic was generally a hindrance to the Irish in their quest for survival in America. When seeking land grants from Catholic Mexico, it was an asset. In the late 1820s, James McGloin and John McMullen, leading several hundred Irish-born Catholics, settled into Texas, initially calling their community San Patricio de Hibernia (St. Patrick of Ireland). On March 17, 1836, San Patricio became the first county recognized in the Republic of Texas.

The town, with a population of about 250, can no longer be found on many maps, but it's worth a visit, especially on St. Patrick's Day when you can tour a few of the original houses and the restored courthouse.

Information: 512-882-5603, Convention and Tourist Bureau, 1201 North Shoreline Drive, Box 2664, 78403.

Utah

Brigham City

P Golden Spike National Historic Site, off I-84 and I-15, 32 miles west of Brigham City. Blood, sweat, and tears of many Irish immigrants were required to fight off the Indians and lay the track which merged the Union Pacific and Central Pacific Railroads, May 10, 1869. Golden and silver spikes mark the spot, along with working, full-size replicas of the engines that met on the newly joined railroad tracks—the *Jupiter* and the *119*. As with much progress, this accomplishment had good and bad ramifications. The uniting of East and West brought an influx of people to the west, hastening the development of many of the Western states. It also brought more serious buffalo hunting and the depletion of the bison herds.

Every year, several celebrations are held commemorating the event. In June, the ceremony which was held in 1869, including the speeches, are repeated, and the second Saturday in August brings the railroaders Festival, highlighted by a spike driving contest. The last weekend of the year, the Railroader's Film Festival is held and the Winter Steam Demonstration. The engines are displayed daily.

The visitor center is open daily 8 a.m.-4:30 p.m. and until 6:00 p.m., Memorial Day-Labor Day. Handicapped facilities. Fee. Information: 801-471-2209.

Lehi

D **John Hutching's Museum of Natural History**, 685 North Center Street. Although there's some question as to where Butch Cassidy ended up, his sawed off shotgun is right here in Lehi, along with a gun collection used to crush the Mormon Rebellion of 1857. The museum houses Indian artifacts and a mineral collection.

Open Monday-Saturday 9:30 a.m. to 5:30 p.m.; closed holidays. Fee. Children's discount. Information: 801-768-8710.

Moab

D You've seen **Moab** many times. It's a popular location for the production of movies. Butch Cassidy and his Wild Bunch were among the many outlaws who roamed this area. There's a question whether Butch really had any Irish blood. It's likely that his real name was Parker. But there weren't many men or women who cared to argue the point.

Set at the foot of red cliffs, overlooking the Colorado River, Moab enjoys a mild climate throughout the year. Oil, potash, and movie production make this a thriving city, but the primary resource is tourism.

Vermont

Franklin

Fenian Monument, Eccles Hill. Located on the border between Franklin and Quebec stands a monument which marks the spot where in 1870 the Canadian militia clashed with invading Fenians. The Irish were making their second aborted effort in four years to take over Canadian territory and exchange it for Ireland's freedom from Britain. General Joseph O'Neill, reported the Plattsburgh, N.Y. *Press-Republican*, claimed 50,000 men and 80,000 rounds of ammunition at his disposal. The Canadians were getting nervous, but the only action they saw involved two tipsy Fenians and one horse. The horse was injured and the Fenians spent a couple of nights in jail.

On May 24, Queen Victoria's birthday, the Canadians marched to Eccles Hill where they encountered O'Neill and 500 of his men crossing the border. Fire was exchanged. O'Neill was about to make a strategic move when he was arrested by a U.S. marshall, shoved into a carriage, and returned to St. Albans and a jail cell. The second and final Fenian invasion ended with the loss of two Irishmen.

Killington

HH **McGrath's Irish Pub**, Route 4, is in the Inn at Long Trail, a setting which attracts hikers and skiers to the mountains of Killington. After you enjoy your Harp, Guinness, or Long Trail Ale in the pub, you may decide to spend the night in one of the fireplace suites.

Open daily. Information: 800-325-2540, 802-775-7181.

St. Albans

G **St. Albans** was the site where the Fenians, the Irish activist group, hatched the ill-fated plan to invade Canada and exchange it for England's revocation of the Treaty of Union. The Treaty was an attempt to incorporate Ireland into Britain.

T **Chester A. Arthur Historic Site,** 10 miles west via VT 36 to Fairfield, follow signs to unpaved road leading to site. The replica of 21st U.S. president Chester A. Arthur's second home islocated next door to the church where his father preached. His father William was born in Dreen, Cullybackey, County Antrim, where the ancestral home is now a national landmark. His mother may, also, have been from Antrim. The site includes an exhibit of Arthur's life and work.

Open Wednesday-Sunday, June to mid-October. Fee. Information: 802-828-3226.

Virginia

Abington

G Daniel Boone camped in the **Abington** area around 1760 and spent some sleepless nights when the wolves attacked his dogs. He named the site Wolf Hill. Boone returned to the area in later years when traveling west with his family. Today the chant of tobacco auctioneers has replaced the howl of wolves in Abington, as the town was renamed.

Alexandria

HH **Ireland's Own,** 132 North Royal Street, honors both Republicans and Democrats. It helps if you're Irish American and have been president of the United States. President Reagan's dinner service, used one St. Patrick's Day, is enshrined on a wall near a bust of JFK. This is a dark, authentic Irish pub with bar and several dining areas, including the patio in summer. Booths are named after Irish families.

Guinness and Harp are on draught, and the soda bread and stew are good reasons for repeat visits. The menu also lists corned beef and cabbage. Live Irish entertainment, offered nightly, has taken the form of music or comics. A few steps away is the Irish Walk, an Irish gift shop. Ireland's Own is very popular with locals and visitors to Old Town and just about anyone who appreciates an exceptional Irish pub.

Open daily. Information: 412-549-4535.

HH Murphy's, 713 King Street, is lively! At all times! Including Saturday afternoon. It's a cheerful, authentic Irish pub that invites you to while away an hour or two or three at the long bar or at a nearby table. Guinness and Harp are on tap along with Murphy's and Mooney's, the latter a private label named for owner Tom Mooney (See Washington, D.C., and Lima, Ohio.) Irish entertainment is presented seven nights a week. No cover. One of the better pubs in the metropolitan Washington area.

Open daily. Information: 703-548-1717.

Arlington

T, G Arlington National Cemetery. An eternal flame glows from the grave of John F. Kennedy, 35th president of the United States; excerpts from his inaugural address are at the gravesite. The grave of Robert F. Kennedy is located next to his brother's. RFK, U.S. senator and attorney general during the Kennedy administration, was assassinated while campaigning for the Democratic presidential nomination sought by the incumbent Lyndon B. Johnson. Admiral Perry and famed orator William Jennings Bryan are also interred here.

Arlington National Cemetery was established in 1864 on the confiscated estate of Confederate General Robert E. Lee and serves as the final resting place for more than 200,000 men and women, including U.S. president William Howard Taft.

Open daily. Tours available. Fee. Information: 703-692-0931.

Ashland

G **Scotchtown**, 11 miles northwest on VA 54, 671, and 685. Built in 1719, Scotchtown was the elegant home to Patrick Henry from 1771 to 1777 and the childhood home of Dolley Payne, later to become First Lady in the administration of James Madison, fourth U.S. president. It was rumored that Henry kept his mentally ill wife in the basement.

Open Tuesday-Saturday 10 a.m.-4 p.m. and Sunday afternoon 1:30-4:30 April-October, other times by appointment. Fee. Children's discount. Information: 804-227-3500.

Brookneal

G **Patrick Henry National Memorial**, 5 miles east on VA 600. Red Hill is the final home and resting place of Irish-American Patrick Henry. The reconstructed home contains family furnishings and memorabilia. Also on the site are Henry's grave and original law office, kitchen, stable, and cook's cabin. His gravestone is inscribed: *His life is his best epitaph. That and his 17 children.*

Open daily 9 a.m.-5 p.m., April-October and 9 a.m.-4 p.m. other months. Fee. Senior and children's discount. Information: 804-376-2044.

Brush Mountain

G **Audie Murphy Monument**, Giles County. Audie Murphy, most decorated hero of World War II, died on May 28, 1971, when his plane crashed into Brush Mountain. The Veterans of Foreign Wars erected a monument in his honor at the crash site. Christiansburg.

Fredericksburg

G **Fredericksburg and Spotsylvania National Military Park,**The park has 6,000 acres, including four Civil War battlefields: Fredericksburg, Chancellorsville, Wilderness, and Spotsylvania

Court House. The Irish Brigade fought at Fredericksburg and Chancellorsville.

G **Fredericksburg Battlefield.** For three weeks, the Confederate Army had prepared for this battle, fortifying their positions while the Union commander, Gen. Ambrose Burnside, watched. Finally, he decided to attack and ordered the Irish Brigade on a known suicide assault on Marye's Heights. Even the embalmers knew what was to happen, and with an aggressive, if insensitive sales approach, they offered their services to themen as they marched by. The men were headed for a stone wall nearthe Sunken Road. As they moved closer to their target, their leader, Irish-born Gen. Thomas Francis Meagher, ordered them to place sprigs of boxwood in their caps to remind them of their duty to Ireland and to their new homeland.

The Confederate troops were lined four deep beyond the wall."Irish Brigade, advance" were the words which led most of the men to their deaths as wave after wave moved forward with courage, determination, and knowledge of the fate that lay ahead. It is reported that after the battle was lost, burial parties found that the bodies closest to the wall bore boxwood sprigs in their caps. The wall can be seen behind the visitor center.

Of the 1,300 Irish sent into battle, fewer than 300 survived. The courage of the Irish was admired even by the enemy. Confederate general George Pickett said, "We forgot they were fighting us and cheer after cheer" arose from the Confederate ranks as the brigade made repeated, futile, and fatal efforts to break through.

G **Fredericksburg Battlefield Visitor Center,** Lafayette Boulevard (US 1) and Sunken Road. Photographs by the War's most celebrated photographer, Matthew Brady, son of Irish immigrants, are displayed. You can also see a film and exhibits on the battle and the Civil War. Tours of the battlefield are offered in the summer.

Open daily, except New Year's and Christmas. Hours vary seasonally. Free. Information: 703-373-6122.

G **Chancellorsville Battlefield.** Robert E. Lee's greatest military success, pitted 60,000 Confederate soldiers against 130,000 Union troops. Lee made a number of brilliant moves which resulted in the near devastation of the Northern forces, until only one battery and the Irish Brigade remained. When it was time for the men to withdraw, the 116th Pennsylvania Infantry of the Irish Brigade was ordered to rescue the weapons from the field under the continuing fire of the Confederacy. The Irish Brigade survivors of Chancellorsville recaptured this land a year later during the Wilderness Campaign.

The visitor center offers exhibits and a film. Open daily 8:30 a.m.-6:30 p.m., mid-June to Labor Day; 9 a.m.-5 p.m., therest of the year; closed New Year's Day and Christmas. Information: 703-373-4461.

HH **The Irish Brigade,** 1005 Princess Anne Street, is named for the famed Civil War Irish Brigade. It consists of a restaurant, club house, and pub. The restaurant, in wood and green, has a small bar and two informal dining areas. The high wood partitions separating the booths have cut out shamrocks. The small upstairs club house is filled with sports memorabilia and loaded with electronic sports games. Four TVs with satellite offer national and international sports events. The pub is very large,with stage and bar.

Food is good and moderately priced. Irish specialties include soda bread, stew, fish, steak, and Irish cream mousse cake served for lunch and dinner. Guinness and Harp are on draught, but you may want to try the Irish Brigade private label dry beer. Music, sometimes Irish, is played in the pub Thursday-Saturday evenings 9:45-1:15 a.m. A good cross-section of Fredericksburg is attracted to this unusual complex, at least in part, because it has one of the friendliest staffs in the Irish business.

Open daily: restaurant, 11 a.m.-10 p.m; pub, club, 5 p.m.-1:30 a.m. Information: 703-371-9413.

G **The Smythe's Cottage and Tavern,** 303 Fauquier Street. No, you're not standing on your head. The Irish-American general and 18th president of the United States is! This restaurant-bar has a picture of Grant hanging upside down. Seems that the general was not very nice to one of the owner's ancestors in years gone by.

Information: 703-373-1645.

Great Falls

𝕳𝕳 **The Old Brogue,** 760 Walker Road, brings in a mixture of blue and white collar workers for food, drink, and entertainment. Irish specialties include Irish salmon and mackerel and corned beef and cabbage. The food is good, service friendly, and prices right. Guinness and Harp are on tap and Happy Hour, 4 p.m.-7 p.m., means cheapie drafts. Live music is played Monday-Saturday, some Irish; special Irish performances are given occasional Sundays. Open mike Monday.

Open daily. Information: 703-759-3309.

Lexington

𝕲 **Stonewall Jackson House,** 8 East Washington Street. "...it was genuine happiness to him to have a home of his own," said hiswife, Mary Anna Jackson. And it was the only home Thomas Jonathan Jackson was ever to own, because he died at the age of 39 from wounds sustained at Chancellorsville. A descendant of Issac Jackson of Antrim, he was given the name he is known by today for his stand at the First Manassas battle.

A modest brick town house, built in 1801, it has a mid-19th century stone addition in the rear. Jackson and his wife moved here in 1859 and stayed until he went to war in 1961. Restored in 1979, it is furnished with many of Jackson's possessions. Guided tours are offered of the house and restored garden. A museum shop specializes in books, prints, and Victoriana.

Open Monday-Saturday 9 a.m.-5 p.m., Sunday afternoon 1-5; open until 6 p.m., June-August. Fee. Information: 703-463-2552.

McLean

𝕳𝕳 **McKeever's Pub,** Old Dominion Road, McLean Square,

proves good things come in small packages. It's an intimate bar with large, comfortable, and private booths. It has an assortment of intriguing artifacts, including a gravity defying Christmas tree hanging upside down from the ceiling, and a curious juxtaposition of curly haired moppet Shirley Temple and nude Marilyn Monroe. Guinness and Harp on draught and a good selection of better-than-average food served by a staff who likes people. The management says they keep busy with a crowd made up of construction workers and professionals.

Open Monday-Thursday, 11 a.m.-12 a.m.; Friday, 11 a.m.-1 a.m.; Saturday, 12 p.m.-12 a.m.; closed Sunday. Information: 703-790-9453.

Manassas

ℋℋ **Brady's** is more modern than traditional, but loaded with green, light wood, and lots of light pouring through the windows. The walls are covered with an assortment of objects and art.

Guinness, Harp, and ten other beers are on draught. You can get them at special prices during Happy Hour, Monday-Friday, 4 p.m.-7 p.m. Half price appetizers on Wednesday. Order lunch, dinner, or pub grub. Good food, but as close as you'll get to Irish is a corned beef sandwich, unless you count the green guacamole served with the Tex-Mex dinners.

Music, some Irish, Thursday-Saturday; electronic darts; free pizza during Monday night football on a 50" TV screen; and an annual ugly bartender contest. Brady's is a pleasant place to spend a little time. Family atmosphere.

Open daily. 8971 Center Street (703-369-1469).

☾ **Manassas National Battlefield Park.** When Col. Michael Corcoran, 69th New York State Militia, noted that the regiment's green flag was drawing the fire of the Confederate soldiers at Bull Run, he told the standard bearer to lower it. "I'll never lower it," responded the soldier whose words were cut off by a Confederate bullet. This incident is reported by Stephen Wright in *The Irish Brigade*. The flag was raised by another. And another as the regiment was ordered to try to achieve an objective which other units had failed to accomplish. When Capt. Thomas Francis Meagher's horse was shot from under him, Meagher, raising the flag shouted, "Boys! Look at the flag. Remember Ireland and Fontenoy." The Regiment was successful in taking the hill, but at a cost of nearly 200 of their men. The gallantry of the regiment is particularly impressive when we consider the fact that their enlistment period had ended the day before the first Battle of Bull Run. They chose to remain and fight.

Open 8:30 a.m.-dusk. See exhibits and a three dimensional map of the battlefield at the Visitor Center, VA 234 between I-66 and US 29. Open daily 8:30 a.m.-6 p.m., mid-June through September 1; until 5 p.m. the remainder of the year; closed Christmas. Fee. Senior, children's, and family discount. Information: 703-361-1865.

Marion

G **Hungry Mother State Park**, 3 miles north on VA 16. The park, containing over 2,180 acres, was named in memory of an Irish-American woman who starved to death when she attempted to escape with her infant child from the Indians. The child, it was said, crawled into town and alerted the townspeople, but they arrived too late to help Molly. One site in the park is labeled Molly's Knob.

The park offers nearly all recreational facilities, including horseback riding, boating, hiking, camping for tents and trailers, and swimming. Cabins available May-September. Fee. General information: 804-786-4484; cabin rental, 804-490-3939.

Orange

T **James Madison Museum**, 129 Caroline Street. The maternal grandparents of Madison, 4th president of the United States, emigrated from County Clare, Ireland. The museum houses exhibits and artifacts associated with Madison's life and work.

Open Monday-Friday 10 a.m.-5 p.m. and Saturday-Sunday afternoon 1-5, March through November; Monday-Friday 10 a.m.-4 p.m. other months; closed major holidays. Fee. Senior and children's discount. Information: 703-672-1776.

T **Montpelier,** 4 miles from Orange on VA 201. The home was begun by James Madison's grandfather, added to by his father, and remodeled by William DuPont. In 1874, following his presidency, Madison and his wife, Dolley Payne Todd, returned to the 2,700-acre plantation, where James remained until his death. The Madisons are buried on the grounds.

Montpelier was the scene of many social affairs. Dolley maintained her reputation as a charming and inventive hostess, receiving many comments on her dessert specialties—brown bread and Parmesan cheese ice cream.

William DuPont purchased the estate in 1901 and added wings to the sides of the home. The grounds include elaborate gardens and a race track added by daughter Marion DuPont Scott, who was married briefly to the movie actor Randolph Scott. Upon her death in 1983, the property was deeded to the National Trust for Historic Preservation.

Montpelier is schizophrenic—part DuPont, part Madison. It is sparsely furnished. Madison had sold much of the original pieces to help cover gambling debts incurred by his step-son. Extensive archeological studies are in progress, and many parts of the mansion cannot be viewed.

Open daily 10 a.m.-5 p.m. Closed major holidays. Fee. Information: 703-672-2728.

Richmond

G **Capitol Square,** between 9th and Governor Streets and Capitol and Bank Streets. Irish Americans Patrick Henry and Hunter McGuire, Confederate surgeon, are represented among the statues of Virginians surrounding the renowned equestrian statue of George Washington sculpted by Thomas Crawford. The visitor center is located at the old bell tower.

Open Monday-Friday 8:15 a.m.-5 p.m. and Saturday-Sunday

from 9:30 a.m.-4:30 p.m., May through October; closed weekends other months. Free. Information: 804-786-4484.

S **Edgar Allan Poe Museum**, 1914 East Main Street. Edgar Allan Poe worked for many years in the Richmond area. The museum consists of 5 buildings, one of which—the Old Stone House—is the oldest building in Richmond, erected about 1737. Housed in the museum are Poe mementos and a slide show. Among the many places Poe lived, his 13 years here were the longest spent in one place. See the drawings based on Poe's "The Raven."

Open Tuesday-Saturday 10 a.m.-4 p.m., Sunday and Monday afternoons 1:30-4; closed Christmas. Fee. Senior and children's discount. Information: 804-648-5523.

G **St. John's Episcopal Church**, 24th and Broad Streets. "Give me liberty, or give me death." These words were spoken by Irish-American Patrick Henry in St. John's at the climax of his impassioned plea for independence for the colonies from Great Britain. Elizabeth Arnold Poe, mother of Edgar Allan, and George Wythe, signer of the Declaration of Independence, are buried here. Re-enactment of the Second Virginia Convention is performed at 2 p.m. Sunday, the last weekend in May and the first weekend in September.

Open daily, except New Year's, Thanksgiving, and December 24-31. Donations. Information: 804-648-5015.

St. John's is set among 70 restored ante-bellum homes, which are sometimes open to the public. Donations. Information: 804-643-7407.

Staunton

B **Augusta Stone Church**, 7 miles north on US 11, Ft. Defiance. Established by Irish Presbyterians in 1740, the church was completed in 1749. Its design enabled it to be used both as a church and as a fort. It served in this latter capacity during Indian raids. The oldest Presbyterian church in Virginia, it contains a museum displaying early church artifacts.

Open by appointment. Information: 703-248-2634.

HI **Museum of American Frontier Culture,** 1 mile west on VA 644, exit 57, has working re-creations of 18th century farms of Northern Ireland, England, Germany, and Appalachia. Each farm raises livestock and crops typical of the 1700s in the Shenandoah Valley. The Irish farm was developed with historic buildings imported from Ulster and reconstructed by Irish tradesmen.

Open daily, except New Year's and Christmas. Handicapped facilities. Fee. Senior citizen discount. Information: 703-332-7850.

T **Woodrow Wilson Birthplace,** 24 North Coalter Street off US 11. Built in 1846, the restored Greek Revival mansion has many original furnishings and Wilson family mementos. You can see a film, a permanent exhibit of his life, and Wilson's 1919 Pierce-Arrow limousine.

Closed Sundays in January and February, New Year's, Thanksgiving, and Christmas. Fee. Senior citizen discount. Information: 703-885-0897.

Steeles Tavern

P **Walnut Grove,** exit 205 off I-81, 1 mile east on 606. Irish American Cyrus McCormick and his father invented and marketed the first grain reaper at the McCormick farm. An original reaper is housed in the blacksmith shop, now a museum.

Open daily 9 a.m.-5 p.m. Free. Information: 703-377-2255.

Tazewell

G **Burke's Garden,** 15 miles from Tazewell via Rt. 623 east and south. In these parts, the tale is told that James Burke, who discovered the valley in 1740, left potato peelings which grew into potatoes and fed the Irish surveyors who came to the area in the late 1740s. Today Burke's Garden, as the Irish named it in honor of its founder, is part of the Virginia Scenic Byway.

Williamsburg

Settled in 1633, **Williamsburg** overflows with colonial history. It was the capital of Virginia from 1699 to 1780. Irish American Patrick Henry made his famous Stamp Act speech here: "If this be treason, make the most of it!" The First and Second Continental Congresses met here, and the Second proposed independence from Britain—a sentiment the Irish could empathize with. After the seat of power moved to Richmond, things settled down, and it looked like Williamsburg had seen its best days. But, in 1926, John D. Rockefeller and W.A.R. Goodwin, rector of Bruton Parish Church, saw the potential of Williamsburg. Through their efforts, abetted by Rockefeller's money, Williamsburg was re-awakened and has become a popular historical attraction for visitors from all over the world.

T Among the numerous sites to enjoy is the **Governor's Palace and Gardens** at the north end of the Palace Green. Erected in 1720, the palace housed the royal governors and the first and second governors of Virginia, Patrick Henry and Thomas Jefferson. The original structure was destroyed by fire in the late 18th century, but has been reconstructed. Set in 10 acres of gardens, it was considered one of the most beautiful of the colonial mansions. The **Capitol**, east end of Duke of Gloucester Street. Built in 1705 and rebuilt in 1751 following a fire, the capitol has been restored to its original appearance and decorated with period furniture. It contains a copy of Patrick Henry's Stamp Act Resolves, approved by the House in 1765, and rare portraits of James Madison, George Washington, Thomas Jefferson, King William, and Queen Mary. The capitol hosts entertainment throughout the year.

T, HH **Raleigh Tavern**, Duke of Gloucester Street. Irish American Patrick Henry, George Washington, and Thomas Jefferson are among the early colonists who met here to socialize, philosophize, and politicize. It is here, in the early 1770s, that his officers honored Col. Patrick Henry with a farewell dinner, and where, in 1776, Phi Beta Kappa was conceived. The tavern was rebuilt after being destroyed by fire in 1859.

The visitor center is open daily 8:30 a.m.-8 p.m., March- December; 9 a.m.-5 p.m. other months. Information: 800-447-9679, or write Colonial Williamsburg Foundation, Box C, 23187 for the various ticket prices, hours, and information for persons with ambulatory limitations.

Washington

Fort Vancouver

℗ **Fort Vancouver National Historic Site**, 612 East Reserve Street. Dr. John McLoughlin directed the building of the Fort in 1825 for the Hudson Bay Company. The Company wanted to retain and expand its control over the fur-trading area. The Site contains seven reconstructed buildings, including a bakery, Indian trade store, the Chief Factor's residence, and formal gardens, located in their original place and surrounded by a 15-foot-high stockade. You can see a film in the visitors center.

Open daily 9 a.m.-5 p.m., Memorial Day-Labor Day; 8 a.m.-4 p.m., the rest of the year; closed Thanksgiving and Christmas. Fee. Information: 206-696-7655.

Seattle

ℋℋ **Kell's Irish Restaurant and Pub**, 1916 Post Alley, is the Irish pub of choice in Seattle. It earns that position through its authentic Irish ambiance which shows up in its friendliness, food, drink, and decor. The owner is Joe Kell. This pub and the one he owns in Portland are a family affair. They keep the Guinness at a perfect 55 degrees and come up with such delectables as Irish stew, which I found particularly enjoyable one cold November evening, and lamb chops. When you visit, ask Joe, who's owned the pub since 1984, about Bloomsday, commemorating Ireland's Easter rebellion of 1916.

Open Wednesday-Saturday 8 a.m.-2 a.m. Cover Friday-Saturday. Information: 207-728-1916.

Spokane

S Crosby Library, East 502 Boone Avenue, Crosby Library, Gonzaga University. Singer-actor Bing Crosby is memoralized by his alma mater with a library containing a collection of his records and memorabilia, including Crosby's Academy Award for "Going My Way." Open Monday-Thursday 8 a.m.-midnight, Friday 8 a.m.- 5 p.m., Saturday 9 a.m.-8 p.m., and Sunday 1 p.m.-8 p.m., September-April; Monday-Friday 9 a.m.-5 p.m., the rest of the year. Free. Some handicapped facilities. Information: 509-328-4220.

West Virginia

Dingess

H1 Ogham Stone, Laurel Lake Park. Stone carvings have been found in West Virginia which may date back to the 5th century. Archaeologist Robert Pyle and language expert Barry Fell believe that they represent Ireland's first written language, Ogham (pronounced *ahm*). Fell has stated that the "West Virginia Ogham texts are the oldest Ogham inscriptions recorded anywhere in the world." Fell hypothesizes that the writers may have been Irish missionaries who followed St. Brendan's visit to the new world.

Philippi

G Philippi Covered Bridge and Museum Col. B. F. Kelley led Union forces in a surprise attack on the Confederate troops on June 3, 1863. It was the first battle of the Civil War, and it was a victory for the North. A covered bridge, used by both sides, is still in use, and the Barbour Historical Museum is near the bridge.

Information: 304-457-4846.

Wisconsin

Appleton

D **Joe McCarthy Bust**, County Courthouse. The bust of U.S. Senator Joe McCarthy is on display in the county courthouse at Appleton. McCarthy, who was born in Appleton, became controversial during the 1950s, when his anti-communist activities led to the blacklisting of many Hollywood personalities, often with no actual ties to the communist movement. Many of Appleton's citizens are happier to claim Harry Houdini, the celebrated magician.

Cedarburg

HIA **Cedarburg**, 20 miles north of Milwaukee on WI 57, was founded in the early 19th century by Irish and German immigrants who, along with the help of limestone and water power of Cedar Creek, provided the vigor to develop a thriving economy. They built dams and mills and used the limestone to construct homes, stores, and churches, many still being used. By the mid-19th century, the trail through Cedarburg, followed by Indians traveling between Green Bay and Milwaukee, was no longer used. The town was a bustling center of activity—industry, quarrying, and milling. Most of the action was in an area called New Dublin, later renamed Hamilton, where you can visit many of the buildings erected in the early days of Cedarburg, including the 1855 mill which sheltered families during the 1862 Great Indian Scare.

While you're in the area, you should drive north about 3 miles on 143 and see one of the few surviving covered bridges.

Information: 414-377-9620; for guided tours, 414-375-1426.

Milwaukee

S **The Milwaukee Art Museum**, Lakefront War Memorial Center, 750 Lincoln Memorial Drive. The museum shows the work of American and European artists from the 19th and 20th centuries.

Among them are Georgia O'Keeffe and Andy Warhol, Picasso, and Miro.

Open Tuesday-Wednesday-Friday-Saturday 10 a.m.-5 p.m., Thursday noon-9 p.m., and Sunday noon-5; closed Monday, New Year's, Thanksgiving, and Christmas. Fee. Senior and children's discount. Free to Milwaukee County residents on Wednesday and Saturday.

Information: 414-271-9508.

Wyoming

Cody

G **Cody**, population 8,000, was founded by William "Buffalo Bill" Cody in 1898. The area is home to many dude- and working ranches. Irish-American Buffalo Bill is remembered by many buildings and a February birthday ball.

G **Buffalo Bill Statue**, west end of Sheridan Avenue. The statue depicts a young Bill Cody on Smoky, his horse.

G **Buffalo Bill Historical Center**, US 14/16/20 at 720 Sheridan Avenue, has 150,000 square feet devoted to art and artifacts of Buffalo Bill and his world of the Wild West.

Open daily, hours vary with season. Fee. Senior and student discount. Information: 307-587-4771.

G **Buffalo Bill Museum**, Buffalo Bill Historical Center (see above). Memorabilia of Buffalo Bill and wife Annie Oakley.

G **Irma Hotel**, 12th and Sheridan Avenue. A $100,000 Buffalo Bill bar is the centerpiece of the hotel. It was a gift to Cody from Queen Victoria in appreciation of Buffalo Bill's Wild West Show. The hotel has served as a gathering spot for locals over the past 80 years.

D **Old Trail Town**, 1 mile west on US 14/16/20. The original site of Cody features reconstructed historic buildings, including a log cabin used by Butch Cassidy, the Sundance Kid, and other members of his Wild Bunch gang. Also at this site is the grave of John "Jeremiah" Johnson and the Museum of the Old West, containing artifacts from prehistoric days and relics of the Plains Indians.

Open daily 8 a.m.-8 p.m., late May through mid-September. Fee. Children's discount. Information: 307-587-5302.

Thermopolis

D **Hot Springs Historical Museum**, 700 Broadway. Among the rooms is a bar which was frequented by Butch Cassidy and his gang. Made of cherrywood, it is fun to consider what devious plans were concocted in this setting. The Montpelier bank robbery? The museum also contains a restored country school, Indian artifacts, and exhibits.

Open Monday-Saturday 8 a.m.-6 p.m., and Sunday afternoon 1-5, June through August; closes 4 p.m. weekdays other months. Fee. Senior and children's discount. Information: 307-864-5183.

G **The Paul Stock Center**, 836 Sheridan Avenue. The center is a replica of Buffalo Bill's T.E. Ranch, which was on the Shoshone River. The Cody Chamber of Commerce is located here.

Information: 307-587-2297, or write Cody Country Chamber of Commerce, PO Box 2777, 836 Sheridan Avenue.

G **Pahaska Tepee,** east entrance to Yellowstone National Park. The tepee was Buffalo Bill's first hunting lodge.

SLÁINTE! HEALTH!
May the wind be always at your back.
The sun shine warm upon your face,
The rain fall soft upon your fields,
And until we meet again,
May God hold you in the hollow of His hand.

An Irish proverb

APPENDICES

And More Irish Pubs
Alabama

Mobile
Callaghan Irish Social Club
916 Charleston
205-433-9374

Arizona

Tucson
Harp and Shamrock
7008 E. Golf Links Rd.
602-790-9439
Open daily. Good, solid, working class neighborhood pub.

California

Los Angeles
Barragan's Irish Mexican Cafe
827 W. Glenoaks
818-240-3129 or -245-3287

Newport Beach
Muldoon's Irish Pub & Restaurant
202 Newport Center Drive
714-640-4110
Open Monday-Saturday
Great Irish stew and shepherd's pie

San Diego
Dublin Pub
5821 Mission Gorge Road
619-280-4698

The Limerick Room
1108 Broadway
619-274-5523

McP's Irish Pub and Grill
1107 Orange Avenue, Coronado
619-435-5280
Live entertainment nightly.

Rosie O'Grady's
3402 Adams Avenue
310-284-7666

San Jose
Finn McCool's
10905 North Wolfe Road
408-253-7111

Stanley's Bar & Grill
2739 S. Winchester Boulevard Campbel
619-378-6484

Santa Monica
Irish Rover
3012 Santa Monica Boulevard
310-828-3960

McGinty's Irish Pub
2615 Wilshire Boulevard
310-453-6220 or -828-9839

Ye Olde King's Head
116 Santa Monica Blvd.
310-451-1402
Open daily.
Is and isn't Irish, is and isn't English; nice combo.

San Francisco

Black Rose
335 Jones
415-441-3585

The Blarney Stone
Geary & 21st Avenue
415-386-2852

Ireland's 32
3920 Geary Boulevard
415-386-6173
Open daily.
For those interested in conversation rather than elegance.

Plough and the Stars
116 Clement Street
415-751-1122
Open daily. Many Irish nationalists.

Toal's Irish Pub
154 9th Street
415-863-7386

South Lake Tahoe
McP's Irish Pub and Grill
4090 Lake Tahoe Boulevard
916-542-4435
Irish specialties including Irish mulligan stew and
corned beef and cabbage.

Colorado

Denver
Shamrock Bar
54 S. Broadway
305-722-2934

Connecticut

Stamford

Shamrock Restaurant
280 Shippan Avenue
203-348-9003

District of Columbia

Emerald Isle
633 Pennsylvania Avenue, SE
202-544-4753
Open daily

Martin's
1304 Wisconsin Avenue, NW
202-338-6144
Calmer than most Irish pubs

Nanny O'Brien's
3319 Connecticut Avenue, NW
202-686-9189
Open daily.

Florida

Ft. Lauderdale

Gallagher's Pub
6234 North Federal Highway
305-491-9784

Ireland's Inn Restaurant
2220 N. Atlantic Boulevard
305-564-2331
Open daily.

Kissimmee

Nolan's Irish Pub
5491 West 192 (Fortune Park)
407-396-8118
Live entertainment

Orlando

Mulvaney's Irish Pub
27 W. Church Street
407-872-3296
Open Monday-Saturday, 11 a.m. - 2 a.m., Sunday 2 p.m.-2 a.m.
Music and entertainment

Mulvaney's Irish Pub
7220 International Drive
407-352-7031
Open Monday-Sunday, 4 p.m.-2 a.m.

Ireland's Inn Restaurant
2220 N. Atlantic Boulevard
305-564-2331
Open daily.

Orlando

Mulvaney's Irish Pub
27 W. Church Street
305-872-3296

St. Petersburg Beach

Harp & Thistle
650 Corey Avenue
813-360-4104
Live Irish music Wednesday-Saturday

Tampa

Irish Pub, The
1721 Seventh Avenue
813-248-2099
Open Monday-Friday, 11:30 a.m. - 3 a.m.,
Saturday-Sunday 12:30 p.m. - 3 a.m.

Georgia

Savannah

Kevin Barry's Pub
117 West River Street
912-233-9626

Restaurant; live Irish music Wednesday-Sunday

Illinois

Chicago

Coogan's Riverside Saloon
180 North Wacker Drive
312-444-1134

Cork and Kerry Pub
10614 South Western Avenue, Beverly
312-445-2675

Dubliner
10910 South Western Avenue
312-238-0784

Dublin's Pub
1030 North State
312-266-6340

✳ Emerald Isle
6686 North New Highway
312-775-2848
Live folk and rock.

Erin's Glen Pub
2434 West Montrose Avenue
312-478-3714

Fitzgeralds's
6615 Roosevelt Road, Berwyn
708-788-2118

Fox's Pub
9240 South Cicero, Oak Lawn
708-499-2233

Glascott's
2158 North Halsted
312-281-1205
Young crowd, 40s bar.

Harp and Shamrock Club
1641 West Fullerton
312-248-0123
Attracts police and bagpipers.

Harrington's Pub
2816 North Halsted
312-248-5933

Innisfree Inn
6800 West Archer
312-229-1199
Irish from here and abroad.

Irish Eyes
2519 North Lincoln
312-348-8548
Irish music Friday/Saturday; cover.

Irish Village
6215 West Diversey
312-237-7555
Open Tuesday-Sunday; full menu and entertainment nightly.

Kitty O'Shea's
720 South Michigan Avenue, Chicago Hilton
312-922-4400
Live music nightly.

Molly Malone's
9908 Southwest Highway, Oak Lawn
708-423-8200
Blue collar Irish American patrons.

Reilly's Daughter's Pub
4010 West 111th Street, Oak Lawn
708-423-1188
Open Monday-Saturday

Remember When
1237 South State Street
312-461-9788
Popular with police—off duty.

Shamrock Club
210 West Kinzie
312-321-9314

Evanston
Tommy Nevin's
1450 Sherman, Evanston
708-869-0450

Indiana

Indianapolis
Kelly's Pub Too
5341 W. 10th Street
317-244-3663
Open daily. Cabbage rolls a specialty.

Iowa

Des Moines
Sully's Irish Pub
110 Grand Avenue, West Des Moines
515-255-9970

Kansas

Wichita
Shamrock Lounge
1724 West Douglas
316-262-9557

Louisiana

New Orleans
Irish Bayou Lounge
Highway 11
504-254-0529

Mick's Irish Pub
4801 Bienville Avenue
504-482-9113

Molly's at the Market Pub
1107 Decatur Street
504-525-5169

Molly's Irish Pub and Restaurant
732 Toulouse
504-568-1915 or 1916

Maryland

Anapolis
McGarvey's Saloon
South Market Space
410-263-5700
Open daily.

Baltimore
The Emerald Taverns
301-752-5835
Open daily. Neighborhood hangout

Irish Pub
249 West Chase Street
301-752-4059
Open Monday-Saturday. Neighborhood pub,
but friendly to strangers.

Irish Pub
418 South Clinton Street
301-276-1164
Open daily. Neighborhood pub with great cheeseburger.

Kavanaugh's
311 West Madison Street
301-462-9585
Open Monday-Friday. Neighborhood pub with
Guinness and Harp on tap.

Catonsville
Molony's
583 Frederick Road
301-744-4030
Open daily

Only Irish bar in Catonsville.

Frederick
Donnelly's Restaurant
103 North Market Street
301-695-5388
Open daily.

Gaithersburg
Gallaghers III
16533 South Frederick Avenue
301-977-9000
Open daily. Blue collar bar.

La Plata-Leonardtown
McIlnenny's
Smallwood Village Shopping Center
St. Charles
301-645-7500 or 843-7500
Open Tuesday-Saturday. Entertainment and dancing.

Marion Station
> Shamrock Bar
> 2 Main Street
> 301-623-3022
> Open daily.

Ocean City
> Duffy's Tavern
> 12933 Coastal Highway
> 301-250-1449
> Open daily during season. A raunchy St. Patrick's Day.

Thurmont
> Shamrock Restaurant
> Rt. 15
> 301-217-2912

Massachusetts

Boston
> Black Rose
> 59 Church Street

Cambridge
> 617-492-8630
> The Black Thorn Bar
> 417 West Broadway
> South Boston
> 617-269-1159
> Open daily. Live music on weekends.

> Brendan Behan Pub
> 378A Centre Street, Jamaica Plain
> Irish seisiun Tuesday
> Center Village Cafe
> 1664 Dorchester Avenue

Dorchester
617-265-1112
Open daily. Guinness, Harp, Irish videos, darts.
Cuchulainns
1445 Dorchester Avenue
617-265-8034
Open daily. Irish newspapers.

Emerald Isle
1501 Dorchester Avenue
617-288-3481
Open daily. Irish music weekends.

The Green Briar
304-308 Washington Street
617-789-4100
Open daily. Food daily, Sunday brunch; live music,
including Irish, most nights.

The Kells
161 Brighton Avenue, Allston
617-782-6172
Open daily. DJ or live Irish music nightly;
lunch/dinner daily; Irish brunch Sunday.

Killarney Tavern
1295 Massachusetts Avenue, Dorchester
617-436-9037

Nash's Pub
1156 Dorchester Avenue
617-436-4134

New Erie Pub
635 Hyde Park Avenue
617-325-1514

The New Quincy Adams
60 Sumner Street, Quincy
617-472-1900
Lunch/dinner daily.

Nostalgia
797 Qunicy Shore Drive, Wollaston Beach
617-479-8989
Live Irish music Sunday.

The Olde Irish Alehouse
2-4 Bridge Street
617-329-6034

O'Leary's
1010 Beacon Street, Brookline
617-734-0049
Irish brunch, including steak and kidney pie and Sunday seisiun.

Pat Flanagan's
79 Parkingway, Quincy Center
617-773-3400
Open daily. Lunch/dinner daily; Sunday brunch;
live Irish music and Karaoke.

Tara Pub
1921 Dorchester Avenue
617-282-5637
Open daily. Live Irish music weekends; traditional
seisiun Sunday.

Braintree

Molly Malone's
37 Forbes Road
617-848-0600
Open daily. Irish entertainment Tuesday-Saturday; no cover.

Dennisport

Clancy's
8 Upper County Road
508-394-6661

Michael Patrick's Publick House
435 Main
508-398-1620

East Falmouth

Irish Embassy Pub
734 Teaticket Highway, Route 28
Cape Cod
508-540-6656
Open daily. Live music nightly.

Framingham

Liam's Irish Tavern
Framingham Centre
508-875-6114
Open daily. Irish beers; lunch/dinner, including lamb
stew and seafood.

Hyannis

The Irish Pub
126 Main, West Harwich
508-432-8808

Hyannisport

Shannon's
251 Iyanough Road
508-775-9122

Malden

My Honey Fitz Irish
142 Pleasant, Malden
508-324-0111

South Easton

The 1882 Irish Embassy
Off Routes 24 or 495, Junction 106 & 123
508-238-1882
Live music nightly, some Irish.

The Irish Whisper Grill
288 East 8th Street
617-269-1927 or 268-6342

The Ringside Inn
332 West Broadway
617-269-9407
Irish entertainment Friday-Sunday.

The Sheebin
332 West Broadway
617-268-1705
Live Irish music Wednesday-Sunday.

West Yarmouth

Cape Cod Irish Village
Rt. 28 508-771-0100
Open daily. Full menu with Irish flair; live Irish entertainment.

Clancy's
175 Rt.
28 508-775-3332

Worcester (508)

Emerald Isle Restaurant
49-53 Millbury
508-798-9747

Michigan

Detroit

Blarney Stone Bar
15224 E. 8 Mile Road
313-371-0166

Dunleavy's Irish Inn
7235 Greenfield
313-584-3282

Emerald Isle Irish Pub
15006 Harper
313-527-4033

Gaelic League Irish American Club
2062 Michigan
313-963-8895

Irish-American Club, Inc.
2068 Michigan
313-964-8700

Irish Saloon of Corktown
1426 Kaline Drive
313-963-2888

Shamrock Lounge
19029 West 7 Mile & Michigan
313-532-7607

Kelly's Irish Pub
3701 South Telegraph, DEA.
313-563-7510

Tipperary Pub
8287 Southfield Road
313-271-5870

Grand Rapids
Flanagan's
139 Pearl Street, NW
616-454-7852
Thursday night jazz.

Minnesota

Minneapolis
Duggan's Bar & Grill
5916 Excelsior Boulevard, St. Louis Park
612-922-6025

Irish Too Pub
201 East Lake
612-823-6016

Missouri

Kansas City
Kelly's Lounge
8245 Wornall Road
816-444-3707

The Shamrock Tavern
301 South 10th
816-621-3513

St. Louis
Blarney Stone
716 North 1st Street
314-231-8171
Open daily. More American fast food than Irish pub.

Emerald Bar
6405 Arsenal
314-647-9659

Emerald Isle Restaurant and Lounge
1824 Brown Road
314-428-0787

Hennessey's Irish Public House
1730 South 8th Street
314-241-8282

Muldoon's Irish Pub
5401 Arsenal
314-781-4436

Nebraska

Omaha

Dubliner Pub
1205 Harney Street
402-342-3555 or 342-5887
Live Irish music.

Nevada

Las Vegas

Blarney Bar
2210 North Las Vegas Boulevard
702-399-7972 Reno

Bugsy Malone's
123 West 1st
702-329-1922

Katie Malone's
1218 B Sparks
702-358-5484

New Hampshire

Jackson

Shannon Door Pub
Route 16
603-383-4211

Manchester

Wild Rover Pub
Block east of Bridge and Elm Streets
603-669-7722
Live Irish music.

Portsmouth-Exeter
The Blarney Restaurant
765 U.S. Rt. 1, York
603-363-5084

New Jersey

Atlantic City
Irish Pub
St. James Place and Boardwalk
609-344-9063
Open daily. Hotel, restaurant, bar.

Bergenfield
The Green's House
52 South Washington Avenue
201-384-1330
Open daily. Live Irish music some weekends.

Camden
Evergreens Irish Pub
601 North White Horse Pike, Somerdale
908-627-9434

Clifton
Harp 'n Bard
363 Lakeview Avenue
201-772-7282
Live Irish music weekends.

Franklin
Sullivan's Gas Light Inn
382 Route 23201-827-8227
Open daily. Irish entertainment Friday-Saturday.

Hoboken

O'Donoghues
205 First Street
201-656-9428
Open daily. Live Irish music weekends; TV Irish sports; pool, darts.

Trenton

Sweeney's Pub & Restaurant
688 South Broad
609-393-6669
Open Monday-Saturday. A popular neighborhood tavern.

Williamstown

Barney's Place
820 N. Blackhorse Pike
609-728-3666
Open daily. Lunch/dinner; live Irish music Sunday evening.

New York

Albany

Shamrock II
109 Everett Road
518-482-0365 or 482-9760

Baldwin

The Irish Pub
734 Sunrise Highway
516-867-9706
Traditional Irish music Sunday.

Brewster

Tom & Jerry's
Rt. 6 & 22
914-278-8900
Lunch, dinner, live entertainment.

Buffalo
Blarney Castle
1856 South Park Avenue
716-824-5858

The Blarney Stone
86 Ledger
716-873-3133

Murray's Irish Pub
127 South Niagara, Tonaivanda
716-692-2093

Blarney Tavern
146-01 Jamaica Avenue
212-526-9272

Irish Hillside Inn
168-02 Hillside Avenue
212-526-9574

Little Neck
Patrick's Pub & Cafe
252-12 Northern Boulevard
718-423-7600
Lunch/dinner; Irish gift shop next door.

Mineola
Kevin Grant's
133 Mineola Boulevard, Long Island
516-746-1316
"Home of Irish music in Mineola"

New York City
Abbey Tavern
Third Avenue at 26th Street
212-532-1978
Open daily noon-4 a.m. Lots of brogues and Irish dishes.

The Archway
2700 Jerome Avenue, The Bronx
212-364-8206
Lunch/dinner; Irish videos Monday; Irish music
Wednesday-Sunday.

The Ashford Arms
2282 Flatbush Avenue
718-377-9169
Open daily. Music weekends, often Irish; lunch daily,
dinner Wednesday-Sunday, brunch Sunday.

Blarney Castle
202-24 Rockway Point Boulevard, Rockaway Point
212-474-9245 (New York)

Blarney Castle
110 Chambers Street
212-474-9245

Blarney Stone Restaurant
106 West 32nd Street
212-502-5139 or 502-5547

Bliss St. Station
47-02 Greenpoint Avenue at 47th Street, Woodside
718-729-6680
Full menu; live Irish music Friday-Saturday.

Bliss Tavern
45-50 46th Street
718-729-9749
Thoroughly Irish patrons, drinks, pub grub, and live
music Wednesday-Saturday.

The Bottom Line
15 West 4th Street
212-228-7880
Live music, some Irish.

Brannigan's
104 Greenwich
212-276-4646

The Breffni
43-45 40th Street, Queens Boulevard, Sunnyside
718-729-9803 or 729-9470
Lunch/dinner; live music, often Irish; televised Irish sports.

Celtic House
5592 Broadway, Bronx
212-548-9410
Live Irish music Saturday-Sunday; televised international sports.

Centerfield's
45-50 46th Street
718-729-9742
Open Monday-Saturday.

The Clubhouse
1586 York Avenue
212-288-3218
Open nightly, Saturday-Sunday afternoons, and for all
major sports events. Televised Irish, other international,
and national sports.

Characters
220 West 242nd Street, the Bronx
212-601-1625
Open daily. Irish music Sunday.

Claddagh Ring
216 West 233 Street
212-548-9747

Costellos'
225 East 44th Street
212-599-9614
Open Monday-Friday 11 a.m.-4 a.m. Local journalists make
this scene, along with business executive types.

Desmond's
327 West 57th Street
212-307-1722
Traditional Irish menu

Desmond's Tavern
433 Park Avenue South
212-684-9472

Dicey Reilly's
620 South Broadway (Yonkers)
914-969-1369
Open daily. Live music.

Dillon's of Woodside
60-04 Roosevelt Avenue, Woodside
718-429-8544
Live music, often Irish, Thursday-Sunday.

Donegal Tavern
93-30 43rd Avenue, Elmhurst
718-639-8804

Doyles Corner
2898 Bailey Avenue, The Bronx
212-948-7512
Live Irish music.

Eamonn Doran's at Madison Square Garden
136 West 33rd Street
212-967-7676
Open daily.
Eamonn Doran's at Marmalade Park

222 East 39th Street
212-687-7803
Open daily

The Emerald Pub
308 Spring Street
212-226-8512
Open daily. Lunch/dinner; Irish seisiun Thursdays, blues Fridays.

Farel O'Toole's
70th Street and Queens Boulevard (Queens)
718-478-6655
Open daily. Televised Irish sports; live music (not Irish)
weekends; Irish brunch Sunday

Fibber Magee's
869 McLean Avenue, Yonkers
914-237-2320
Open daily. Live music Wednesday-Monday, often Irish;
Irish brunch Saturday and Sunday.

Fiddler's Green
58 West 48th Street
212-819-0095
Open daily. No frills, but friendly brogue behind the bar.

Fireside Pub
4272 Katonah Avenue, Woodlawn
212-655-9516
Open daily until 4 a.m. Local and imported Irish music weekends.

Fitzgerald's Pub
43-16 Queens Blvd., Sunnyside
718-784-9552
Open daily. Entertainment Friday-Sunday; Irish videos.

Fitzgerald's Pub
336 Third Avenue
212-532-3071 or 3453
Pub grub; owners are Fitzgeralds of Killarney.

Flannery's
14th Street & Seventh Avenue
212-929-9589
$1 draughts; live music, sometimes Irish, and no cover.

Frenchy's
790 McLean Avenue, Yonkers
914-237-9920
Open daily. Full menu; Sunday Irish breakfast; live music,
often Irish, Friday-Sunday.

Glocca Morra
304 Third Avenue
212-473-9638
Lunch/dinner daily; music and sing-along Wednesday-Saturday.

Grandstand Bar and Restaurant
85-35 Grand Avenue, Elmhurst
718-651-4996
Open daily. Lunch/dinner daily, Irish Brunch Saturday-Sunday;
live Irish entertainment.

Green Derby Restaurant & Bar
994 Second Avenue
212-688-1250
Live Irish traditional, ballad, and folk music Wednesday-
Saturday; no cover.
Greenfields
2081 Flatbush Avenue, Brooklyn
718-692-4266

Gregory's
116-34 Metropolitan Avenue, Kew Gardens
718-849-7319
Live music Saturday.

Hibernian Bar
102-14 Roosevelt Avenue, Corona, Queens
718-429-8940

Hickey's Bar
139 West 33rd Street
212-244-6120
Open daily. Video screens show all sports events.

The Hide Out
143 East 233 Street, Woodlawn
212-655-8042
Live Irish music.

Innisfree
3178 Bainbridge Avenue, The Bronx
212-655-2748
Open daily. Music Friday-Sunday, Irish videos Monday-Sunday.

Irish Cottage
54-20 Roosevelt Avenue
718-429-9426
Brogues here, there, and everywhere as Irish newcomers meet
Irish staff.

The Irish Pub
839 7th Avenue
212-664-9364

Joyce's Steak and Lobster House
948 2nd Avenue
212-759-6780
Full menu; many calm and quiet patrons.

Kate Kearney's
251 East 50th Street
212-935-2045
Live traditional Irish music Saturday.

Keane's Recovery Room
171 Gunhill Road, Bronx
212-655-9946
Lunch/dinner daily; brunch Saturday-Sunday.

Kennedy's
978 2nd Avenue
212-759-4242
Popular with neighbors; look for the leprechaun! Breezy Point

Kennedy's on the Bay
406 Bayside Avenue
718-945-0202

Kerry Hills Pub
113-24 Rockaway Beach Boulevard
718-474-9317
Open daily. Live Irish music weekends.

Krayz
54-20 Roosevelt Avenue
718-429-9426
Open Thursday-Sunday. Only adults over 23.

Lavelle's
46th Street & Broadway, Astoria, Queens
718-278-9071
Live Irish music weekends; Irish videos daily.

Leydon's
362 West 23rd Street
212-989-2500
Open daily. Gentlemen from Galway promise
"Reasonable prices, luxury and ambience."

Limerick's Restaurant and Bar
575 2nd Avenue
212-683-4686
Open daily.

McCarron's Pub
2414 149th Street, Whitestone, Queens
718-762-8674
Irish music Friday-Saturday

McGovern's Pub
49th Street & Skillman Avenue, Woodside
Live Irish music weekends.

McLoughlin's Pub
44-23 Queens Boulevard
718-729-9617

McMahon's
357 East 20th Street, The Bronx
212-655-6726
Open daily. Irish sports on video Monday; live Irish music
weekends.

McSorley's Old Ale House
15 East 7th Street
212-473-9148
Open daily noon-1 a.m.

Maguire's Cafe
800 2nd Avenue
212-370-5454

Morley's
123/129 Lake Avenue
914-969-9336
Thursday is Irish night.

Mountain Dew Tavern
7-9 Bedford Park Blvd, The Bronx
212-364-6096
Open daily. Irish television; music Friday-Sunday.

O'Casey's
22 East 41st Street
212-685-6807

Paddy Reilly's
495 2nd Avenue
212-686-1210
Open daily. One of Ireland's top entertainers.

Peggy Gordon's
52-13 Roosevelt Avenue, Woodside, Queens
718-429-9863
Live music, often Irish; Irish newspapers.

The Phoenix
367 East 204th Street, The Bronx
212-655-9525
Live contemporary and traditional entertainment; TV sports.

Pier 92
377 Beach 92nd Street, Rockaway
718-945-2200

P.J. Carney's
906 7th Avenue
212-664-0056

P.J. Clarke's
915 Third Avenue at 65th Street
212-355-8857
Open daily 11 a.m.-4 a.m. A very "today" crowd mixes
with 19th-century decor.

P.J. Moran's
3 East 48th Street
212-753-6440

Possibilities
320 East 204th Street, The Bronx
212-655-9233 or 655-9102
Open daily. Music Friday-Saturday, sometimes Irish.

Potcheen Still Pub
72-08 Broadway, Jackson Heights
718-429-8979

Power's Court
221 East 58th Street
212-486-1818
Elegant dining in a pub setting.

The Raintower Tavern
108-03 Rockaway Beach Drive, Rockaway Park
718-318-6107
Guinness, Harp, and Murphy's draught

Reilly's
2nd Avenue at 28th Street
212-686-1210
Live Irish music

Revels
54-20 Roosevelt Avenue (Woodside)
718-429-9426
Live Irish music.

Roaring 20s
336 East 204th Street, The Bronx
212-655-8337
TV Irish sports; live music weekends; pool table.

Rosie O'Grady's
211 Pearl Street
212-425-7912

Rumours
641 McLean Avenue, Yonkers
914-969-7436
Live Irish music; TV sports.

Ryan's Irish Pub
151 Second Avenue
212-979-9511
Open daily. Live Irish music, seisiun Sunday night; Irish
brunch Saturday-Sunday

Sally O'Brien's
45-52 46th St., Woodside
718-729-9870
Open daily. Live Irish TV and videos; music Friday-Sunday;
Irish newspapers.

Sam Maguire's
6697 Broadway, The Bronx
212-549-9730
Open daily. Music Thursday-Sunday, some Irish.

Sarsfield's
320 East 204th Street, The Bronx
212-655-9233 or 655-9102
Open daily. Monday night Irish sports videos; Cross
Channel Soccer; music Friday-Sunday; singles.

Scruffy Duffy's
743 8th Avenue
212-245-9126
"Coolest place in Hell's Kitchen"

Shamrock Inn
66-19 Woodhaven Boulevard, Rego Park, Queens
718-830-9097

Shillelagh Tavern
47-22 30th Avenue, Astoria, Queens
718-728-9028

Sidetracks
45-08 Queens Boulevard, Sunnyside
716-786-3570
Open daily. Lunch/dinner daily; brunch and live Irish
music weekends.

Stephen's Green
46th Street & Queens Boulevard, Sunnyside
718-786-5737
Live televised Irish sports; live music, some Irish.

Taegerhouse
97-11 Queens Boulevard
718-897-3035
Open daily.

Tara Restaurant
840 Midland Avenue, Yonkers
914-423-1234
Open daily. Music Tuesday-Sunday, some Irish.

Terminal Bar
5987 Broadway, The Bronx
212-549-6713 or 548-9761
Televised Irish sports; live music (sometimes Irish) weekends;
"ample taxi service"

Village Pub
3207 Bainbridge Avenue
212-652-9829
Live music weekends.

Nyack
>   Saints & Scholars
>   116½ Main Street
>   914-358-8540
>   Thursday is Celtic night.

Poughkeepsie
>   O'Neill's Irish Castle
>   313 ManchesterRoad, Route 55
>   914-454-5848
>   Open daily. Irish music weekends, full menu.

Schenectady
>   Shamrock Restaurant
>   157 Clinton
>   518-382-9553

Yonkers
>   Morley's
>   123/129 Lake Avenue
>   914-969-9336
>   Thursday is Irish night.

North Carolina

Winston Salem
>   O'Casey's Place
>   1314 South Hawthorne Road
>   919-723-5550
>   Open daily.

North Dakota

Black Hills
>   Shamrock Cafe
>   Junction of Highways 85 & 385, Deadwood
>   605-578-3576

Sioux Falls
  Irish Pub
  Montrose
  605-363-5313

Ohio

Cincinnati
  Crowley's Highland House Cafe
  958 Pavillion, ME Adams
  513-721-7704
  No Irish music, but Guiness and Harp

Cleveland
  Blarney Stone
  13334 Lorain Avenue
  216-941-6972
  Madden's Irish Village Lounge

  1817 East 13th Street
  216-696-5229

  Pride of Erin
  12228 Lorain Avenue
  216-215-2922

  Shamrock Tavern
  11922 Madison Avenue
  216-521-9740

Lima
  Murphy's
  318 North Main Street
  419-227-0670

Oklahoma

Oklahoma City
Harrigan's
6420 NW Expressway
405-728-1329

O'Brien's
103 East California, Bricktown
405-235-3434

O'Shaughnessy Irish Grill
5336 East Admiral Place
405-832-0860

Norman
O'Connell's Irish Pub and Grill
120 East Lindsey
405-364-8454

Oregon

Portland
Dublin Pub
3104 S.E. Belmont
503-230-8817

Dublin Pub at Raleigh Hills
6821 SW Beaverton-Hillsdale Highway
503-297-2889

Dublin Pub at St. John's
8203 North Ivanhoe
503-283-6880

Kell's Irish Restaurant and Pub
112 SW 2nd Street
503-227-4057

Pennsylvania

Allentown

The Limerick Restaurant & Bar
3900 Hamilton Boulevard
215-820-0851
Open Monday-Saturday.

Ardmore

Annie's Cafe
98 Cricket Avenue
215-649-0283
Open daily. Entertainment all week.

Bethlehem

Shamrock Inn
409 Wyandotte
215-866-5535
Open Monday-Saturday.

Erie

Irish Cousins
3924 Main Street
814-899-2050
Open Monday-Saturday.

Hazelton

O'Donnell's Tavern
North East on PA 940
717-636-2387

Johnstown

Blarney Stone Restaurant & Lounge
RD 6, Old Rt. 22, East of Mundy's Corner
814-749-7853
Open Tuesday-Sunday (r), daily (l). Drinks, food, and imported
gifts from Ireland.

Norwood
Erin Pub
35 West Winona
215-461-0991
Open daily. Irish entertainment Friday-Saturday.

Philadelphia
Bridget Foy's
200 South Street
215-922-1813
Open daily. Nice fireplace in small dining area.

Cavanaugh's
23 & Sansom
215-386-4889
Open daily. Irish entertainment Saturday, Sunday, and Tuesday.

C.J. McGee's
Springfield Shopping Center
Routes 1 and 320, Springfield
215-543-7161
Live Irish music Wednesday and Saturday.

Devine's Pub & Restaurant
5813 Rising Sun Avenue
215-728-9327
Open daily. A traditional Irish pub owned by Roscommon-born Tom Devine.

Emmett's
Levic & Frankfort
215-625-9500
Open Tuesday-Saturday

Garvin's Irishmen's Inn
5450 Large Street
215-537-9929
Open daily.

Loretta's
7681 Frankford Avenue
215-338-4188
Open daily.

Moriarty's Pub & Restaurant
1116 Walnut Street
215-627-7670
Open daily. Very popular with after work crowd.

New Deck Tavern
3408 Sansom
215-386-4600
Open daily. Lunch, dinner, late night music Tuesday-Saturday.

O'Cunnigan's Who's on First
700 South 3rd Street
215-625-2835
Open Wednesday-Saturday.

O'Malley's Bar & Restaurant
2227 Pine Street
215-546-2547
Open daily.

O'Neal's
611 S. 3rd Street
215-574-9495
Open daily.

Ryan's Pub
607 South Braddock Avenue
412-241-0464
Open daily.

Shamrock Pub
965 East Ontario
215-634-7558
Open daily.

Rhode Island

Newport
O'Brien's Pub
501 Thames
849-6623

Providence
Patrick's Pub
381 Smith Street
401-751-1553
Live Irish music weekends; Irish videos shown weekly.

Texas

Dallas
Birraporetti's
9100 North Central Expressway
214-692-0565
Open daily 11 a.m.-2 a.m. Another in the chain of Irish pubs with Italian kitchens.
Also: 2031 North Collins, Arlington
817-265-0555

Tipperary Inn
2818 Greenville Avenue
214-823-7167

Utah

Salt Lake City
Leprechaun Inn
4700 South, 900 East, Holladay
801-268-3294

Shenanigan's
274 South West Temple
801-364-3663
Open daily.

Shenanigan's
7176 South, 900 East
801-565-8400

Washington

Seattle

Murphy's Pub
Meridian & N. 45th Street, Wallingford
207-634-2110
Open daily. Authentic and college; nightly Irish music.

Wisconsin

Milwaukee

Irish Castle
1328 W. Lincoln Avenue
414-643-9654
Dancing and live Irish music.

Shamrock Grove
4813 West National Avenue
414-671-5455

St. Patrick's Day Parades

California
Beverly Hills
Mission Viejo
Oakland
Sacramento
San Diego
San Francisco

Colorado
Denver

Connecticut
Greenwich
Hartford
Meridan
New Haven

Delaware
Wilmington

Florida
Delray Beach
Forth Lauderdale
Jacksonville
Miami

Georgia
Atlanta
Dublin
Savannah

Hawaii
Honolulu

Illinois
Chicago
Decatur
Waukegan

Iowa
Cedar Rapids
Dyersville
Emmetsburg

Kentucky
Bardstown
Lexington
Louisville

Louisiana
New Orleans

Maryland
Baltimore
Ocean City

Massachusetts
Boston
Brookline
Holyoke
Lawrence

Michigan

Bay City
Detroit

Minnesota
Belle Plaine
Minneapolis
St. Paul
Waseca

Missouri
Kansas City
Rolla
St. Louis
Springfield

Montana
Anaconda

Nebraska
O'Neill

Nevada
Las Vegas

New Jersey
Belmar
Jersey City
Kedasborg
Kearny
Newark
Norwood
Nutley
South Amboy
Trenton
West Orange
Wharton
Woodbridge

New Mexico
Albuquerque

New York

Albany
Binghamton
Brentwood
Buffalo
East Islip
Elmira
Garden City
Greenville
Huntington
Mahopac
New Paltz
New York
Brooklyn
Manhattan
Staten Island
Pearl River
Rochester
Syracuse
Troy
Utica
Westhampton Beach
Yonkers

Ohio
Akron
Cincinnati   *involved during parade?*
Cleveland
Columbus

Oklahoma
Shamrock

Pennsylvania
Allentown
East Stroudsburg
Freeland
Limeport
Philadelphia

Pittsburgh
Pottsville
Scranton
Springfield
Upper Darby
Wilkes-Barre

Rhode Island
Newport
Providence
West Warwick

South Dakota
Clear Lake
Deadwood
Sioux Falls

Texas
Corpus Christi
Dallas
Dublin
Houston
San Antonio

Shamrock

Utah
Salt Lake City

Virginia
Alexandria
Richmond

Washington
Seattle
Spokane

Wisconsin
Beloit
La Crosse
Milwaukee

District of Columbia

Puerto Rica
San Juan

Irish American Organizations

Irish Americans have thoroughly established themselves as a community in every part of the U.S. For an Irish American, or anyone interested in learning, teaching, researching or just socializing amid Irish culture and heritage, there are Irish American Gaelic and Celtic Leagues, Historic Societies, Fraternal Organizations, Tourist and Travel Offices for Ireland and the U.S., Libraries, Institutes, Clubs, Committees, Caucuses and Conferences. In fact, they have been so widespread that these groups and organizations are difficult to document with accuracy. To become involved in the Irish American activities and groups in a specific location or theme of interest, contact an established Irish American organization that can direct you toward the most current information. A few are listed below.

The Embassy of Ireland

2234 Massachusetts Avenue, NW
Washington, DC 20008
(202) 462-3939
Contact: Noel Kilkenny

Consulates General

The Consulates General provide not only Irish visa information, but have information regarding Irish American organizations in their region. It is recommended to first contact the consulates with requests for information (be specific) by letter.

New York:

345 Park Avenue
New York, NY 10154-0037
(212) 319-2555

Chicago:
400 North Michigan Avenue,
Room 911
Chicago, IL 60611
(312) 337-1868

Boston:
535 Boylston Street
Boston, MA 02159
(617) 267-9330

San Francisco:
681 Market Street
San Francisco, CA 94105
(415) 392-4214

Ancient Order of Hibernians in America

The Hibernians are an Irish Catholic organization that promotes Irish culture and causes, such as immigration. There are local chapters in 38 states across the country; listed below is the national contact who can provide up-to-date information on each chapter. The group was founded in 1836.

31 Logan street
Auburn, NY 13201
(315) 252-4872
Contact: Thomas D. McNabb

The Gaelic League-Irish American Clubs, Inc.

Promotes Irish culture and activities in the greater Detroit area. There are Gaelic Leagues established across America to promote Irish culture and activities in greater metropolitan areas.

2068 Michigan Avenue
Detroit, MI 48216
(313) 963-8895
Contact: Kathleen O'Neil

American Irish Historical Society

Founded 1897, the Society presents an annual medal to an outstanding American of Irish lineage. Maintains Irish and Irish American information in a library and archives of about 25,000 volumes. Open to the public by appointment only.

991 Fifth Avenue
New York, NY 10028
(212) 288-2263
Contact: Alec Ormsby

Irish American Cultural Institute

This independent (though it is associated with the College of St. Thomas) nonprofit research organization works to encourage research in the field of Irish and Irish American studies, and produces a monthly newsletter and a quarterly journal of Irish Studies, gives awards, presents lectures, and offers other educational programs. Their new offices in New Jersey have a reading room open to members and the public.

Administrative Offices:
University of St. Thomas
2115 Summit Avenue, Mail #5026
St. Paul, MN 55105-1096
(612) 962-6040 phone, (612) 962-6043 fax

Executive Offices:
Plaza Building
3 Elm Street, Suite 204
Morristown, NJ 07960
(201) 605-1991 phone, (201) 605-8875 fax
Chairman: John Walsh
Founded 1964

Irish American Heritage Center

Subscribe

The center is a meeting place for all kinds of Irish cultural events sponsored by different area organizations. A newsletter listing upcoming events is published every other month.

4626 N. Knox
Chicago, IL 60630
(312) 282-7035

United Irish Cultural Center
San Francisco, CA
(See Reference, Research, and Multi-Media Appendix)

Irish American Reference, Research and Multi-Media Sources

A good place to find books, films, and material about Irish American points of interest across the North American landscape is a library with Irish and Irish American concentrations. An ultimate guide to these wealthy stores of Irish information is *The Irish in America* by Patrick J. Blessing, a cloth-bound book published 1992 by the Catholic University Press of America in Washington, DC. Blessing's book is a tremendous bibliography of collections, libraries, and archives in 48 states, and the literature, dictionaries, and other publications held within them. Here are a few listings that suggest the large amount of information available.

Burns Library

This already extensive Irish collection recently acquired original letters, notebooks, and manuscripts of poet W.B. Yeats from Michael Yeats. While most of the collection is open to the public, certain materials must be viewed by appointment.

Boston College Irish Collection
Chestnut Hill, MA 02167
Reference Librarian: John Atteberry
(617) 552-3282

Duane Library

Library open to public with restrictions. Primary Irish holdings include Gaelic translations of literature written in English.

Fordham University—Special Collections
Bronx, NY 10458
Chief Reference Librarian: Patrice Kane
(718) 933-2233

Ellen Clarke Bertrand Library
Founded 1846, the library is open to public for reference use only.
Bucknell University
Lewisburg, PA 17837
(717) 524-1557
Director: Ann DeKlerk

Feehan Memorial Library
Founded in 1929, open to the public for reference use only.
Saint Mary of the Lake Seminary
Mundelein, IL 60060
(708) 566-6401
Librarian: Brother Henry Baldwin

Irish Family Historical Society Library
Publishes a newsletter five times a year. Concentrates on geneology. Library open to public.
173 Tremont Street
Newton, MA 02158
(617) 965-0939

McLaughlin Library
Founded in 1958, the MacManus collection is open to the public with the permission of the librarian.
MacManus Collection
Seton Hall University
South Orange, NJ 07979
(201) 761-9435
Director: Julie Andrews Allen

Miller Library
This collection, begun in 1938, consists mainly of books, letters, journals and manuscripts dating from the Irish literary renaissance. Open to the public.

Colby College—Special Collections
Healy Collection of Irish Literature
Waterville, ME 04901

O'Shaughnessy Library
Collection is open to qualified users.
College of Saint Thomas Celtic Library
St. Paul, MN 55105
(612) 647-5720

United Irish Cultural Center
Founded in 1975, one of largest Irish libraries in North America, the United Irish Cultural Center conducts lecture series, classes, guided tours, and shows films. On weekends, doors are opened and visitors can enjoy the lounge, dining room and Irish music.
2700 45th Avenue
San Francisco, CA 94116
(415) 661-2700
Library Director: Tom Carey

Irish Travel

Many people who have traveled the world (both Irish and non-Irish) claim that the country is the most picturesque and lovely they have visited. There are many reasons to travel there, whether on a vacation or a visit to the relatives, and many different areas and attractions to consider. For aid in getting to Ireland, getting around in Ireland and getting to know Ireland, there's the **Irish Tourist Board**, 345 Park Avenue, New York, NY 10154, (212) 869-5500. For those outside the city a toll-free number is available: 1-800-223-6470. The Irish Tourist Board can supply a wealth of information on many different aspects of traveling around Ireland.

Indeed, anyone going to the Emerald Isle will need advice. Two books published by Hippocrene Books, Inc., 171 Madison Avenue, New York, NY 10016, fill the need for Irish language instruction and tour and cultural information. First, the *Companion Guide to Ireland, Second Edition* (paperback, $14.95), by Henry Weisser, offers travel tips and complete information regarding geography, history, politics, economic issues, as well as the circumstances and contemporary implications of Ireland's history. Weisser teaches classes at Colorado State University and conducts study tours in Ireland and the U.K. for Americans. Also see the *Irish-English/English-Irish Dictionary and Phrasebook* (paperback, $7.95), which is not only a "practical" dictionary, but lists Gaelic (Irish) phrases covering travel, sight-seeing, shopping, and recreation with notes on pronunciation, grammar, and dialect. If you can't find these gems at your local bookstore, contact the publisher.

Selected Readings

American Automobile Association, *Tour Book*. Heathrow, FL: American Automobile Association (1993).

Birmingham, Stephen, *Real Lace: America's Irish Rich*. New York: harper & Row, Publishers (1973).

Callahan, Bob, *The Big Book of American Irish Culture*. New York: Penguin Books (1989).

Clark, Dennis, *The Irish in Pennsylvania*, University Park, PA: The Pennsylvania Historical Association (1991).

Colum, Padraic, *A Treasury of Irish Folklore*. New York: Wing Books (1992).

Cooper, Brian E., *The Irish American Almanac and Green Pages*. New York: Harper & Row, Publishers (1990).

Cure, Karen, *Sunday in New York*. New York: Fodor's Travel Publications, Inc. (1993).

Flannery, John Brendan, *The Irish Texans*. San Antonio: The University of Texas Institute of Texan Cultures (1980).

Greeley, Andrew, *Irish Americans*. New York: Time Books (1981).

Griffin, William D., *The Book of Irish Americans*. New York: Random House (1990).

Ludberg, Richard, *Ethnic Chicago*. Lincolnwood, IL: Passport Books (1993).

Mobile Travel Guide. New York: Prentice Hall (1993).

Moody, T.W. and F.X. Martin, *The Course of Irish History*. Dublin: The Mercier Press (1984).

Reilly, Robert T., *Irish Saints*. New York: Avenel Books (1981).

Robb, Diane Burton, *Book of Famous Places*. Grand Rapids, MI: Gollehon (1990).

Watts, J.F., *The Irish Americans*. New York: Chelsea House Publishers (1988).

Wood, Ernest, *The Irish Americans*. New York: Mallard Press (1922).

Index

COMPANION GUIDES FROM HIPPOCRENE BOOKS

COMPANION GUIDE TO AUSTRALIA, *by Graeme and Tamsin Newman*
With helpful tips on preparing for your trip, this cheerful guide outlines the distinctive characters and main attractions of cities, describes picturesque countryside, and links the things tourists like to do with the history and character of the Australian people.
_____294 pages • b/w photos and 4 maps • 0-87052-034-2 • $16.95

COMPANION GUIDE TO BRITAIN, *by Henry Weisser*
Highlights are cited and explained clearly, describing what is best to see in London and the provinces: castles cathedrals, stately homes, villages, and towns. This essential practical guide lists history, geography, politics, culture, economics, climate and language use.
_____250 pages • 0-7818-0147-8 • $14.95

COMPANION GUIDE TO MEXICO, *by Michael Burke*
Along with the usual tips on sites, this guide outlines contemporary realities of Mexican society, religion and politics.
_____320 pages • b/w photos • 0-7818-0039-0 • $14.95

COMPANION GUIDE TO POLAND (Revised), *by Jill Stephenson and Alfred Bloch*
"This quaint and refreshing guide is an appealing amalgam of practical information, historical curiosities, and romantic forays into Polish culture."—*Library Journal*
_____179 pages • b/w photos, maps • 0-7818-0077-3 • $14.95

COMPANION GUIDE TO PORTUGAL, *by T.J. Kubiak*
Learn about the land, the people, their heritage and much more with this guide to the unexpected bounty of Portugal.
_____260 pages • maps • 0-87052-739-8 • $14.95

COMPANION GUIDE TO ROMANIA, *by Lydle Brinkle*
Written by a specialist in Eastern European geography, this modern guide offers comprehensive historical, topographical, and cultural overviews.
_____220 pages • 0-87052-634-0 • $14.95

COMPANION GUIDE TO SAUDI ARABIA, *by Gene Lindsey*
Gene Lindsey, an American who has spent much of the last decade in Saudi Arabia, traces the history of the region, religion, development, harsh environment, foreign policy, laws, language, education, technology, and underlying it all, its mindset.
_____368 pages • maps • 0-7818-0023-4 • $11.95

HIPPOCRENE U.S.A.
ETHNIC TRAVEL SERIES

Hippocrene Books, a renowned travel guide publisher, has established the Ethnic Travel Series to recognize the contributions of all races to the heritage of America and its colorful and varied landscape, as well as providing for a fun travel experience. For a catalog and other ethnic titles, write to Hippocrene Books, 171 Madison Avenue, New York, New York 10016.

BLACK AMERICA
Marcella Thum
"A useful acquisition for all travel collections."—*Library Journal*
"An admirable guide."—*Choice Magazine*
Organized by state, this fully indexed guide describes more than 700 historic homes, art and history museums, parks, monuments, landmarks of the civil rights movement, battlefields, colleges and churches across the U.S., all open to the public.
_____325 pages • ISBN 0-87052-045-8 • $11.95

BLACK WASHINGTON
Sandra Fitzpatrick and Maria Goodwin
"The authors provide a much-needed corrective and show how black Washingtonians affected not only this city but the nation and indeed, the world."—*The Washington Post Book World*
Explore over 200 sites in our nation's capital, central to the African-American experience. Gain insight into the heritage that had a profound impact on African-American culture and American society at large, including information about such pivotal figures as Frederick Douglas, Ralph Bunche, Anna J. Cooper, Duke Ellington, and Senator Edward Brooke. From Capitol Hill to Shaw to Lafayette Square to Georgetown, the authors systematically cover the entire city.
_____288 pages • ISBN 0-87052-832-7 • $14.95

HISTORIC BLACK SOUTH
Joann Biondi and James Haskins
"The book provides some wonderful reading and inspires tourists to go and explore a part of the South that has not been emphasized in travel."—*Library Journal*
This unique guide describes over 1,000 sites which pay tribute to the significant and often overlooked contribution of the southern African-American community. Read about, then visit, churches, art galleries and jazz clubs, beaches and barbershops, as this guide opens doors to a new appreciation of the historic Black South for all. Includes a description of attractions open to the public, listing hours, fees, directions, and phone numbers.
_____300 pages • ISBN 0-7818-0140-0 • $14.95

HISTORIC HISPANIC AMERICA
Oscar and Joy Jones
"This is an unusual guide that any serious traveler to the southwest would find informative."—*Library Journal*
This guide focuses on uncovering the living heritage in the Southwestern U.S. for historians and travelers alike. Both Spanish and Indian presence is still felt in the language, religion, customs, and attitudes that reflect a deep respect for a passionate heritage in the United States. Landmarks and historic sites are listed with hours of operation and directions.
_____300 pages, ISBN 0-7818-0141-9 • $14.95

POLISH HERITAGE TRAVEL GUIDE TO USA & CANADA
Jacek Galazka and Albert Juszczak
"A very useful contribution to an understanding of the Polish heritage in North America."—*Zbigniew Brzezinski*
For travelers seeking to visit important Polish points of interest in North America. Includes directions for 195 sites in 90 locations throughout North America. "This is a terrific guide for everyone who wants to learn about Polish heritage in the USA and Canada. It is filled with fun facts and easy to follow directions. Now everyone can find the places where history was made and where Polish culture is thriving," says Senator Barbara Mikulski.
_____272 pages, 90 photographs, ISBN 0-7818-0035-8 • $14.95

HIPPOCRENE GUIDE TO THE UNDERGROUND RAILROAD
Charles Blockson
The first of its kind on the subject, this ready-reference lists and describes sites by city and county of each state or province. The Underground Railroad is among the most popular topics of interest at tourist bureaus. Over one hundred fifty entries follow the covert salvation operation that involves over 25 mid-western, southern and eastern states.

As the chair of the advisory committee to the National Park Service, author Charles Blokson has been a key participant in the formation of a National Trail of historical markers identifying sites that have been soundly verified for historical accuracy.
_____300 pages, maps, b&w photos, ISBN 0-7818-0253-9 • $14.95

HIPPOCRENE U.S.A. GUIDE TO BLACK NEW YORK
Joann Biondi and James Haskins
New York City carries the highest population of African-Americans in the United States. Therefore it follows that New York should be rich in Black heritage. *Black New York* takes you by the hand into the heart of the city's Black communities and explains the significant contributions that African-Americans have made. Newspapers, jazz joints, festivals, radio shows, and historic sites are just a few of the contributions to American society New Yorkers have made.
_____250 pages, b&w photos, maps, ISBN 0-7818-0172-9 • $14.95

HIPPOCRENE INSIDER'S GUIDES

Hippocrene Insider's Guides provide you with tips on traveling to not-too-familiar lands. You'll be guided to the most interesting sights, learn about culture and be assured of an eventful stay when you visit with the Insider's Guide.

INSIDER'S GUIDE TO THE DOMINICAN REPUBLIC, by Jack Tucker and Ursula Eberhard
212 pages • b/w photos, maps • 0-7818-0075-7 • $14.95

INSIDER'S GUIDE TO HUNGARY, by Nicholas Parsons
366 pages • b/w photos, 20 maps • 0-87052-976-5 • $16.95

INSIDER'S GUIDE TO JAVA AND BALI, by Jerry LeBlanc
222 pages • b/w photos, maps • 0-7818-0037-4 • $14.95

INSIDER'S GUIDE TO ROME, by Frances D'Emilio
376 pages • b/w photos, map • 0-7818-0036-6 • $14.95

INSIDER'S GUIDE TO NEPAL, by Prakash Raj
136 pages • illustrated, maps • 0-87052-026-1 • $9.95

INSIDER'S GUIDE TO POLAND, 2nd revised edition, by Alexander Jordan
233 pages • 0-87052-880-7 • $9.95

(Prices subject to change.)

TO PURCHASE HIPPOCRENE BOOKS contact your local bookstore, or write to: HIPPOCRENE BOOKS, 171 Madison Avenue, New York, NY 10016. Please enclose check or money order, adding $4.00 shipping (UPS) for the first book and .50 for each additional book.